Teaching and Learning in Higher Education with Generative AI

This interdisciplinary book demonstrates how generative artificial intelligence (GenAI) changes higher education across diverse academic fields, including philology, management, engineering, and psychology. Drawing on empirical case studies, surveys, and experiments, this book combines theoretical and practical perspectives to explore AI's impact on learning and cognitive development. Each chapter offers discipline-specific analysis of how GenAI reshapes pedagogy – supporting multilingual education, enhancing reflective thinking, fostering self-regulated learning, and encouraging ethical awareness. By comparing case studies from varied academic and cultural contexts, this book highlights the opportunities and challenges of AI adoption, emphasizing responsible, creative, and critically informed approaches to academic innovation. It will appeal to researchers of AI in Higher Education across disciplines. Key features:

- Explains how GenAI transforms higher education across a variety of disciplines, from logistics to psychology.
- Includes practical and theoretical insights into AI's role in reshaping pedagogy, fostering critical thinking, and supporting multilingual education.
- Provides a global perspective on the opportunities and challenges of AI adoption through diverse case studies and empirical research.

Ida Skubis is an Assistant Professor at the Silesian University of Technology. A linguist with a PhD and MA degrees in four languages, she combines academic and international managerial experience. Her work focuses on interdisciplinary AI research, ethics, and management. She has received prestigious fellowships abroad, including 10-month fellowships under Marie Skłodowska-Curie agreement in France and Israel, and numerous awards, including the scholarship of The Minister of Education and Science for Outstanding Young Scientists.

Jolanta Wodarska, PhD, DSc (Habilitation), Eng., is a Professor at the Silesian University of Technology in Poland. Her research interests focus on investment project planning, with particular emphasis on evaluating financial performance and implementation risk, as well as on methods and concepts for managing contemporary organizations. She is currently engaged in research on the application of artificial intelligence, including its use in education.

Krzysztof Wodarski, PhD, DSc (Habilitation), Eng., is a Professor at the Silesian University of Technology in Poland. His work includes strategic management and project management and more recently the application of artificial intelligence in business and education. He has extensive experience in higher education management and in business and science support institutions that foster entrepreneurship and investment.

Teresa Sánchez-Gutiérrez, PhD is an Associate Professor at the University of Córdoba, Spain, specializing in psychology and psychopharmacology. She has extensive experience in national and European research projects, international research stays, and academic leadership. Her work focuses on psychosis, adolescent cannabis use, biopsychosocial risk factors, and psychoeducational interventions, with contributions to innovative mental health research and applied clinical psychology.

Teaching and Learning in Higher Education with Generative AI

Interdisciplinary Case Studies from Engineering, Management, Linguistics, and Psychology

Ida Skubis, Jolanta Wodarska,
Krzysztof Wodarski, and
Teresa Sánchez-Gutiérrez

CRC Press
Taylor & Francis Group
Boca Raton London New York

CRC Press is an imprint of the
Taylor & Francis Group, an informa business

First edition published 2026
by CRC Press
2385 NW Executive Center Drive, Suite 320, Boca Raton FL 33431

and by CRC Press
4 Park Square, Milton Park, Abingdon, Oxon, OX14 4RN

CRC Press is an imprint of Taylor & Francis Group, LLC

ISBN: 9781041350910 (hbk)
ISBN: 9781041350743 (pbk)
ISBN: 9781003795926 (ebk)

DOI: 10.1201/9781003795926

Typeset in Times
by codeMantra

Contents

Introduction vii

1 Generative AI and German pluricentrism: ChatGPT and advancing language education **1**

2 Diversity of use and attitudes toward generative AI in academic teaching **21**

3 Critical thinking competences and the use of generative AI **86**

4 Attitudes, perceptions, and self-regulated learning in the use of AI in psychology education **112**

Conclusions **126**

Reference 135
Index 145

Introduction

Generative artificial intelligence (GenAI), particularly large language models such as ChatGPT, Claude, and Gemini, is now being widely used in higher education settings. Researchers and educators are examining how these tools affect teaching practices, student learning behavior, and disciplinary expectations (Pérez et al., 2025; Testa et al., 2025). The use of GenAI in academic environments is no longer limited to isolated disciplines. It has become a topic of interest across fields including language education, management, engineering, and psychology.

At the same time, higher education discussions increasingly emphasize how people interact with GenAI systems through prompts and how these systems respond under ethical and policy constraints. Research based on prompt-response analysis demonstrates that GenAI tools can be both academically useful and operationally limited when users ask for sensitive, controversial, or potentially harmful information (Skubis et al., 2024). In particular, the analysis of human–ChatGPT interaction shows that model outputs are shaped not only by user intent but also by safety rules and embedded ethical boundaries, which can lead to refusals, partial answers, or responses that redirect the user toward broader societal, legal, or ethical dimensions rather than explicit details (Skubis et al., 2024). These dynamics are relevant in higher education because they affect what students can realistically obtain from GenAI tools, how they learn to formulate prompts, and how they interpret the reliability and completeness of AI-generated content. This dynamic resembles adoption processes in other AI domains, where decision-makers tend to focus on perceived usefulness, operational efficiency, and risks before integrating AI tools into real practice (Skubis, 2025a).

Recent comparative research further refines this perspective by demonstrating that different generations of large language models respond to controversial prompts in systematically different ways. A comparative analysis of ChatGPT 3.5 and GPT-4.0 shows that while both models emphasize ethical considerations and compliance with usage policies, they differ in their prompt sensitivity, linguistic flexibility, and response strategies (Skubis et al., 2025). ChatGPT 3.5 tends to adopt a more conservative and avoidance-oriented stance, frequently declining to engage with sensitive content, whereas GPT-4.0 displays a more nuanced contextual understanding and greater willingness to engage, albeit sometimes at the cost of reduced factual accuracy. Research on AI highlights that algorithmic decision-making can optimize workflows and strategic planning, yet still requires clear human oversight due to limitations in emotional intelligence, ethical reasoning, and accountability (Skubis, 2025b, 2025c). These findings highlight that GenAI use in education is not static but depends on the specific model, its training, and its ethical alignment mechanisms.

This book presents case studies from several disciplines to document how students and teachers engage with GenAI in practical settings. These studies are based on empirical methods such as surveys, experimental tasks, and classroom observation. The aim is to document how GenAI tools are being applied, what expectations students and teachers hold, and what types of cognitive and pedagogical effects are being reported.

In language learning and teaching, the research on GenAI is largely concentrated on English as a Foreign Language (EFL) contexts and higher education. It demonstrates that GenAI tools can support personalized learning, enhance writing development, foster learner motivation, and streamline teachers' workload through automated feedback, material generation, and assessment support (Law, 2024).

Castany (2025) examined translation classes where AI-generated outputs are compared with human translations to highlight both strengths and errors. These comparisons help students recognize dialectal variation and explore questions of stylistic consistency and lexical accuracy.

Recent systematic evidence reinforces these trends. Li et al. (2025), in a two-year review of 144 empirical studies published between 2023 and 2024, found that research on GenAI in language education has expanded exponentially, changing from exploratory work to more robust, data-driven investigations. Their analysis shows that higher education and EFL contexts continue to dominate the field, with writing, particularly AI-supported drafting and feedback, emerging as the most extensively studied skill. Mixed-methods research has become increasingly common, reflecting a growing interest in understanding how GenAI affects learners' cognitive, affective, and behavioral dimensions.

Recent studies show that GenAI is beginning to influence both the content and format of teaching in management and business education. Csaszar et al. (2025) argue that AI's ability to match or exceed student performance in analytical tasks is pushing business schools toward a strategic rethinking of their pedagogical models, marking a possible "third epoch" of management education. At the student level, Nawaz and Ong (2025) found that postgraduate business learners are not only using GenAI for literature synthesis, academic writing, and research planning but also warn of risks such as diminished critical thinking and ethical uncertainties. In a more applied context, Meepung (2025) developed and tested a creative learning model integrated with GenAI, demonstrating improvements in innovation-related skills, including creativity, design thinking, problem-solving, and digital literacy among undergraduate students in business and information technology.

In the context of logistics and production engineering education, Reider and Lang (2025) present a system architecture that enables students and practitioners to use GenAI for simulation modeling tasks that would traditionally require deep domain expertise. Their framework combines natural language input with structured modeling tools, allowing users to describe scenarios in plain language, which are then converted into simulation models. This setup lowers technical barriers, making it useful for educational settings where students can experiment with factory planning and logistics without needing advanced simulation skills.

Halliday et al. (2025) conducted a scoping review to explore how GenAI can be incorporated into assessment practices in tertiary psychology education. The review identified three main opportunities: using GenAI as a personal tutor, designing authentic assessment tasks involving GenAI, and asking students to critique AI-generated outputs to build digital literacy and ethical awareness. While only a few studies currently address this topic, the findings suggest that GenAI, if used thoughtfully, can support pedagogical goals without compromising accreditation standards. The authors emphasize the need for evidence-based assessment models that reflect the growing presence of AI in professional psychological practice.

The contributions in this book provide comparative perspectives across different academic cultures and disciplines. By focusing on specific use cases, the chapters avoid abstract claims and instead concentrate on the actual conditions under which GenAI tools are used. The topics range from student attitudes and ethical concerns to writing support, reflective learning, and disciplinary norms. Studies have shown that there is no uniform way in which students adopt GenAI tools, differences appear across subject areas, course levels, and institutional policies (Chamorro-Mera, 2025; Hayes et al., 2025).

Rather than presenting GenAI as either a threat or a solution, this volume collects findings from varied teaching contexts. It offers empirical documentation and structured analysis of GenAI use, emphasizing academic practice over theoretical speculation. Readers will find that the chapters address both the everyday uses of AI tools in higher education and the long-term questions related to educational responsibility, student learning habits, and disciplinary change.

This volume is organized into four chapters that collectively examine the use of GenAI in higher education from interdisciplinary, empirical, and pedagogical perspectives.

Chapter 1 focuses on language education, specifically on German as a Foreign Language, by examining the role of GenAI in addressing German pluricentrism. It analyzes students' awareness of linguistic varieties and evaluates ChatGPT's capacity to recognize and generate diverse language forms, illustrating how AI tools can support multilingual competence, intercultural awareness, and applications relevant to international business and communication.

Chapter 2 presents the results of a survey conducted among students of STEM disciplines, such as logistics, production engineering, biomedical engineering, and social sciences, such as management and project management. In particular, this chapter shows the results of research relating to students' affective and motivational attitudes toward GenAI in the learning process and to the frequency, scope, and methods of using GenAI tools by students in the learning process, depending on their demographic and educational characteristics. In addition, the relationships between students' attitudes and their intention to continue using GenAI in the learning process and their willingness to recommend it to other students are presented. The results of research on students' perceptions of the impact of GenAI on learning effectiveness, productivity, creativity, and the development of educational and professional competences, while being aware of its limitations and potential risks, were also presented.

Chapter 3 expands on this analysis, focusing on critical thinking skills in the context of AI-assisted learning. Based on an experiment conducted with a group of students majoring in Project Management, this chapter answers two questions:

- Does the use of AI in a long-term teaching project strengthen or weaken students' reflective thinking?
- Does the condition of limited AI use allow for a beneficial balance between technological support and students' intellectual autonomy?

Chapter 4 addresses psychology education and explores students' attitudes, perceptions, and self-regulated learning practices in relation to GenAI. Using the Technology Acceptance Model, the Unified Theory of Acceptance and Use of Technology, and Self-Regulated Learning frameworks, the chapter analyzes ethical reflection, metacognitive awareness, and cognitive engagement as key dimensions of responsible and effective AI-supported learning.

Finally, the concluding chapter synthesizes findings across all empirical studies, providing an integrated overview of how GenAI is being incorporated into higher education. It identifies recurring patterns, disciplinary variations, and shared challenges while reflecting on ethical considerations, cognitive development, and ongoing pedagogical transformation. The chapter concludes by offering evidence-based recommendations for the responsible, reflective, and innovative use of GenAI in academic contexts.

1 Generative AI and German pluricentrism

ChatGPT and advancing language education

According to Statista, approximately 130 million people worldwide speak German as either a first or second language, around 15.4 million people are learning German as a foreign language (GFL), and about 7.5 million people belong to a German-speaking minority. In the USA, 45 million people claim German-speaking heritage, including 1.4 million native German speakers.[1]

For years, Poland has been at the top with 1.95 million learners according to data from 2020.[2] According to Statista, in 2022, more than 846,000 middle school students in Poland were studying GFL. In contrast, the number of elementary school pupils learning German was significantly lower, with nearly 77,000 students enrolled.[3] The results of the study "Deutsch als Fremdsprache in der Welt", presented in Berlin by the German Foreign Ministry in cooperation with Deutsche Welle (DW), the Goethe Institute, the German Academic Exchange Service (Deutscher Akademischer Austauschdienst – DAAD), and the Central Agency for Schools Abroad (Zentralstelle für das Auslandsschulwesen – ZfA) have proved that this number has decreased by 15% since 2015. Despite this declining trend, the German language remains one of the most popular foreign languages in the world.

In German-speaking countries, there are different variants of the language, as German is a pluricentric language. A pluricentric language has

DOI: 10.1201/9781003795926-1

at least two national varieties (Skubis, 2016a, 2020). Ammon (1995) states that every language can be considered pluricentric if it has several standard variants that are used in different countries, although they do not necessarily need to have the status of an official language.

German is the only national official language in Germany and Austria, whereas in Switzerland it functions alongside French, Italian, and Romansh. On the one hand, there is standard grammar, orthography, and vocabulary, but on the other hand, there are linguistic differences depending on the region in which it is used (Russ, 1994).

Duden (2011) defines the standard variety as "a generally binding language form that stands above dialects, local colloquial languages, and group languages, and can be used in both spoken and written forms". The standard is represented by individuals with established cultural roles within a society.

Ammon (1995) identifies three full centers and four semi-centers of the German language. The full centers are Germany, Austria, and the German-speaking part of Switzerland, each having a linguistic code (also called the linguistic codex or simply codex): the linguistic code is the norm-setting body of a standard variety, usually the easiest to identify, easier than model texts, the corrective behavior of norm authorities, or the judgments of language experts (Retti, 1999).

For each full center of German, the following codes exist (Ammon, 1995):

- The 12-volume Duden series for Germany;
- Österreichisches Wörterbuch für Österreich;
- Unser Wortschatz: Schweizer Wörterbuch der deutschen Sprache für die deutschsprachige Schweiz.

In contrast to full centers, semi-centers do not have codices. In this paper, we deal with full centers, which can be also called national norms or national varieties. The semi-centers of the German language include Luxembourg (where German is a national official language alongside French and Luxembourgish), Liechtenstein (where German is the only national official language), South Tyrol (where German is a regional official language in the province of Bolzano-South Tyrol alongside Italian and, in some areas, Ladin), and the German-speaking community in eastern Belgium (where German is a regional official language in the area of the German-speaking community) (Ammon et al., 2004).

The full centers determine the varieties of the German language, meaning that German has three varieties:

- German variety;
- Austrian variety;
- Swiss variety.

It should also be noted that the spoken standard differs from the written standard in all full- and semi-centers.

National and regional variants play an important role in the process of learning a foreign language. Students should be sensitized to the different variants because, as users of the language, they will often have to deal with various varieties. If they only acquire one variety, they will likely experience a shock abroad. This situation is also illustrated by the words of Ehnert et al. (2000):

> Somewhere in the world they are taught, they learn a German that does not exist. When they come to Austria, Germany, or Switzerland, depending on where they land, they believe they have arrived in a country where the German they thought they knew is not spoken.

The above-mentioned quote reflects the learner's encounter with reality. Skubis (2020, 2022a) emphasizes that the German language should be understood not only as the standard language in foreign language teaching but also as a language with all its national and regional variants. Therefore, teachers should prepare their students for real communication in the real world.

This chapter investigates the role of pluricentrism in DaF education and highlights the need for increased focus on national varieties within language instruction. Through an empirical study comparing the knowledge of German language students and the artificial intelligence (AI) model GPT-5 in recognizing and identifying German national varieties, this research aims to showcase the existing knowledge gap and propose ways to enrich language education. By doing so, the study highlights the importance of exposing students to the full spectrum of German linguistic diversity to foster better comprehension and adaptability in authentic language environments.

Moreover, in the field of management, effective multilingual communication is a key factor in global business success. AI-driven tools such as GPT-5 can be applied to international management, assisting in overcoming language barriers, optimizing translation accuracy in corporate settings, and facilitating intercultural communication. Businesses operating across multiple linguistic regions must ensure consistency in messaging and terminology, which AI can support by providing real-time, region-specific language adaptation.

1.1 CHATGPT AND ITS CHARACTERISTICS

Recent advancements in AI, particularly in natural language processing (NLP), have reshaped human-computer interaction (Botha & Pieterse, 2020; Clayton, 2023; Wołk et al., 2021, 2022). ChatGPT, developed by OpenAI, is a notable example of these advancements, representing a significant step forward in conversational AI. Built on the Generative Pre-trained Transformer (GPT) architecture, ChatGPT uses deep learning models that understand and generate human-like text responses based on user input. OpenAI's training approach combines unsupervised pre-training with supervised fine-tuning, optimizing the model for coherence and relevance in output (Radford & Narasimhan, 2018; Radford et al., 2019; Roumeliotis & Tselikas, 2023). This has led to broad applications in sectors ranging from customer service automation to healthcare (Brynjolfsson et al., 2023; Guo et al., 2023).

OpenAI's best practices for prompt engineering, the process of crafting specific inputs to guide ChatGPT's responses, include using clear instructions, providing examples, and specifying desired formats (Skubis & Kołodziejczyk, 2024; White et al., 2023). Despite its capabilities, ChatGPT also faces challenges, such as mathematical errors, common-sense reasoning issues, and hallucinations – instances where the model generates unsubstantiated content (Bang et al., 2023). These weaknesses highlight the need for ongoing evaluation frameworks and improvements.

From a disciplinary perspective, linguistic applications of AI can be regarded as comparatively low risk for users when contrasted with AI systems deployed in fields such as robotics, autonomous vehicles, or electronics, where software failures may directly endanger human life and health. In language-related AI, typical errors, such as grammatical inaccuracies, imperfect translations, or pragmatic mismatches, remain correctable by human users and do not usually lead to irreversible physical harm. Consequently, linguistics emerges as a relatively safe domain for empirical AI research, provided that human oversight, data protection, and ethical standards are maintained (Skubis, 2020).

Ethical concerns around ChatGPT's deployment are extensive, particularly regarding safety, responsibility, and potential misuse in sectors like academia, where it could enable plagiarism (Skubis, 2021, 2024a; Zhou et al., 2022). In terms of bias, ChatGPT's training data can inadvertently encode social and linguistic biases, leading to potential unfairness and underrepresentation for specific groups (Zhuo et al., 2023).

To mitigate these concerns, Zhuo et al. (2023) emphasize the need for diverse training data and regular updates. Key ethical categories – bias, robustness, reliability, and toxicity –form the basis for assessing generative AI models like ChatGPT. For instance, robustness requires models to maintain performance under varied inputs, while reliability ensures that the outputs are accurate and current. Transparency, especially in informing users when they are interacting with AI, is also a priority under the EU's AI Act (The European Union, (2024), Artificial Intelligence Act (AI Act). Hacker et al., 2023; Skubis, 2024b).

Regulatory frameworks like the AI Act and GDPR, along with proposals from scholars like The AI Act, categorize general-purpose AI models like ChatGPT as limited-risk AI systems but mandate transparency, especially when users engage with these systems in ways that could lead to misinterpretation or undue influence. These regulatory recommendations also include clarifying roles between AI developers, deployers, and users to ensure shared accountability across the AI lifecycle. In terms of teaching and learning, ChatGPT can be a useful source of information, and in this chapter, we are going to check its ability to deal with German national varieties which are a big obstacle for language learners.

1.2 GERMAN LANGUAGE IN THE CONTEXT OF DAF LESSONS

The consideration of national and other (supra-regional and dialectal) variants is an important aspect of teaching. Language plays a central role in individual, regional, and national identification processes, i.e. language is not just a means of communication, its spectrum is much broader. This is also an important argument in favor of GFL (German as a Foreign Language – DaF in German) lessons but also in GSL (German as a Second Language – DaZ in German).

Pluricentrism is an important aspect of foreign language teaching, but it is still very much neglected and the teaching of German varieties is limited to a few well-known words from the Austrian variety, such as *Paradeiser (A) – Tomaten (D); Erdäpfel (A) – Kartoffeln (D); Obers (A) – Sahne (D); Jänner – Januar; Feber (A) – Februar (D); heuer (A) – dieses Jahr (D); Trafik (A) – Kiosk (D)* (Skubis, 2016b). Standard Swiss German is usually omitted. The concept of German pluricentrism in GFL lessons has been investigated by researchers such as de Cilia (2006), Ransmayr (2006), Hägi (2007), Radzik (2012, 2013), Jarząbek (2013), Skubis (2020), and Utri (2013). The study shows that some approaches to integrating German diversity into GFL lessons and textbooks point to national differences. Nevertheless, the number of these approaches is still insufficient (Skubis, 2022a).

It is important to harness learners' awareness of varieties at a relatively early stage. Hägi (2007) emphasizes the role of national variants, especially in receptive skills, which are useful in examinations such as the Austrian German Language Diploma or the Zertifikat Deutsch. According to Hägi (2007), this is linked to the development of perceptual tolerance. The authors of Profile Deutsch (in Hägi, 2007) are also of the opinion that tolerance and understanding of varieties play a central role in GFL lessons and that more attention should be paid to them.

Pusswald (2007) analyzed textbooks from a pluricentric perspective. She interviewed 105 teachers of GFL from the USA, Ireland, and the UK and came to a critical conclusion. Although many current GFL textbooks appear pluricentric at first glance, as they refer to the 'German-speaking countries' and include the DACHL map on the inside cover, Germany dominates the content. Switzerland and Austria are often only mentioned in specific, tourist-oriented, or clichéd lessons. According to Pusswald (ibid.), this superficial and inadequate presentation of the linguistic situation in the DACHL region contributes to the consolidation of a monocentric image.

Interestingly, Pusswald (ibid.) found that basic level textbooks contain more and more systematic vocabulary variants than intermediate level textbooks. Nevertheless, the textbooks are written from the perspective of the dominant (West German) variety. The scientist summarizes that teaching and learning materials for GFL, apart from exceptions such as 'Dimensions' and 'Memo', pay too little attention to the pluricentricity of German, especially in the area of standard phonological variation. Similar to Ransmayr and Hägi, Pusswald also notes that there is often a mixture of non-standard and standard varieties and variants (Shafer, 2018).

Radzik (2012, 2013) emphasizes the importance of national variants in GFL lessons in her works. The researcher believes that students should learn about both regional dialects and national varieties in class. Teaching this competence should be a significant factor because learners, as the future teachers and translators or interpreters, should become aware of the numerous differences between German centers in order to avoid mistakes and understand the intentions of native speakers of centers outside Germany (Skubis, 2020:93).

Jarząbek (2013) claims that there is not enough information about the Austrian and Swiss language varieties in books for GFL teaching and she assumes that the reason for this is the lack of Austrian and Swiss native speakers who could contribute to the preparation of such teaching materials in Poland. It is important to note that native speakers and learners often have similar challenges in perceiving varieties.

Utri (2013, 2014) emphasizes that representatives of different varieties should work together to create valuable and information-rich textbooks.

This would also increase the prestige and success of the German language compared to other languages. The researcher highlights that teachers should first and foremost also be trained to teach the varieties, as they have usually only acquired the German variety in Germany in their academic career and training this is why they also have difficulties in teaching German varieties.

Skubis (2022b) suggests the cooperation of teachers who specialize in certain varieties – i.e. co-teaching. Co-teaching can be defined as follows: "the collaboration of two or more people who share responsibility for the whole teaching process: planning, instruction, evaluation and general classroom management" (Villa, Thousand and Nevin in Skubis, 2022b).

1.3 METHODOLOGY

This study aimed to verify the proficiency of GPT-5, an advanced language model developed by OpenAI, and that of German language students in recognizing and understanding the pluricentric nature of the German language and its national varieties. The methodology involved parallel analyses of GPT's responses and those of the students to a set of linguistic tasks designed to assess their knowledge of German national varieties – specifically, Germanisms (D), Austricisms (A), and Helvetisms (CH).

Data collection focused on the following:

- Exposure to German-speaking regions
- Recognition of Germanisms (D), Austricisms (A), and Helvetisms (CH)
- Ability to generate examples of national varieties
- Awareness of linguistic structures affected by pluricentrism

1.4 PARTICIPANTS

For the student analysis, 62 students enrolled in Applied Linguistics (German and English) and German Philology programs at a university in Poland participated in the study. These students had intermediate to advanced proficiency in GFL but limited exposure to the linguistic nuances of Austria and Switzerland. Many had not traveled to German-speaking countries, which may have influenced their familiarity with the national varieties.

For the GPT analysis, we used GPT-5, which has been trained on a diverse range of internet text up to its knowledge cutoff in September 2021. This model is capable of understanding and generating text in multiple languages, including German and its regional variations. The questionnaire consisted of six questions (Appendix 1) and the topic was German national varieties.

1.5 PROCEDURE

For the students, the questionnaire was administered during a scheduled class session. Participation was voluntary, and the survey was conducted anonymously to ensure privacy and encourage honest responses. Students were given clear instructions for each task and were asked to complete the questionnaire individually without external assistance.

In the identification task, students wrote the appropriate abbreviation (D, A, CH) next to each word based on their knowledge or intuition. In the own examples task, they attempted to provide words that are characteristic of each national variety, filling them into the respective columns for Germany, Austria, and Switzerland. Finally, they selected what they believed to be the correct answer in the multiple-choice question.

For the GPT analysis, the same questionnaire was presented to GPT-5 through a series of prompts that mirrored the instructions given to the students. The interaction was conducted in English to align with the model's primary language of interaction, but the German words and phrases were used as necessary. GPT was asked to identify the national varieties for each word, provide its own examples of words differing among the varieties, and answer the multiple-choice question.

1.6 SURVEY RESULTS AMONG STUDENTS

The first question was designed to give the overview of the students' experience of different countries. This was a general question, which was meant to check which German-speaking countries they had been to so far. Spending time in German-speaking countries has a positive influence on the acquisition of the foreign language, which is why the answers to this question were very important, as they influence the results of the next questions.

If someone has already been to Austria or Switzerland, then they have certainly noticed that there are many differences between the German varieties. However, the results associated with this question were not satisfactory. Out of 62 students, 20 people had never been to a German-speaking country and only 38 had visited Germany. Twenty-four people have been to Austria and only eight to Switzerland. Two students mentioned Liechtenstein and one mentioned Belgium.

The following pie chart shows the students' reactions to the first question (Figure 1.1):

The answers to this question have provided us with the information that the other questions cannot be answered by most students. However, another possibility emerges here – if they have not been to any of those countries, they could perhaps have been taught some examples of the German varieties in foreign language classes. However, the number of students who have been abroad to practice and improve their foreign language skills is disappointing. Their answers indicate that they only learn the language in Poland and they have not had the opportunity to try out their knowledge in real life and speak with native speakers. All their knowledge is based on GFL books and foreign language teachers. However, nowadays, learners have many ways to read and listen to authentic texts such as television and YouTube.

In the answer to the second question, students should write whether they have lived in German-speaking countries, for how long and where. Two people have lived in Germany as children – one student for 6.5 years and the other for 7 years. The third student has worked in Germany twice, first for 6 months, then for a year and now she has been living in Germany again for 1.5 years.

In the third question, the students were asked to note the national varieties they knew. Twenty-seven students gave no answer, seventeen named the German variety, fifteen the Austrian variety, and twelve the Swiss variety.

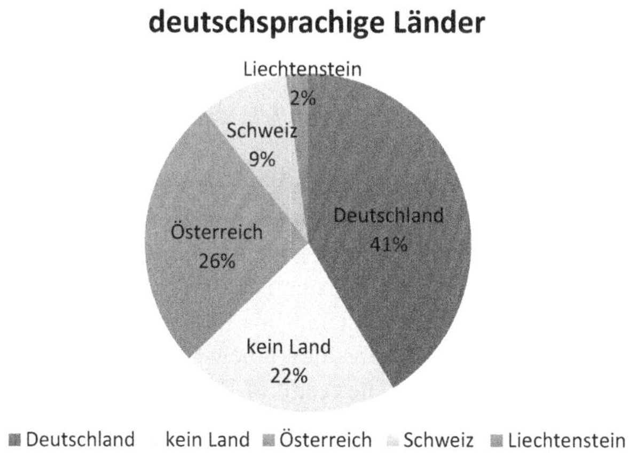

FIGURE 1.1 Pie chart with students' visited destinations

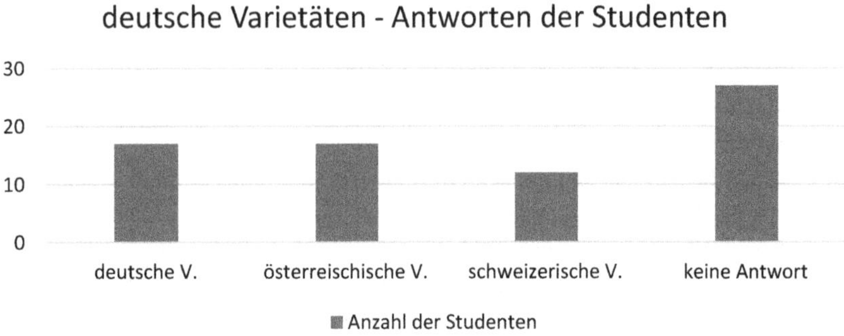

FIGURE 1.2 Bar chart with students' answers about their knowledge of German national varieties

Some of them confused variety with dialect and wrote Bavarian or Saxon and some did not give any examples but mentioned that they know that different dialects are used in different regions in Germany. The answers to this question confirm that the majority of students have no idea about the existence of the different varieties of the German language. They learn at school or at the university the German variety used in Germany and cannot name the other ones. Most of them do not know the concept of variety, and if they already have a limited knowledge, they cannot distinguish the term 'variety' from a 'dialect'.

The following bar chart shows the information provided by the students (Figure 1.2):

The fourth task of the survey was as follows: Write whether the given words are Austriacisms (A), Helvetisms (CH), or Germanisms (D). There were some examples as pairs of words in the left column – two words that have the same meaning but are used in other centers, e.g. *das Obers, die Sahne, das Billet, die Fahrkarte*. In the right-hand column there were stand-alone examples, e.g. *der Erdapfel, die Marille, der Jänner, die Treppe*.

The students achieved better results with the word pairs. After the survey, they also admitted that they had compared these words and thus determined which word belonged to which variety. They first labeled the words that they knew that are Germanisms (D) and afterward assigned the other examples to either Austriacisms (A) or Helvetisms (CH). And here they also found a solution – they labeled the words they had never seen or heard as Helvetisms. The result of this way of thinking is shown below – next to each word in brackets is the correct answer and the number of students (out of a total of 62 students) who correctly assigned these words:

a) Die Fleischbrühe – (D) – 14/62
b) Der Kren – (A) – 9/62
c) Das Obers – (A) – 18/62
d) Die Sahne – (D) – 31/62
e) Das Portmonee/Portemonnaie – (CH) – 10/62
f) Der Geldbeutel – (D) – 20/62
g) Die Matura – (A, CH) – 29/62
h) Das Abitur – (D) – 38/62
i) Das Billet – (CH) – 8/62
j) Die Fahrkarte – (DE) – 32/62
k) der Erdapfel – (A) – 15/62
l) die Marille – (A) – 11/62
m) der Tumbler – (CH) – 9/62
n) das Häuserl – (A) – 10/62
o) das Salär – (CH) – 10/62
p) die Apfelsine (D) – 8/62
q) der Bub – (A, CH) – 12/62
r) der Nidel – (CH) 7/62
s) die Treppe – (D) – 31/62
t) der Jänner – (A) – 14/62

There were two correct answers for *Bub* and *Matura*, so this answer was counted as correct if someone only gave one correct answer. In general, it can be observed that the students' knowledge of the national varieties of German is low. The following words, which come from the German variety in Germany, received the highest scores: *Sahne, Abitur, Fahrkarte*, and *Treppe. Matura* also achieved a fairly good score, as the students compared the word *Matura* with the word *Abitur* and then concluded that they always used the word *Abitur,* so the word *Matura* must belong to a different variety. Many students simply did not give an answer.

The fifth task was the most difficult for all students. They had to fill in a table with their own examples. There were three columns: Germany, Austria, and Switzerland. Only six students took part in this challenge. It is much easier when the examples are given than when they have to come up with something themselves. The examples they mentioned for Germany were: *Hallo, Fahrrad, Krankenhaus, Brötchen, Straßenbahn, Quark, Blumenkohl*; for Austria: *Grüß Gott, Tram, Semmel, Topfen, Karfiol;* for Switzerland: *Grüezi, Vélo, Spital.*

It seems to be more difficult to find own variants instead of assigning parts of word pairs to the countries of origin. This could be a general phenomenon where it is more difficult to generate creative examples. Furthermore, it is relevant to consider that even native speakers might have difficulties with this task. This shows that the identification and selection of linguistic variants can be a challenging task, even for people who speak the language fluently.

The last question was a multiple-choice question. Students were asked to tick one correct answer out of four given and the question was as follows:

The differences between German varieties concern:

a. Vocabulary and grammar
b. Vocabulary, orthography, and phonetics
c. Vocabulary and pragmatics
d. All answers are correct

Fourteen students chose point B in this task: Vocabulary, spelling, and phonetics, and twenty students chose point D: all answers are correct. Six students marked answer C: vocabulary and pragmatics. Surprisingly, 22 of them did not mark any answer.

The correct answer is point D – all answers are correct. The differences between German varieties concern vocabulary, grammar, spelling, phonetics, and also pragmatics. They are present at all these levels of the language. However, their number is most visible in the area of vocabulary (Skubis, 2016b, 2017). It can be concluded that students are not sure which levels of the language are influenced by a national variety.

This survey shows that the students have little knowledge about German varieties. When completing these questions, they used their intuition and realized that they would have difficulties with the translation into Polish. The examples in this survey come from everyday language and even these terms have already caused problems for learners, but as Skubis (2020) points out, the degree of difficulty only increases with specialized translations because students are not prepared to work with documents from different German centers.

1.7 CHATGPT AND GERMAN NATIONAL VARIETIES

In this study, GPT-5 was tasked with identifying the national varieties of German words and providing explanations where necessary. The model's responses were analyzed to assess its understanding of the pluricentric nature of the German language, particularly in comparison to human learners – students of GFL.

GPT-5 demonstrated a high level of accuracy in identifying whether words were Germanisms (D), Austricisms (A), Helvetisms (CH), or belonged to multiple varieties. For instance, it correctly identified *die Fleischbrühe* as a Germanism (D), *der Kren* as an Austricism (A), and *das Billet* as a Helvetism (CH). When words were used in more than one national variety, such as *die Matura,* GPT accurately noted that it is used in both Austria and Switzerland (A, CH). Moreover, GPT provided nuanced explanations for its classifications. For example, regarding *Portmonee/Portemonnaie*, GPT classified it as both D and CH, acknowledging its use in Germany and Switzerland.

It explained that while dictionaries often list this term as Swiss, it is also commonly used in Germany, especially in certain regions; however, marking this option as Germanism in terms of national varieties is not the appropriate choice. However, GPT noted that in Austria, other terms like *Brieftasche* or *Geldtasche* are more prevalent. This reflects a sophisticated understanding of regional language use that extends beyond national borders into dialectal variations.

Below are the answers given by ChatGPT-5:

a. die Fleischbrühe – D
b. der Kren – A
c. das Obers – A
d. die Sahne – D
e. das Portmonee/Portemonnaie – D, CH
f. der Geldbeutel – D
g. die Matura – A, CH
h. das Abitur – D
i. das Billet – CH
j. die Fahrkarte – D
k. der Erdapfel – A
l. die Marille – A
m. der Tumbler – CH
n. das Häuserl – A
o. das Salär – CH
p. die Apfelsine – D
q. der Bub – A, CH
r. der Nidel – CH
s. die Treppe – D
t. der Jänner – A

When asked to provide its own examples of words unique to each national variety, GPT generated the following examples:

1. Brötchen (D) – Semmel (A) – Brötli (CH)
2. Kartoffel (D) – Erdapfel (A) – Härdöpfel (CH)
3. Tomate (D) – Paradeiser (A) – Tomate (CH)
4. Schlagsahne (D) – Schlagobers (A) – Schlagrahm (CH)
5. Aprikose (D) – Marille (A) – Aprikose (CH)
6. Pflaume (D) – Zwetschke (A) – Zwetschge (CH)
7. Mais (D) – Kukuruz (A) – Mais (CH)
8. Krapfen (D) – Faschingskrapfen (A) – Berliner (CH)
9. Anzug (D) – Gewand (A) – Anzug (CH)
10. Schornstein (D) – Rauchfang (A) – Kamin (CH)
11. Müll (D) – Mist (A) – Abfall (CH)

12. Gurke (D) – Gurkerl (A) – Guggumere (CH)
13. Tüte (D) – Sackerl (A) – Säckli (CH)
14. Sahne (D) – Obers (A) – Rahm (CH)

In response to the multiple-choice question regarding the linguistic aspects affected by German national varieties, GPT-5 correctly selected option d) "all the answers are correct" admitting that differences encompass vocabulary, grammar, orthography, phonetics, and pragmatics. This indicates a comprehensive understanding of the multifaceted nature of linguistic variation within pluricentric languages.

GPT's adeptness at handling the pluricentric aspects of the German language suggests significant potential for applications in language education and linguistic research:

1. Educational tool:
   GPT can serve as a valuable resource for learners seeking to understand the regional differences within the German language. Its ability to provide explanations and examples can enhance comprehension of national varieties.
2. Curriculum development:
   The model's knowledge can inform the creation of educational materials that accurately represent the linguistic diversity of German, aiding in developing more inclusive curricula.
3. Language processing applications:
   GPT's proficiency indicates that AI language models can effectively handle pluricentric languages, which is beneficial for translation services, localization, and NLP tasks that require sensitivity to regional variations.

   There are also some limitations, because as an AI language model, GPT does not possess personal experiences or cultural immersion, which can influence language understanding. Its knowledge is based solely on the data it was trained on.

1.8 CHATGPT VS NATIONAL VARIETIES AND LANGUAGE LEARNING

The initial survey question aimed to gauge students' exposure to German-speaking countries, a factor influencing their familiarity with German language varieties. Out of 62 students, 20 had never visited any German-speaking country, and most of those who had visited had only been to Germany. This limited exposure likely contributed to their lack of awareness regarding Austrian and Swiss linguistic nuances. The lack of international exposure underscores the importance of classroom-based resources for teaching pluricentric language knowledge.

In contrast, GPT does not rely on physical immersion but instead on its vast training data, allowing it to recognize national varieties without personal experience. Students can thus use GPT to bridge gaps in exposure, offering a way to explore language variations digitally.

In the third question, students were asked to list the German national varieties they were aware of. Most students could name only the German variety (17 students), with much smaller numbers recognizing the Austrian (15) and Swiss (12) varieties. Additionally, students often confused "variety" with "dialect", indicating conceptual misunderstandings. This shows a lack of formal instruction on the distinctions between language varieties and dialects, suggesting a need for more structured inclusion of these concepts in the curriculum.

GPT, in contrast, accurately distinguishes varieties and dialects due to its exposure to structured linguistic information. This capability makes GPT a useful tool for clarifying these concepts for students and enhancing their understanding of the German language's pluricentric nature.

In the identification task, students had to assign given words to specific varieties (Germanisms, Austricisms, Helvetisms). The data reveal that students tended to guess, particularly for unfamiliar terms, and generally performed better with word pairs than with single terms. For example, only 31 students correctly identified *die Sahne* as a Germanism (D). The difficulty students faced here illustrates the complexity of national variations, even in everyday vocabulary, highlighting the need for exposure to authentic language use across German-speaking regions.

GPT's performance was markedly higher, accurately identifying each word's origin and providing explanations based on regional usage. Students could benefit from using GPT to confirm their guesses and receive additional context for challenging terms, enhancing their knowledge of lexical variety.

This task to provide own examples required students to generate their examples of words specific to German, Austrian, and Swiss varieties. Only six students attempted this, demonstrating the difficulty of recalling region-specific vocabulary. This low participation rate indicates a lack of familiarity and confidence, reinforcing the need for more targeted practice in generating examples independently.

GPT, conversely, generated multiple accurate examples for each variety, reflecting its robust handling of lexical diversity. Students can use GPT to explore a range of examples they might not otherwise encounter, improving their ability to recognize and use these variety-specific lexical items appropriately in different linguistic and cultural contexts, as well as strengthening their overall communicative competence in pluricentric German.

The final multiple-choice question assessed students' understanding of the different linguistic levels affected by German national varieties. The correct answer (all levels: vocabulary, grammar, orthography, phonetics, and pragmatics) was chosen by only 20 students, with many others leaving the question unanswered. The results suggest that students lack comprehensive knowledge of how national variations affect different language structures, underscoring a gap in holistic language education.

GPT-5 selected the correct answer, demonstrating an understanding of the breadth of linguistic variation. By using GPT, students can gain insights into these structural differences and better appreciate the nuances of pluricentric languages.

This study highlights that GPT, a large language model developed by OpenAI, can be an effective support tool for students learning German varieties. Through its extensive training on diverse language data, GPT can identify, distinguish, and provide context for words and phrases unique to different German-speaking regions. This capacity makes it a particularly useful resource for students looking to improve their understanding of regional linguistic nuances in the absence of direct exposure or native speakers. By incorporating GPT as a supplementary tool in DaF instruction, students can access practical examples of German national varieties and better prepare for real-world language use.

1.9 RESULTS AND DISCUSSION

1. Student awareness vs. GPT performance: students showed limited recognition of German pluricentric variations, with only 15 recognizing Austrian German and 12 recognizing Swiss German. Many confused varieties with dialects, indicating a conceptual gap in their linguistic education. In contrast, GPT correctly classified 96% of national varieties and provided nuanced explanations, highlighting its potential as a supplementary educational tool.
2. Challenges in lexical and grammatical distinctions: students performed better in tasks involving word pairs but struggled with individual lexical items. This suggests that context aids in distinguishing varieties but is insufficient for developing a comprehensive understanding. GPT, by comparison, consistently identified distinctions, demonstrating how AI can support lexical exposure. This challenge becomes even more consequential in specialized communication, where the correct selection of nationally appropriate equivalents

matters. Research on German pluricentrism stresses that lexical differentiation is particularly extensive and that national-terminology mismatches may cause misinterpretation or "fatal" translation consequences in domains such as law and administration, where terms cannot be substituted freely and must match the national legal and institutional context (Skubis, 2016b).

3. Broader implications for pluricentric language education and management: the findings suggest that AI tools like GPT can be integrated into curricula for pluricentric languages beyond German. Similar challenges exist in English, Spanish, and Arabic, where learners often acquire one dominant variety but struggle with others. AI models can help bridge this gap by providing diverse linguistic exposure, real-time feedback, and personalized learning.

   In addition to language education, these findings have strong implications for global business operations and international management. Multinational corporations often face difficulties when adapting brand communication, contracts, and customer service across different linguistic regions. AI-assisted language adaptation can improve corporate efficiency, reducing misunderstandings in multilingual interactions and ensuring compliance with regional linguistic standards. AI tools can further support business negotiations and leadership communication by providing accurate, real-time translations that reflect national varieties, enhancing cultural sensitivity in global markets.

1.10 CONCLUSIONS

Pluricentrism is a very important aspect of foreign language learning. There are numerous differences at different levels of the language, but the largest number is determined by lexical differences. GPT-5's performance indicates that it handles everyday language usage varieties effectively, making it a valuable support tool in language learning. Students can use GPT to explore and understand language variations, especially in contexts where access to native speakers or regional materials is limited. However, they should do so with limited trust in its outputs, verifying with dictionaries and authoritative resources to ensure accuracy.

This cautious approach reflects broader findings from linguistic AI research, which emphasize that although machine learning and NLP offer substantial support for language learning, translation, and corpus-based analysis, human control remains indispensable. The main risks associated with linguistic AI concern data security, potential bias in training data, and the quality of generated content, rather than direct threats to users' safety. Therefore, maintaining the guiding and supervisory role of the human user is essential for ensuring trust and responsible use of generative AI in language education (Skubis, 2020).

The results of this survey among students of Applied Linguistics (German and English) and German Philology in Poland demonstrate some interesting findings. The survey among students showed that they have little knowledge of the differences between the three German national varieties. Many of them have also not all traveled to German-speaking countries, so they have not had the opportunity to practice and deepen what they have learnt at school. This may explain the limited exposure to different German varieties. Above all, they have learnt nothing about German varieties and often do not know the term '(national) variety' or confuse it with the term 'dialect'.

The task of providing their own examples of German varieties was seen as particularly challenging. Only a small number of students took part in this task. This may indicate that finding examples of varieties can be a general problem, not only for learners of a foreign language but also in relation to native speakers.

The last question showed that many students had difficulty recognizing the variety of differences between German varieties. This was also confirmed in relation to the multiple-choice question, where some students had difficulty recognizing all relevant aspects of the differences between the varieties.

It needs to be underlined that more time should be devoted to German varieties during lessons and, above all, textbooks should be designed to provide knowledge about national varieties. It also seems essential to train teachers as they are often unfamiliar with the subject. Teachers should first master the knowledge of the varieties themselves in order to pass it on to the students later.

The consideration of German varieties not only in GFL lessons but also in GSL lessons affects all levels, i.e. teaching content, didactics and methodology, the design of textbooks and materials, performance assessment, examinations and tests, teacher training and further training (de Cilia, 2006). As we mentioned at the beginning, a differentiated and realistic approach to the varieties prevents unpleasant surprises abroad, so that one not only understands the basic language and the practiced dialogues but also finds one's way in a complex language environment that is authentic and goes beyond the reality of the book.

When it comes to GPT's responses, it demonstrates a good understanding of the pluricentric nature of the German language and its national varieties. The model accurately identifies regional lexical differences, provides nuanced explanations, and generates appropriate examples across different varieties. Its performance indicates that AI language models can effectively process and comprehend the complexities of pluricentric languages, offering valuable support for language learners and educators.

The analysis underlines the potential for integrating AI tools like GPT into language education to enhance learners' exposure to and understanding of linguistic diversity. Using AI tools like GPT as supplementary aids in language education could provide students with an expanded, nuanced view of language use across regions, albeit with the caution to verify AI outputs. By leveraging such technology, educators can supplement traditional teaching methods, providing students with richer, more comprehensive language experiences, while students can deepen their understanding of German varieties, bridge gaps in regional knowledge, and enhance their linguistic flexibility in pluricentric language contexts.

Future research should explore AI's role in other pluricentric languages, assessing how generative models can facilitate cross-linguistic understanding. Additionally, longitudinal studies examining AI-assisted learning over time could provide deeper understanding about its impact on linguistic competency. From a management perspective, further investigation is needed into the role of AI-based language adaptation in global corporate communication, leadership, and brand consistency. Understanding the business applications of pluricentric language processing will be critical for companies aiming to enhance their international presence. AI-based learning offers a promising avenue for enhancing language education, promoting adaptability, and fostering global communication skills in an increasingly interconnected world.

APPENDIX 1: DEUTSCHE NATIONALE VARIETÄTEN - FRAGEBOGEN

1. In welchen deutschsprachigen Ländern sind Sie gewesen?
2. Haben Sie in deutschsprachigen Ländern gewohnt? Falls ja, wie lange und wo?
3. Welche deutschen nationalen Varietäten kennen Sie?
4. Schreiben Sie, ob die gegebenen Wörter Austriazismen (A), Helvetismen (CH) oder Germanismen (D) sind.

a) die Fleischbrühe -
b) der Kren -

k) der Erdapfel -
l) die Marille -

c) das Obers -
d) die Sahne -
e) das Portmonee/Portemonnaie -
f) der Geldbeutel -
g) die Matura -
h) das Abitur -
i) das Billet -
j) die Fahrkarte -
m) der Tumbler -
n) das Häuserl
o) das Salär
p) die Apfelsine
q) der Bub
r) der Nidel
s) die Treppe
t) der Jänner

5. Geben Sie andere Beispiele, die die deutsche, österreichische und schweizerische Varietät betreffen.

DEUTSCHLAND	ÖSTERREICH	SCHWEIZ

6. Die Unterschiede zwischen deutschen Varietäten betreffen:
   a. Wortschatz und Grammatik
   b. Wortschatz, Orthographie, und Phonetik
   c. Wortschatz und Pragmatik
   d. Alle Antworten sind korekt

NOTES

1 Statista: https://de.statista.com/statistik/daten/studie/1119851/umfrage/deutschsprachige-menschen-weltweit/; Christina Iglhaut, 31.05.2025 - Deutschland.de: https://www.deutschland.de/pl/topic/wiedza/szesc-zabawnych-faktow-o-jezyku-niemieckim?utm_source=chatgpt.com.

2 Deutsche Welle: https://www.dw.com/pl/polacy-przodują-w-nauce-niemieckiego/a-53699376.

3 Statista: https://www.statista.com/statistics/1255847/poland-pupils-learning-german/.

2 Diversity of use and attitudes toward generative AI in academic teaching

Research on artificial intelligence (AI) in education has been going on for over 35 years. The first publications in this field appeared with the launch of *The International Journal of Artificial Intelligence in Education*, followed by the International AI in Education Society. Although the journal and association generated excitement, enthusiasm for AI did not last long. It was not until 20 years later, around 2010, that interest in AI was rekindled, driven in part by advances in data mining, the Internet of Things, smart homes, and chatbots, and in education, by intelligent teaching systems and adaptive learning platforms. However, it should be emphasized that it was only the latest advances in generative artificial intelligence (GenAI) that caused a big surprise, among other things, in connection with the release of OpenAI's ChatGPT in November 2022. (Farrelly & Baker, 2023; Hidayat-ur-Rehman & Ibrahim, 2024; Huang et al., 2023; Muthukrishnan et al., 2020; Williamson & Eynon, 2020; Zawacki-Richter et al., 2019;).

The latest GenAI technologies are free and publicly available, so their use by students is becoming widespread. This is significantly changing academic education, as GenAI is becoming an integral part of the learning and teaching process, opening up new opportunities for students, and offering them many benefits (Farrelly & Baker, 2023; Hidayat-ur-Rehman & Ibrahim,

DOI: 10.1201/9781003795926-2

2024). However, it should be emphasized that GenAI technologies also pose many problems that determine research challenges. These include, among others:

1. Student attitudes toward GenAI – in particular, it is challenging to examine the relationship between students' affective and motivational attitudes toward GenAI in the learning process, depending on their demographic and educational characteristics;
2. Frequency and methods of GenAI use by students – a particular challenge is to examine the frequency, scope, and methods of GenAI use by students in the learning process, depending on their demographic and educational characteristics;
3. Intentions to continue using GenAI and willingness to recommend it – in particular, it is challenging to examine the relationship between students' attitudes and their intention to continue using GenAI in the learning process and their willingness to recommend it to other students as a useful academic tool;
4. Perceived benefits and limitations of using GenAI – a particular research challenge is to capture how students perceive the impact of GenAI on learning effectiveness, productivity, creativity, and the development of educational and professional competencies, while being aware of its limitations and potential risks.

2.1 RESEARCH METHODOLOGY

2.1.1 Research objective and hypotheses

This chapter presents the results of research and considerations whose main purpose was to contribute to answering the research challenges posed. To achieve this goal, four research hypotheses were formulated, relating to specific challenges, as shown in Table 2.1.

2.1.2 Theoretical basis of the research

The research was based on the Affective–Behavioral–Cognitive (ABC) model and the Unified Theory of Acceptance and Use of Technology (UTAUT) and Extended Unified Theory of Acceptance and Use of Technology (UTAUT2).

TABLE 2.1 Link between research challenges and specific objectives and research hypotheses

RESEARCH CHALLENGE	*RESEARCH HYPOTHESIS*
1. Students' attitudes toward GenAI	1. Students' affective and motivational attitudes toward GenAI are determined by their demographic and educational characteristics.
2. Frequency and methods of GenAI use by students	2. Students differ in the frequency and methods of using GenAI, depending on their demographic and educational characteristics.
3. Intentions to continue using GenAI and recommend it to others	3. Attitudes toward GenAI are related to the intention to continue using it and recommending it to other students.
4. Perceived benefits, competencies, and limitations of GenAI	4. Students perceive GenAI as a tool that supports learning effectiveness and competence development, while being aware of its limitations.

Own study.

The foundation for researching students' attitudes toward GenAI was the ABC model, which derives from classical concepts of social psychology. Within this framework, D. Katz pointed to the functional nature of attitudes, emphasizing the importance of the affective and motivational components in regulating individual behavior (Katz, 1960). Subsequently, M. Fishbein developed a multi-component approach to attitudes, describing in detail their structure and methods of measuring cognitive, affective, and behavioral components (Fishbein, 1967). Shortly thereafter, M. Rokeach defined attitude as a relatively stable organization of beliefs, emotions, and tendencies to act, integrating earlier concepts and giving them a theoretical framework (Rokeach, 1968). Subsequently, I. Ajzen precisely described the mechanisms of attitude functioning and their relationship to intentions and behaviors, which makes it possible to predict an individual's actions based on attitudes (Ajzen, 2001). Together, the work of these authors created the theoretical basis for the ABC model. Currently, this model is widely used in research on attitudes toward technology, innovation, and social change, as it allows for the simultaneous capture of users' emotional reactions, beliefs, and behaviors. It is also worth noting that it has repeatedly served as the basis for research on student attitudes, for example, research on the relationship between ABC components in the context of attitudes toward educational technologies (Svenningsson et al., 2022), studies of students directly related to cognitive-affective attitudes and behaviors toward ChatGPT (Acosta-Enríquez et al., 2024a; 2024b), and studies analyzing cognitive and affective components separately in students (Wang et al., 2023).

Adopting the ABC model as the basis for this study, it was assumed that students' attitudes toward GenAI consist of three interrelated components:

- Affective, which refers to students' emotional responses related to the use of GenAI tools in the learning process (it includes positive responses such as enthusiasm, pleasure, inspiration, interest, and satisfaction, as well as a general emotional attitude toward the inclusion of GenAI in academic teaching);
- Behavioral, which refers to students' declared or actual actions, tendencies to act, and behavioral intentions toward GenAI and concerns the frequency and specific ways in which students use GenAI, both in individual learning processes and in teamwork;
- Cognitive, which refers to students' beliefs and assessments of GenAI, including its usefulness, effectiveness, limitations, and consequences of its use in learning processes, competence development, productivity, creativity, and future professional functioning.

The ABC model was chosen for this study because of its characteristics, which allow for a comprehensive description of students' attitudes toward GenAI, taking into account their educational diversity (technical and social fields of study, at the Bachelor's and Master's levels) as well as demographic diversity (age and gender). However, it should be noted that ABC does not provide detailed explanatory mechanisms – it does not answer the question of how these attitudes translate into intentions to continue using the technology and into actual user behavior. This gap is filled by the Unified Theory of Acceptance and Use of Technology (UTAUT and UTAUT2).

UTAUT was proposed by V. Venkatesh, M. G. Morris, G. B. Davis, and F.D. Davis (Venkatesh et al., 2003), integrating eight previous theories to explain the determinants of technology use intentions and actual use. These include the following:

- Performance expectancy, which in this study refers to the degree to which students believe that using GenAI will improve learning outcomes, such as better understanding of content, higher academic performance, time savings, and the development of educational and professional competencies;
- Effort expectancy, which refers to the extent to which students perceive the use of GenAI as easy, intuitive, and not requiring excessive cognitive effort;
- Social influence, which refers to the extent to which students perceive that people who are important to them (from the academic community) expect or approve of the use of GenAI;

- Facilitating conditions, which refer to students' belief that they have the appropriate resources, competencies, and knowledge to use GenAI effectively and safely.

UTAUT constructs indicate that people are more likely to adopt technology if they believe it will improve their performance, it is easy to use, and their social environment supports its use and if the technical and organizational conditions for its effective use are in place. An extension of UTAUT is the UTAUT2 model proposed by V. Venkatesh, J. Y., L. Thong, and X. Xu (Venkatesh et al., 2012). New constructs have been added to this model, among which the following are relevant to this study:

- Hedonic motivation, which refers to the pleasure and satisfaction derived from using technology,
- Habit, which describes the degree of automation of behavior resulting from previous experiences.

UTAUT2 is widely used in various research contexts, and its constructs are used to study not only the organizational use of technology but also educational behaviors, including mobile technologies, e-learning, and AI systems in education (Tamilmani et al., 2021).

As mentioned, in the context of this study on students' use of GenAI, the UTAUT and UTAUT2 models serve as interpretive frameworks that extend the classic ABC attitude model. For example, the constructs of hedonic motivation and habit usually correlate with the affective and behavioral components of the ABC model, while also extending them to include aspects such as enjoyment of using the technology or automatic behavior resulting from previous experiences. This may provide a more complete understanding of not only why students perceive technologies such as GenAI as useful or enjoyable but also why they declare their intention to continue using them or actually use them. In addition, UTAUT2 allows for social influences to be taken into account, which is particularly important in the context of students, who often base their decisions on the opinions of their peers or the academic community. Facilitating conditions, in turn, help explain the extent to which technical and environmental conditions are conducive to their use. As a result, combining ABC with UTAUT/UTAUT2 creates a multidimensional interpretive framework for analyzing students' attitudes, intentions, and behaviors toward GenAI.

As part of the conceptual combination of the indicated model and theory, ABC operationalizes how students perceive GenAI emotionally and cognitively, while UTAUT/UTAUT2 explains why and how intentions and contextual factors influence their usage behavior. Thanks to this, the comprehensive theoretical framework (ABC+UTAUT/UTAUT2) will enable a multidimensional interpretation of the research results.

2.1.3 Research tool

The research tool was a survey questionnaire developed for the purposes of this study, taking into account ABC and UTAUT/UTAUT2. It consisted of two parts: I. Personal details, II. Attitudes toward GenAI. The questionnaire is presented in Table 2.2. Part II additionally indicated the relationship with the components of the ABC model and the UTAUT and UTAUT2 constructs.

2.1.4 Nature and course of the research

The research was quantitative, cross-sectional, and diagnostic-exploratory in nature.

The quantitative nature of the research means the use of numerical data and statistical methods to describe and analyze students' attitudes, declared behaviors, and intentions toward GenAI. The quantitative approach is used in educational and social research, especially in situations where the goal is to identify relationships between variables and compare groups of respondents (Williams, 2007; Creswell & Creswell, 2022).

The cross-sectional nature of the research means that the data were collected once, at a single point in time, and the results obtained reflect the attitudes and practices of students regarding the use of GenAI at that time. Cross-sectional studies enable the diagnosis of social and educational phenomena in their current form and are used in analyses of the acceptance and use of new technologies (Creswell & Creswell, 2022; Majer et al., 2023).

At the same time, the research was diagnostic and exploratory in nature. The diagnostic aspect consisted of identifying current attitudes, methods of use, and declared intentions of students related to the use of GenAI in the learning process. The exploratory aspect, on the other hand, referred to the identification of new patterns of behavior emerging with the dynamic development and dissemination of GenAI tools (Saka et al., 2023; Creswell, Creswell, 2022).

The research was conducted in three stages.

In stage I, a survey questionnaire was developed, as presented in Table 2.2, which was then transferred to Google Forms. In stage II, the survey was used to conduct anonymous research on a group of 309 students from a Polish university, diverse in terms of demographic characteristics (age and

TABLE 2.2 Survey questionnaire template

PART I. PERSONAL DETAILS

Demographic characteristics:

1. Age: ☐ ≤20 ☐ 21–30 ☐ 31–40 ☐ >40
2. Gender: ☐ Female ☐ Male

Educational characteristics:

1. Fields of study
   Technical: ☐ Logistics ☐ Production engineering ☐ Biomedical engineering
   Social sciences: ☐ Management ☐ Project management
2. Degree level: ☐ B ☐ M

PART II. ATTITUDES TOWARD GENAI

1 – Strongly disagree 2 – Disagree 3 – Neither agree nor disagree
4 – I agree 5 – I strongly agree

ITEM	*COMPONENT ABC*	*UTAUT/UTAUT2 CONSTRUCTS*
1. I feel enthusiastic when using GenAI tools while learning	Affective	Hedonic motivation
2. I enjoy using GenAI	Affective	Hedonic motivation
3. I feel inspired by the possibilities that GenAI offers in education	Affective	Hedonic motivation
4. Using GenAI makes learning more interesting for me	Affective	Hedonic motivation
5. I feel confident using GenAI	Affective	Effort expectancy
6. Using GenAI increases my motivation to learn	Affective	Hedonic motivation
7. I feel satisfied when GenAI helps me complete my academic tasks	Affective	Performance expectancy
8. I like experimenting with new features of GenAI tools	Affective	Hedonic motivation
9. I have a positive attitude toward incorporating AI into the teaching process	Affective	Hedonic motivation
10. Using GenAI makes me feel more engaged in learning	Affective	Hedonic motivation
11. I regularly use GenAI in my studies and project preparation	Behavioral	Habit
12. I often use GenAI to search for and analyze information	Behavioral	Performance expectancy

(*Continued*)

TABLE 2.2 (*Continued*) Survey questionnaire template

ITEM	*COMPONENT ABC*	*UTAUT/UTAUT2 CONSTRUCTS*
13. I use GenAI to create notes or summaries of materials	Behavioral	Performance expectancy
14. I experiment with various GenAI tools (e.g., ChatGPT, Claude, Gemini)	Behavioral	Hedonic Motivation
15. I use GenAI to organize my learning (e.g., planning, reminders)	Behavioral	Performance expectancy
16. I explore new ways to use GenAI effectively	Behavioral	Habit
17. I use GenAI to solve problems in group projects	Behavioral	Social Influence Performance expectancy
18. I implement GenAI in my daily learning tasks	Behavioral	Habit
19. I intend to use GenAI more often in the future	Cognitive	Performance expectancy
20. I recommend GenAI to other students	Cognitive	Social Influence
21. I believe that GenAI improves learning effectiveness	Cognitive	Performance expectancy
22. I believe that GenAI facilitates academic tasks	Cognitive	Effort expectancy
23. I believe that GenAI can support the development of my competencies	Cognitive	Performance expectancy
24. I believe that the ability to use GenAI is essential in my future work	Cognitive	Performance expectancy
25. I am aware that GenAI can make mistakes, so it requires critical evaluation	Cognitive	Performance expectancy
26. I believe that GenAI can support creativity in problem solving	Cognitive	Performance expectancy Hedonic motivation
27. I believe that GenAI provides valuable information in the learning process	Cognitive	Performance expectancy

(*Continued*)

TABLE 2.2 (*Continued*) Survey questionnaire template

ITEM	*COMPONENT ABC*	*UTAUT/UTAUT2 CONSTRUCTS*
28. I believe that GenAI increases my productivity	Cognitive	Performance expectancy
29. I am aware of how to use GenAI tools safely in my studies	Cognitive	Facilitating conditions
30. I believe that GenAI will play an increasingly important role in education	Cognitive	Performance expectancy

Own study.

TABLE 2.3 Characteristics of the research sample, N = 309

DEMOGRAPHIC CHARACTERISTICS	*AGE*	*NUMBER OF RESPONDENTS*	
Age	≤20	17	
	21–30	232	
	31–40	38	
	>40	22	
Gender	Women	160	
	Men	149	
EDUCATIONAL CHARACTERISTICS	*FIELD OF STUDY*	*NUMBER OF RESPONDENTS*	
STEM technical fields	Production engineering	12	102
	Biomedical engineering	26	
	Logistics	64	
Social sciences	Management	83	207
	Project management	124	
Degrees	Bachelor's	175	
	Master's	134	

Own study.

gender) and educational characteristics (fields of study: technical and social sciences as well as degree level: Bachelor's and Master's). The total population of students in the fields of study surveyed was 1,245. The characteristics of the respondents are presented in Table 2.3. The required number of respondents was 294, assuming a maximum error of 5%. Taking this into account, the number of responses obtained from the surveys (309) constituted a representative group for the given student population.

In stage III of the research, which consisted of four steps, statistical analyses were carried out, the results of which formed the basis for verifying the hypotheses.

2.2 RESEARCH RESULTS

2.2.1 Step 1: verification of hypothesis 1

Statistical analyses were conducted to verify hypothesis 1, which assumed that students' affective and motivational attitudes toward GenAI are determined by their demographic and educational characteristics.

The calculations took into account the respondents' answers to all items in Part I of the survey: Personal details and items 1–10 in Part II: Attitudes toward GenAI.

The data analysis began with descriptive statistics, including measures of central tendency and dispersion (mean, median, standard deviation, minimum, and maximum). This was followed by a Shapiro-Wilk normality test (Field, 2018). For the purposes of statistical analysis, an additional Composite Index (CI) was also calculated: the overall average of affective-motivational attitudes toward GenAI (based on items 1–10 from Part II).

The statistics were performed taking into account data from Part I. Metrics, concerning demographic characteristics (age and gender) and educational characteristics (field of study: technical and social, degree: Bachelor's and Master's) as well as items 1–10 from Part II. The results of the calculations are presented in Table 2.4: a) age, b) gender, c) field of study, and d) degree level.

The data were characterized by completeness, a moderately positive response rate, full use of the adopted Likert scale (Boone & Boone, 2012; DeVellis, 2017), and distributions deviating from normality, which justified the use of non-parametric tests. For this reason, Spearman's non-parametric correlation was used (Hollander et al., 2014), which is based on monotonic relationships. The results of the analysis of correlations between demographic and educational characteristics and items 1–10 from Part II are presented in Table 2.5.

In accordance with the conventions adopted in the social sciences, ρ values in the range of 0.50–0.69 were interpreted as moderate correlations, while values ≥ 0.70 were interpreted as strong correlations (Hinkle et al., 2003). The use of these thresholds is consistent with classic recommendations for

TABLE 2.4 Selected descriptive statistics

A) STUDENTS' AFFECTIVE-MOTIVATIONAL ATTITUDES BY AGE																						
	ITEMS FROM PART II OF THE SURVEY																					
MEASURES OF ANALYSIS	*1.*				*2.*				*3.*				*4.*				*5.*				*6.*	
AGE/YEARS	*≤20*	*21–30*	*31–40*	*>40*	*≤20*	*21–30*	*31–40*	*>40*	*≤20*	*21–30*	*31–40*	*>40*	*≤20*	*21–30*	*31–40*	*>40*	*≤20*	*21–30*	*31–40*	*>40*	*≤20*	*21–30*
Valid	17	232	38	22	17	232	38	22	17	232	38	22	17	232	38	22	17	232	38	22	17	232
Missing	0	0	0	0	0	0	0	0	0	0	0	0	0	0	0	0	0	0	0	0	0	0
Median	3.000	3.000	3.000	4.000	3.000	3.000	3.000	4.000	3.000	4.000	4.000	4.000	3.000	3.000	3.000	4.000	2.000	3.000	3.000	3.000	3.000	3.000
Mean	2.941	3.017	2.974	3.273	2.765	3.237	3.132	3.500	3.059	3.578	3.395	3.955	2.941	3.220	2.868	3.727	2.176	3.026	3.026	3.136	2.412	2.819
Std. Deviation	1.088	1.036	1.026	1.202	0.903	0.993	1.044	0.964	1.144	1.046	1.028	0.899	1.088	1.060	0.906	0.985	0.728	1.105	1.052	0.889	0.795	1.090
Shapiro-Wilk	0.846	0.900	0.900	0.855	0.850	0.900	0.879	0.861	0.765	0.887	0.848	0.758	0.922	0.910	0.839	0.850	0.809	0.915	0.901	0.890	0.715	0.914
P-value of Shapiro-Wilk	0.009	< .001	0.002	0.004	0.011	< .001	< .001	0.005	< .001	< .001	< .001	< .001	0.160	< .001	< .001	0.003	0.003	< .001	0.003	0.019	< .001	< .001
Minimum	1.000	1.000	1.000	1.000	1.000	1.000	1.000	1.000	1.000	1.000	1.000	1.000	1.000	1.000	1.000	1.000	1.000	1.000	1.000	1.000	1.000	1.000
Maximum	5.000	5.000	5.000	5.000	4.000	5.000	5.000	5.000	4.000	5.000	5.000	5.000	5.000	5.000	4.000	5.000	3.000	5.000	5.000	5.000	3.000	5.000

	ITEMS FROM PART II OF THE SURVEY																					
	6		*7*				*8.*				*9.*				*10.*				*CI*			
AGE/YEARS	*31–40*	*>40*	*≤20*	*21–30*	*31–40*	*>40*	*≤20*	*21–30*	*31–40*	*>40*	*≤20*	*21–30*	*31–40*	*>40*	*≤20*	*21–30*	*31–40*	*>40*	*≤20*	*21–30*	*31–40*	*>40*
Valid	38	22	17	232	38	22	17	232	38	22	17	232	38	22	17	232	38	22	17	232	38	22
Missing	0	0	0	0	0	0	0	0	0	0	0	0	0	0	0	0	0	0	0	0	0	0
Median	3.000	3.000	3.000	3.000	3.000	4.000	3.000	3.000	3.000	3.500	3.000	4.000	3.000	4.000	2.000	3.000	3.000	3.000	2.930	3.280	3.065	3.540
Mean	2.711	3.136	3.176	3.276	2.868	3.500	2.882	3.297	3.079	3.500	2.765	3.388	3.237	3.364	2.294	2.918	2.684	3.227	2.764	3.204	3.021	3.463
Std. Deviation	1.011	0.889	1.015	1.078	0.963	0.740	1.269	1.214	1.171	0.673	0.970	1.013	1.051	1.002	0.849	1.092	0.904	1.066	0.607	0.796	0.765	0.716
Shapiro-Wilk	0.835	0.890	0.915	0.894	0.832	0.836	0.873	0.904	0.907	0.823	0.880	0.893	0.864	0.810	0.881	0.916	0.852	0.897	0.892	0.989	0.947	0.929
P-value of Shapiro-Wilk	< .001	0.019	0.123	< .001	< .001	0.002	0.024	< .001	0.004	0.001	0.032	< .001	< .001	< .001	0.033	< .001	< .001	0.026	0.050	0.083	0.072	0.116
Minimum	1.000	1.000	1.000	1.000	1.000	2.000	1.000	1.000	1.000	2.000	1.000	1.000	1.000	1.000	1.000	1.000	1.000	1.000	1.410	1.000	1.000	1.520
Maximum	4.000	5.000	5.000	5.000	4.000	5.000	5.000	5.000	5.000	5.000	4.000	5.000	5.000	5.000	4.000	5.000	4.000	5.000	3.640	5.000	4.400	5.000

(Continued)

TABLE 2.4 (*Continued*) Selected descriptive statistics

B) STUDENTS' AFFECTIVE-MOTIVATIONAL ATTITUDES BY GENDER (W = WOMEN, M = MEN)																						
MEASURES OF ANALYSIS	*ITEMS FROM PART II OF THE SURVEY*																					
	1.		*2.*		*3.*		*4.*		*5.*		*6.*		*7.*		*8.*		*9.*		*10.*		*CI*	
GENDER	*W*	*M*	*W*	*M*	*W*	*M*	*W*	*M*	*W*	*M*	*W*	*M*	*W*	*M*	*W*	*M*	*W*	*M*	*W*	*M*	*W*	*M*
Valid	160	149	160	149	160	149	160	149	160	149	160	149	160	149	160	149	160	149	160	149	160	149
Missing	0	0	0	0	0	0	0	0	0	0	0	0	0	0	0	0	0	0	0	0	0	0
Median	3.000	3.000	3.000	3.000	4.000	4.000	3.000	3.000	3.000	3.000	3.000	3.000	3.000	3.000	3.000	4.000	3.000	4.000	3.000	3.000	3.130	3.330
Mean	2.862	3.201	3.131	3.309	3.481	3.631	3.138	3.262	2.869	3.114	2.756	2.859	3.181	3.295	3.050	3.490	3.269	3.403	2.900	2.852	3.089	3.268
Std. Deviation	1.049	1.020	0.998	0.993	1.070	1.022	1.049	1.055	1.076	1.075	1.051	1.066	1.126	0.955	1.233	1.088	1.026	1.013	1.083	1.055	0.808	0.754
Shapiro-Wilk	0.894	0.903	0.897	0.896	0.883	0.871	0.906	0.904	0.913	0.911	0.910	0.911	0.904	0.870	0.900	0.901	0.900	0.878	0.915	0.913	0.973	0.992
P-value of Shapiro-Wilk	< .001	< .001	< .001	< .001	< .001	< .001	< .001	< .001	< .001	< .001	< .001	< .001	< .001	< .001	< .001	< .001	< .001	< .001	< .001	< .001	0.004	0.530
Minimum	1.000	1.000	1.000	1.000	1.000	1.000	1.000	1.000	1.000	1.000	1.000	1.000	1.000	1.000	1.000	1.000	1.000	1.000	1.000	1.000	1.000	1.210
Maximum	5.000	5.000	5.000	5.000	5.000	5.000	5.000	5.000	5.000	5.000	5.000	5.000	5.000	5.000	5.000	5.000	5.000	5.000	5.000	5.000	5.000	5.000

C) STUDENTS' AFFECTIVE-MOTIVATIONAL ATTITUDES BY FIELD OF STUDY (T = STEM; S = SOCIAL SCIENCES)																						
MEASURES OF ANALYSIS	*ITEMS FROM PART II OF THE SURVEY*																					
	1.		*2.*		*3.*		*4.*		*5.*		*6.*		*7.*		*8.*		*9.*		*10.*		*CI*	
FIELD OF STUDY	*T*	*S*	*T*	*S*	*T*	*S*	*T*	*S*	*T*	*S*	*T*	*S*	*T*	*S*	*T*	*S*	*T*	*S*	*T*	*S*	*T*	*S*
Valid	102	207	102	207	102	207	102	207	102	207	102	207	102	207	102	207	102	207	102	207	102	207
Missing	0	0	0	0	0	0	0	0	0	0	0	0	0	0	0	0	0	0	0	0	0	0
Median	3.000	3.000	3.000	3.000	4.000	4.000	3.000	3.000	3.000	3.000	3.000	3.000	3.000	3.000	3.000	3.000	4.000	3.000	3.000	3.000	3.330	3.230
Mean	3.069	3.005	3.294	3.179	3.637	3.512	3.147	3.222	3.000	2.981	2.804	2.807	3.255	3.227	3.324	3.232	3.451	3.275	2.922	2.855	3.217	3.155
Std. Deviation	0.859	1.130	0.863	1.058	0.888	1.119	0.979	1.088	1.034	1.106	1.025	1.075	1.041	1.053	1.101	1.224	0.840	1.096	1.021	1.092	0.647	0.847
Shapiro-Wilk	0.874	0.907	0.864	0.907	0.867	0.881	0.892	0.907	0.911	0.917	0.910	0.908	0.872	0.900	0.906	0.902	0.863	0.900	0.910	0.912	0.975	0.987
P-value of Shapiro-Wilk	< .001	< .001	< .001	< .001	< .001	< .001	< .001	< .001	< .001	< .001	< .001	< .001	< .001	< .001	< .001	< .001	< .001	< .001	< .001	< .001	0.050	0.064
Minimum	1.000	1.000	1.000	1.000	1.000	1.000	1.000	1.000	1.000	1.000	1.000	1.000	1.000	1.000	1.000	1.000	1.000	1.000	1.000	1.000	1.520	1.000
Maximum	5.000	5.000	5.000	5.000	5.000	5.000	5.000	5.000	5.000	5.000	5.000	5.000	5.000	5.000	5.000	5.000	5.000	5.000	5.000	5.000	4.550	5.000

D) STUDENTS' AFFECTIVE–MOTIVATIONAL ATTITUDES BY DEGREE LEVEL (B = BACHELOR'S, M = MASTER'S)																						
MEASURES OF ANALYSIS	ITEMS FROM PART II OF THE SURVEY																					
	1.		2.		3.		4.		5.		6.		7.		8.		9.		10.		CI	
DEGREE LEVEL	B	M	B	M	B	M	B	M	B	M	B	M	B	M	B	M	B	M	B	M	B	M
Valid	134	175	134	175	134	175	134	175	134	175	134	175	134	175	134	175	134	175	134	175	134	175
Missing	0	0	0	0	0	0	0	0	0	0	0	0	0	0	0	0	0	0	0	0	0	0
Median	3,000	3.000	3.000	3.000	4.000	4.000	3.000	3.000	3.000	3.000	3.000	3.000	3.000	3.000	3.000	3.000	3.500	3.000	3.000	3.000	3.230	3.230
Mean	3.052	3.006	3.261	3.183	3.597	3.520	3.239	3.166	3.037	2.949	2.948	2.697	3.284	3.200	3.358	3.189	3.351	3.320	2.903	2.857	3.228	3.135
Std. Deviation	1.159	0.956	1.069	0.941	1.104	1.005	1.118	1.001	1.179	1.002	1.119	0.997	1.073	1.028	1.235	1.142	1.119	0.941	1.123	1.027	0.894	0.693
Shapiro-Wilk	0.907	0.891	0.911	0.874	0.879	0.870	0.910	0.898	0.914	0.908	0.910	0.903	0.898	0.885	0.898	0.904	0.900	0.875	0.916	0.909	0.986	0.971
P-value of Shapiro-Wilk	< .001	< .001	< .001	< .001	< .001	< .001	< .001	< .001	< .001	< .001	< .001	< .001	< .001	< .001	< .001	< .001	< .001	< .001	< .001	< .001	0.180	0.001
Minimum	1.000	1.000	1.000	1.000	1.000	1.000	1.000	1.000	1.000	1.000	1.000	1.000	1.000	1.000	1.000	1.000	1.000	1.000	1.000	1.000	1.000	1.000
Maximum	5.000	5.000	5.000	5.000	5.000	5.000	5.000	5.000	5.000	5.000	5.000	5.000	5.000	5.000	5.000	5.000	5.000	5.000	5.000	5.000	5.000	4.550

Own study.
Legend:
Valid: number of valid observations included in the analysis for a given item and synthetic indicator.
Missing: number of missing data (unanswered responses).
Median: middle value of the distribution – half of the observations have values less than or equal to the median, and half have values greater than or equal to the median.
Mean: arithmetic mean, average value of responses.
Std. Deviation: standard deviation, a measure of the variation of responses around the mean.
Shapiro–Wilk: Shapiro–Wilk test statistic, which checks how close the data distribution is to normal. The closer to 1, the closer the distribution is to normal.
P-value of Shapiro-Wilk: significance level of the test.
Minimum: the lowest observed value (the lowest category on the scale).
Maximum: the highest observed value (the highest category on the scale).

TABLE 2.5 Spearman's correlation coefficients

A) STUDENTS' AFFECTIVE-MOTIVATIONAL ATTITUDES BY AGE

≤20 YEARS

ITEMS	*1*	*2*	*3*	*4*	*5*	*6*	*7*	*8*	*9*	*10*	*CI*
1	NaN	NaN	NaN	NaN	NaN	NaN	NaN	NaN	NaN	NaN	NaN
2	NaN	NaN	NaN	0.65	NaN	NaN	0.49	NaN	NaN	NaN	0.64
3	NaN	NaN	NaN	NaN	NaN	NaN	NaN	NaN	NaN	NaN	NaN
4	NaN	0.65	NaN	NaN	0.48	NaN	NaN	NaN	NaN	NaN	0.51
5	NaN	NaN	NaN	0.48	NaN	0.53	0.48	0.60	NaN	0.72	0.70
6	NaN	NaN	NaN	NaN	0.53	NaN	NaN	NaN	NaN	0.63	0.59
7	NaN	0.49	NaN	NaN	0.48	NaN	NaN	0.50	NaN	NaN	NaN
8	NaN	NaN	NaN	NaN	0.60	NaN	0.50	NaN	NaN	0.56	0.77
9	NaN	NaN	NaN	NaN	NaN	NaN	NaN	NaN	NaN	0.65	0.64
10	NaN	NaN	NaN	NaN	0.72	0.63	NaN	0.56	0.65	NaN	0.76
CI	NaN	0.64	NaN	0.51	0.70	0.59	NaN	0.77	0.64	0.76	NaN

21–30 YEARS

ITEMS	*1*	*2*	*3*	*4*	*5*	*6*	*7*	*8*	*9*	*10*	*CI*
1	NaN	0.69	0.56	0.48	0.45	0.49	0.53	0.45	0.53	0.43	0.75
2	0.69	NaN	0.60	0.55	0.45	0.56	0.48	0.39	0.50	0.47	0.76
3	0.56	0.60	NaN	0.57	0.40	0.50	0.49	0.42	0.49	0.49	0.75
4	0.48	0.55	0.57	NaN	0.46	0.59	0.38	0.38	0.45	0.58	0.73
5	0.45	0.45	0.40	0.46	NaN	0.47	0.37	0.36	0.45	0.48	0.67
6	0.49	0.56	0.50	0.59	0.47	NaN	0.46	0.39	0.45	0.65	0.75
7	0.53	0.48	0.49	0.38	0.37	0.46	NaN	0.40	0.52	0.45	0.68
8	0.45	0.39	0.42	0.38	0.36	0.39	0.40	NaN	0.47	0.37	0.63
9	0.53	0.50	0.49	0.45	0.45	0.45	0.52	0.47	NaN	0.54	0.73
10	0.43	0.47	0.49	0.58	0.48	0.65	0.45	0.37	0.54	NaN	0.74
CI	0.75	0.76	0.75	0.73	0.67	0.75	0.68	0.63	0.73	0.74	NaN

31–40 YEARS

ITEMS	*1*	*2*	*3*	*4*	*5*	*6*	*7*	*8*	*9*	*10*	*CI*
1	NaN	0.36	NaN	NaN	NaN	0.35	0.44	0.46	0.38	NaN	0.44
2	NaN	NaN	0.36	NaN	NaN	NaN	NaN	0.42	0.38	NaN	0.36
3	NaN	NaN	NaN	NaN	NaN	NaN	NaN	NaN	NaN	NaN	NaN
4	0.34	NaN	NaN	NaN	NaN	NaN	NaN	NaN	NaN	NaN	NaN
5	NaN	0.37	NaN	NaN	0.47	NaN	NaN	0.49	0.45	NaN	0.36
6	0.36	0.37	0.43	0.34	NaN	NaN	NaN	0.54	0.38	0.32	0.47
7	NaN	0.68	0.57	0.68	0.42	NaN	0.60	0.42	0.60	NaN	0.73

(Continued)

TABLE 2.5 (*Continued*) Spearman's correlation coefficients

8	0.68	NaN	0.59	0.74	0.41	0.51	0.54	0.46	0.67	0.51	0.81
9	0.57	0.59	NaN	0.68	NaN	NaN	0.41	0.45	0.50	NaN	0.65
10	0.68	0.74	0.68	NaN	0.40	0.55	0.62	NaN	0.54	0.50	0.81
CI	0.42	0.41	NaN	0.40	NaN	0.37	0.35	0.47	0.49	NaN	0.61
						>40 YEARS					
ITEMS	*1*	*2*	*3*	*4*	*5*	*6*	*7*	*8*	*9*	*10*	*CI*
1	NaN	0.92	0.70	0.64	NaN	0.71	NaN	NaN	NaN	0.50	0.80
2	0.92	NaN	0.71	0.69	NaN	0.69	NaN	NaN	0.45	0.55	0.83
3	0.70	0.71	NaN	0.72	NaN	NaN	NaN	0.47	0.48	NaN	0.67
4	0.64	0.69	0.72	NaN	NaN	NaN	NaN	0.45	0.46	NaN	0.65
5	NaN	NaN	NaN	NaN	NaN	NaN	NaN	NaN	NaN	NaN	NaN
6	0.71	0.69	NaN	NaN	NaN	NaN	0.56	NaN	0.55	0.62	0.79
7	NaN	NaN	NaN	NaN	NaN	0.56	NaN	NaN	0.60	0.72	0.62
8	NaN	NaN	0.47	0.45	NaN	NaN	NaN	NaN	0.66	0.53	0.57
9	NaN	0.45	0.48	0.46	NaN	0.55	0.60	0.66	NaN	0.67	0.77
10	0.50	0.55	NaN	NaN	NaN	0.62	0.72	0.53	0.67	NaN	0.80
CI	0.80	0.83	0.67	0.65	NaN	0.79	0.62	0.57	0.77	0.80	NaN
						B) STUDENTS' AFFECTIVE-MOTIVATIONAL ATTITUDES BY GENDER (W = WOMEN, M = MEN)					
						W					
ITEMS	*1*	*2*	*3*	*4*	*5*	*6*	*7*	*8*	*9*	*10*	*CI*
1	NaN	0.63	0.54	0.42	0.40	0.42	0.47	0.42	0.48	0.43	0.69
2	0.63	NaN	0.64	0.57	0.41	0.54	0.45	0.41	0.54	0.51	0.75
3	0.54	0.64	NaN	0.53	0.42	0.42	0.51	0.46	0.54	0.51	0.76
4	0.42	0.57	0.53	NaN	0.43	0.55	0.37	0.40	0.47	0.63	0.71
5	0.40	0.41	0.42	0.43	NaN	0.50	0.40	0.40	0.44	0.47	0.66
6	0.42	0.54	0.42	0.55	0.50	NaN	0.47	0.40	0.41	0.64	0.72
7	0.47	0.45	0.51	0.37	0.40	0.47	NaN	0.42	0.50	0.49	0.69
8	0.42	0.41	0.46	0.40	0.40	0.40	0.42	NaN	0.48	0.40	0.65
9	0.48	0.54	0.54	0.47	0.44	0.41	0.50	0.48	NaN	0.52	0.73
10	0.43	0.51	0.51	0.63	0.47	0.64	0.49	0.40	0.52	NaN	0.76
CI	0.69	0.75	0.76	0.71	0.66	0.72	0.69	0.65	0.73	0.76	NaN
						M					
ITEMS	*1*	*2*	*3*	*4*	*5*	*6*	*7*	*8*	*9*	*10*	*CI*
1	NaN	0.72	0.52	0.58	0.43	0.51	0.52	0.37	0.49	0.37	NaN
2	0.72	NaN	0.56	0.59	0.47	0.57	0.51	0.38	0.50	0.46	0.72

(*Continued*)

TABLE 2.5 (*Continued*) Spearman's correlation coefficients

3	0.52	0.56	NaN	0.58	0.35	0.52	0.42	0.40	0.44	0.42	0.52
4	0.58	0.59	0.58	NaN	0.46	0.57	0.47	0.32	0.42	0.49	0.58
5	0.43	0.47	0.35	0.46	NaN	0.43	0.30	0.34	0.48	0.48	0.43
6	0.51	0.57	0.52	0.57	0.43	NaN	0.45	0.37	0.47	0.67	0.51
7	0.52	0.51	0.42	0.47	0.30	0.45	NaN	0.41	0.53	0.42	0.52
8	0.37	0.38	0.40	0.32	0.34	0.37	0.41	NaN	0.49	0.44	0.37
9	0.49	0.50	0.44	0.42	0.48	0.47	0.53	0.49	NaN	0.59	0.49
10	0.37	0.46	0.42	0.49	0.48	0.67	0.42	0.44	0.59	NaN	0.37
CI	0.75	0.79	0.70	0.75	0.66	0.76	0.67	0.62	0.74	0.73	0.75

C) STUDENTS' AFFECTIVE-MOTIVATIONAL ATTITUDES BY FIELD OF STUDY (T = STEM; S = SOCIAL SCIENCES)

T

ITEMS	*1*	*2*	*3*	*4*	*5*	*6*	*7*	*8*	*9*	*10*	*CI*
1	NaN	0.65	0.42	0.41	0.31	0.43	0.55	NaN	0.48	0.36	0.69
2	0.65	NaN	0.50	0.40	0.32	0.37	0.53	0.25	0.34	0.29	0.67
3	0.42	0.50	NaN	0.38	0.25	0.38	0.39	0.26	0.31	0.32	0.61
4	0.41	0.40	0.38	NaN	0.44	0.49	0.34	0.24	0.36	0.62	0.70
5	0.31	0.32	0.25	0.44	NaN	0.45	0.22	NaN	0.41	0.38	0.62
6	0.43	0.37	0.38	0.49	0.45	NaN	0.44	0.26	0.31	0.64	0.73
7	0.55	0.53	0.39	0.34	0.22	0.44	NaN	0.27	0.39	0.36	0.66
8	NaN	0.25	0.26	0.24	NaN	0.26	0.27	NaN	0.28	0.28	0.49
9	0.48	0.34	0.31	0.36	0.41	0.31	0.39	0.28	NaN	0.48	0.63
10	0.36	0.29	0.32	0.62	0.38	0.64	0.36	0.28	0.48	NaN	0.71
CI	0.69	0.67	0.61	0.70	0.62	0.73	0.66	0.49	0.63	0.71	NaN

S

ITEMS	*1*	*2*	*3*	*4*	*5*	*6*	*7*	*8*	*9*	*10*	*CI*
1	NaN	0.69	0.57	0.54	0.46	0.48	0.48	0.50	0.49	0.41	0.74
2	0.69	NaN	0.64	0.66	0.50	0.63	0.46	0.46	0.58	0.56	0.81
3	0.57	0.64	NaN	0.63	0.45	0.52	0.50	0.50	0.57	0.52	0.78
4	0.54	0.66	0.63	NaN	0.46	0.61	0.45	0.42	0.49	0.53	0.75
5	0.46	0.50	0.45	0.46	NaN	0.47	0.41	0.47	0.48	0.51	0.68
6	0.48	0.63	0.52	0.61	0.47	NaN	0.47	0.44	0.50	0.66	0.75
7	0.48	0.46	0.50	0.45	0.41	0.47	NaN	0.48	0.55	0.49	0.68
8	0.50	0.46	0.50	0.42	0.47	0.44	0.48	NaN	0.57	0.46	0.70
9	0.49	0.58	0.57	0.49	0.48	0.50	0.55	0.57	NaN	0.58	0.77
10	0.41	0.56	0.52	0.53	0.51	0.66	0.49	0.46	0.58	NaN	0.75
CI	0.74	0.81	0.78	0.75	0.68	0.75	0.68	0.70	0.77	0.75	NaN

(*Continued*)

TABLE 2.5 (*Continued*) Spearman's correlation coefficients

D) STUDENTS' AFFECTIVE–MOTIVATIONAL ATTITUDES BY DEGREE LEVEL (B = BACHELOR'S, M = MASTER'S)

B											
ITEMS	*1*	*2*	*3*	*4*	*5*	*6*	*7*	*8*	*9*	*10*	*CI*
1	NaN	0.65	0.44	0.43	0.29	0.34	0.49	0.31	0.39	0.27	0.66
2	0.65	NaN	0.54	0.51	0.39	0.46	0.46	0.37	0.38	0.33	0.73
3	0.44	0.54	NaN	0.40	0.29	0.40	0.37	0.29	0.33	0.36	0.64
4	0.43	0.51	0.40	NaN	0.41	0.50	0.34	0.29	0.32	0.47	0.67
5	0.29	0.39	0.29	0.41	NaN	0.46	0.26	0.33	0.40	0.42	0.63
6	0.34	0.46	0.40	0.50	0.46	NaN	0.40	0.33	0.36	0.62	0.72
7	0.49	0.46	0.37	0.34	0.26	0.40	NaN	0.42	0.46	0.41	0.67
8	0.31	0.37	0.29	0.29	0.33	0.33	0.42	NaN	0.40	0.36	0.60
9	0.39	0.38	0.33	0.32	0.40	0.36	0.46	0.40	NaN	0.52	0.66
10	0.27	0.33	0.36	0.47	0.42	0.62	0.41	0.36	0.52	NaN	0.70
CI	0.66	0.73	0.64	0.67	0.63	0.72	0.67	0.60	0.66	0.70	NaN

M											
ITEMS	*1*	*2*	*3*	*4*	*5*	*6*	*7*	*8*	*9*	*10*	*CI*
1	NaN	0.71	0.63	0.58	0.56	0.60	0.50	0.54	0.60	0.53	0.79
2	0.71	NaN	0.67	0.67	0.52	0.67	0.50	0.44	0.66	0.65	0.82
3	0.63	0.67	NaN	0.73	0.49	0.55	0.57	0.59	0.67	0.59	0.83
4	0.58	0.67	0.73	NaN	0.50	0.66	0.50	0.45	0.58	0.66	0.80
5	0.56	0.52	0.49	0.50	NaN	0.49	0.47	0.42	0.53	0.53	0.70
6	0.60	0.67	0.55	0.66	0.49	NaN	0.53	0.43	0.53	0.70	0.78
7	0.50	0.50	0.57	0.50	0.47	0.53	NaN	0.42	0.56	0.51	0.69
8	0.54	0.44	0.59	0.45	0.42	0.43	0.42	NaN	0.59	0.46	0.68
9	0.60	0.66	0.67	0.58	0.53	0.53	0.56	0.59	NaN	0.58	0.81
10	0.53	0.65	0.59	0.66	0.53	0.70	0.51	0.46	0.58	NaN	0.78
CI	0.79	0.82	0.83	0.80	0.70	0.78	0.69	0.68	0.81	0.78	NaN

NaN: Not a Number – indicates that the calculated correlation coefficient is not statistically significant (e.g., due to a weak relationship between the variables or high data variability)

interpreting effect sizes in social research (Field, 2018). It is also worth noting that correlations > 0.70 are rare in these sciences (Tabachnick & Fidell, 2019).

The statistical significance of correlations was tested at the level (alpha = 0.05) and only statistically significant correlations were considered. The results of the correlation analysis indicate the following:

- Students' affective-motivational attitudes toward GenAI show moderate internal correlations ($\rho \approx 0.50$–0.65) and are stable across groups: gender, age, field of study (but not degree level, whose role is weaker and less clear than that of the other groups).

- There are no systematic structural differences in the correlation patterns between groups.

Therefore, it is not possible to confirm unequivocally the diversity of attitudes between the groups studied but rather to point to the universal nature of students' attitudes toward GenAI.

Based on the results obtained, it can be concluded that hypothesis 1 has only been partially confirmed. The affective-motivational attitudes of the studied group of students toward GenAI exist and vary individually, but there is no evidence of strong differentiation based on demographic and educational characteristics. Therefore, in order to fully confirm hypothesis 1, additional difference tests should be conducted.

Additional difference tests were performed. For demographic characteristics related to age and gender, the Kruskal-Wallis test was first used (Field, 2018; Hollander et al., 2014). The Kruskal-Wallis test showed that age significantly differentiates students' affective-motivational attitudes toward GenAI ($H(3) = 10.525$; $p = 0.015$), as shown in Table 2.6. However, no significant differences were found based on gender. Due to the significant result for age, post hoc analyses were performed using Dunn's test (Hollander et al., 2014; Field, 2018), the results of which are presented in Table 2.7. These analyses showed that there is a significant difference after correction between students ≤20 years of age and those >40 years of age (pholm = 0.014). Students >40 years of age obtained higher ranks, which indicates more positive affective-motivational attitudes toward GenAI in this group. The remaining pair comparisons did not reach significance after correction.

Due to the previously obtained results regarding gender and the lack of normal distributions in the subgroups, another analysis was performed using the non-parametric Mann-Whitney U test (Sheskin, 2020). The results of the calculations presented in Table 2.8 showed that gender differentiates only selected aspects of students' affective-motivational attitudes toward GenAI. Significant differences were noted in the enthusiasm for using GenAI (item 1),

TABLE 2.6 Kruskal-Wallis test results: demographic characteristics and affective-motivational attitudes

FACTOR	*STATISTIC (H)*	*DF*	*P*
Metric [Age]	10.525	3	0.015
Personal details [Gender]	3.327	1	0.068

Note: Tests are conducted separately for each variable, without accounting for multivariate effects.
Legend:
Factor: grouping factor
Statistic: Kruskal–Wallis test statistic (H)
df: degrees of freedom = number of groups – 1
p: significance level.

TABLE 2.7 Results of Dunn's post hoc comparisons test: demographic characteristics and affective-motivational attitudes

A) AGE							
COMPARISON	*Z*	W_I	W_J	R_{RB}	*P*	P_{BONF}	P_{HOLM}
21–30 years – ≤20 years old	2.373	157.681	104.471	0.338	0.018	0.106	0.088
21–30 years – 31–40 years old	1.142	157.681	139.842	0.115	0.253	1.000	0.349
21–30 years – >40 years old	−1.721	157.681	191.955	0.216	0.085	0.511	0.256
≤20 years – 31–40 years old	−1.358	104.471	139.842	0.226	0.174	1.000	0.349
≤20 years – >40 years old	−3.035	104.471	191.955	0.642	0.002	0.014	0.014
31–40 years – >40 years old	−2.179	139.842	191.955	0.342	0.029	0.176	0.117
B) GENDER							
Women-men	−1.824	146.063	164.597	0.120	0.068	0.068	0.068

Note: Rank-biserial correlation based on individual Mann-Whitney tests.
Legend:
Comparison: indicates which two groups are being compared.
z: standardized test statistic that indicates the direction of the difference (+ / – sign), the strength of the rank difference ("–" sign means that the first group – women has lower ranks than the second group – men.
W_i: mean rank for the first group in the comparison – women.
W_j: mean rank for the second group in the comparison – men.
r_{rb}: rank-biserial correlation – a measure of the effect size for comparing two groups, which indicates how large the difference is, regardless of the sample size (~0.10 small effect, ~0.30 medium effect, ≥0.50 large effect).
p: raw level of statistical significance.
p_{bonf}: p after Bonferroni correction (conservative).

TABLE 2.8 Mann-Whitney U test results: students' affective-motivational attitudes and their gender

ITEMS RELATED TO AFFECTIVE-MOTIVATIONAL ATTITUDES	*U*	*P*
1. I feel enthusiastic when I use GenAI tools while studying.	9796.000	0.004
2. I enjoy using GenAI.	10749.500	0.116
3. I feel inspired by the possibilities that GenAI offers in education.	10986.500	0.210

(Continued)

TABLE 2.8 (*Continued*) Mann-Whitney U test results: students' affective-motivational attitudes and their gender

ITEMS RELATED TO AFFECTIVE-MOTIVATIONAL ATTITUDES	*U*	*P*
4. Using GenAI makes learning more interesting for me.	11081.000	0.265
5. I feel confident using GenAI.	10539.000	0.068
6. Using GenAI increases my motivation to learn.	11250.500	0.373
7. I feel satisfied when GenAI helps me with my academic tasks.	11320.500	0.424
8. I like experimenting with new GenAI tool features.	9646.500	0.003
9. I have a positive attitude toward incorporating GenAI into the teaching process.	10937.000	0.188
10. Using GenAI makes me feel more engaged in learning.	12241.500	0.670
Overall average for affective-motivational attitudes	10490.000	0.068

Note: Mann-Whitney U test.

Legend:

U: Mann–Whitney test statistic, determining the degree of difference between the ranks of two independent groups (women and men). The smaller the value of U, the greater the difference between the compared groups. U is used to calculate the significance level (p).

p: p-value, indicating the probability of obtaining such (or greater) a difference between groups if there is no real difference in the population. Interpretation: $p < 0.05$ → the difference is statistically significant; $p \geq 0.05$ → no basis for concluding that there are significant differences.

TABLE 2.9 Mann-Whitney U test results

A) STUDENTS' AFFECTIVE-MOTIVATIONAL ATTITUDES AND FIELD OF STUDY		
ITEMS RELATED TO AFFECTIVE-MOTIVATIONAL ATTITUDES	*U*	*P*
1. I feel enthusiastic when I use GenAI tools while studying.	10844.000	0.682
2. I enjoy using GenAI.	11155.500	0.393
3. I feel inspired by the possibilities that GenAI offers in education.	10931.000	0.594

(*Continued*)

TABLE 2.9 (*Continued*) Mann-Whitney U test results

A) STUDENTS' AFFECTIVE-MOTIVATIONAL ATTITUDES AND FIELD OF STUDY		
ITEMS RELATED TO AFFECTIVE-MOTIVATIONAL ATTITUDES	*U*	*P*
4. Using GenAI makes learning more interesting for me.	10125.000	0.542
5. I feel confident using GenAI.	10614.000	0.937
6. Using GenAI increases my motivation to learn.	10548.000	0.990
7. I feel satisfied when GenAI helps me with my academic tasks.	10803.000	0.727
8. I like experimenting with new GenAI tool features.	10889.000	0.643
9. I have a positive attitude toward incorporating GenAI into the teaching process.	11348.000	0.260
10. Using GenAI makes me feel more engaged in learning.	10797.000	0.736
Overall average for affective-motivational attitudes (CI)	11107.000	0.456
B) AFFECTIVE-MOTIVATIONAL ATTITUDES OF STUDENTS AND DEGREE OF STUDY		
1. I feel enthusiastic when I use GenAI tools while studying.	12008.000	0.701
2. I enjoy using GenAI.	12142.000	0.572
3. I feel inspired by the possibilities that GenAI offers in education.	12377.500	0.377
4. Using GenAI makes learning more interesting for me.	12164.500	0.556
5. I feel confident using GenAI.	12291.000	0.451
6. Using GenAI increases my motivation to learn.	13160.500	0.054
7. I feel satisfied when GenAI helps me with my academic tasks.	12242.500	0.486
8. I like experimenting with new GenAI tool features.	12728.500	0.183
9. I have a positive attitude toward incorporating GenAI into the teaching process.	12069.000	0.643
10. Using GenAI makes me feel more engaged in learning.	11880.500	0.836
Overall average for affective-motivational attitudes (CI)	12297.000	0.462

Note: Mann-Whitney U test.
Legend: As in Table 2.8

as well as a trend in the tendency to experiment with new AI tool features (item 8) – the results prove that men feel more enthusiasm and indicate that they like to experiment with GenAI more than women.

Similar analyses were performed for educational characteristics. Based on statistical calculations, including the Mann-Whitney U test, it can be concluded that students' affective-motivational attitude toward GenAI does not depend on the field of study or the level of study, as shown in Table 2.9. Analyses at the level of individual items showed only isolated, unsystematic differences that did not affect the overall result of the scale. Based on the results obtained in the in-depth analyses, it can be concluded that hypothesis 1 has not been fully confirmed.

2.2.2 Step 2: verification of hypothesis 2

The research process was similar to step 1. First, statistical analyses were performed to verify hypothesis 2, which assumed that students differ in the frequency and methods of using GenAI, depending on their demographic and educational characteristics.

The calculations took into account the respondents' answers to the items in Part I of the survey: Personal details and items 11–18 in Part II: Attitudes toward GenAI. It should be noted that the frequency and methods of using GenAI (items 11–18) constitute a behavioral component of attitudes toward GenAI, referred to hereinafter as "GenAI usage patterns".

Similar to step 1 of the study, the data analysis began with descriptive statistics, including measures of central tendency and dispersion, the Shapiro-Wilk normality test, and the development of an additional CI: the overall average GenAI usage patterns (based on items 11–18 from Part II). The results of the calculations are presented in Table 2.10: a) age, b) gender, c) field of study, and d) degree of study.

As in step 1, the descriptive statistics results showed distributions deviating from normality, which justified the use of Spearman's nonparametric correlation. The results of the analysis of correlations between demographic and educational characteristics and items 11–18 from Part II are presented in Table 2.11.

To verify hypothesis 2 using Spearman's rank correlation coefficient, as in step 1 of the study, the following correlation strength thresholds were adopted: $\rho = 0.50$–0.69 (moderate correlation), $\rho \geq 0.70$ (strong correlation). The results obtained indicate that all statistically significant correlations between items 11–18 (and their CI mean) and the analyzed demographic and educational characteristics of students reached values not exceeding $\rho = 0.21$. This means that their strength did not meet the criteria for moderate or strong correlation.

Consequently, it can be concluded that, at the adopted thresholds, hypothesis 2 has not been confirmed. The results do not provide evidence of

TABLE 2.10 Selected descriptive statistics results

A) GENAI USAGE PATTERNS BY AGE																				
MEASURES OF ANALYSIS	*ITEMS FROM PART II OF THE SURVEY*																			
	11.				*12.*				*13.*				*14.*				*15*			
Age/years	≤20	21–30	31–40	>40	≤20	21–30	31–40	>40	≤20	21–30	31–40	>40	≤20	21–30	31–40	>40	≤20	21–30	31–40	>40
Valid	38	17	232	22	38	17	232	22	38	17	232	22	38	17	232	22	38	17	232	22
Missing	0	0	0	0	0	0	0	0	0	0	0	0	0	0	0	0	0	0	0	0
Median	3	2.9	4	3.5	4	4	4	4	3	3	4	3	3	4	3	3	2	3	2	2
Mean	2.921	2.741	3.634	3.318	3.5	3.412	3.724	3.682	2.974	3.294	3.797	3.045	3	3.471	3.147	3.364	2	2.824	2.591	2.403
Std. Deviation	1.239	0.603	1.069	0.945	1.268	1.176	0.959	0.839	1.325	0.772	1.06	1.133	1.273	1.231	1.243	1.049	0.9	1.334	1.319	1.093
Shapiro-Wilk	0.832	0.89	0.87	0.87	0.856	0.915	0.862	0.866	0.904	0.859	0.84	0.927	0.902	0.87	0.904	0.917	0.849	0.878	0.88	0.902
P-value of Shapiro-Wilk	< .001	0.046	< .001	0.008	< .001	0.124	< .001	0.007	0.003	0.015	< .001	0.107	0.003	0.022	< .001	0.066	< .001	0.029	< .001	0.032
Minimum	1	1.4	1	1	1	1	1	2	1	2	1	1	1	1	1	1	1	1	1	1
Maximum	5	3.6	5	5	5	5	5	5	5	5	5	5	5	5	5	5	4	5	5	5
MEASURES OF ANALYSIS	*ITEMS FROM PART II OF THE SURVEY*																			
	16.				*17*				*18*				*CI*							
Age/years	≤ 20	21–30	31–40	> 40	≤ 20	21–30	31–40	> 40	≤ 20	21–30	31–40	> 40	≤ 20	21–30	31–40	> 40				
Valid	38	17	232	22	38	17	232	22	38	17	232	22	38	17	232	22				
Missing	0	0	0	0	0	0	0	0	0	0	0	0	0	0	0	0				
Median	2	3	3	3	2	2	3	3	3	3	3	3	2.755	3	3.25	3.38				
Mean	2.395	2.647	2.828	3.182	2.421	2.471	3.009	3.091	2.605	2.882	3	3.273	2.729	2.647	3.218	3.173				
Std. Deviation	1.175	1.057	1.183	1.097	1.154	1.281	1.252	0.921	1.198	1.219	1.238	0.883	0.928	1.115	0.812	0.758				
Shapiro-Wilk	0.873	0.88	0.911	0.913	0.842	0.897	0.889	0.906	0.832	0.912	0.901	0.873	0.946	0.915	0.991	0.939				
P-value of Shapiro-Wilk	< .001	0.032	< .001	0.054	< .001	0.06	< .001	0.04	< .001	0.107	< .001	0.009	0.065	0.121	0.187	0.188				
Minimum	1	1	1	1	1	1	1	1	1	1	1	1	1	1	1	1.25				
Maximum	5	4	5	5	4	5	5	5	4	5	5	5	4.25	5	5	5				

(Continued)

TABLE 2.10 (*Continued*) Selected descriptive statistics results

B) GENAI USAGE PATTERNS BY GENDER (WOMEN = W, MEN = M)																		
	ITEMS FROM PART II OF THE SURVEY																	
MEASURES OF ANALYSIS	*11.*		*12.*		*13.*		*14.*		*15.*		*16.*		*17.*		*18.*		*CI*	
Gender	W	M	W	M	W	M	W	M	W	M	W	M	W	M	W	M	W	M
Valid	160	149	160	149	160	149	160	149	160	149	160	149	160	149	160	149	160	149
Missing	0	0	0	0	0	0	0	0	0	0	0	0	0	0	0	0	0	0
Median	4	4	4	4	4	4	3	3	2	2	3	3	3	3	3	3	3.13	3.25
Mean	3.494	3.53	3.606	3.738	3.65	3.597	3.019	3.242	2.525	2.49	2.681	2.886	2.844	3.034	2.938	2.966	3.097	3.188
Std. Deviation	1.099	1.124	0.997	0.975	1.139	1.162	1.266	1.201	1.303	1.212	1.236	1.136	1.247	1.205	1.217	1.21	0.854	0.814
Shapiro-Wilk	0.875	0.874	0.872	0.863	0.846	0.875	0.892	0.91	0.878	0.888	0.901	0.913	0.897	0.885	0.906	0.895	0.988	0.976
P-value of Shapiro-Wilk	< .001	< .001	< .001	< .001	< .001	< .001	< .001	< .001	< .001	< .001	< .001	< .001	< .001	< .001	< .001	< .001	0.21	0.011
Minimum	1	1	1	1	1	1	1	1	1	1	1	1	1	1	1	1	1	1.13
Maximum	5	5	5	5	5	5	5	5	5	5	5	5	5	5	5	5	5	5
C) GENAI USAGE PATTERNS BY FIELD OF STUDY (STEM = T, SOCIAL SCIENCES = S) OPPOSITE TO EARLIER																		
	ITEMS FROM PART II OF THE SURVEY																	
MEASURES OF ANALYSIS	*11.*		*12.*		*13.*		*14.*		*15.*		*16.*		*17.*		*18.*		*CI*	
Field of study	T	S	T	S	T	S	T	S	T	S	T	S	T	S	T	S	T	S
Valid	102	207	102	207	102	207	102	207	102	207	102	207	102	207	102	207	102	207
Missing	0	0	0	0	0	0	0	0	0	0	0	0	0	0	0	0	0	0
Median	4	4	4	4	4	4	3	3	2	2	3	3	4	3	3	3	3.38	3.13
Mean	3.696	3.42	3.814	3.599	3.804	3.536	3.147	3.116	2.598	2.464	2.892	2.725	3.275	2.768	3.088	2.884	3.292	3.067
Std. Deviation	0.973	1.163	0.887	1.028	1.126	1.152	1.181	1.268	1.229	1.272	1.125	1.221	1.145	1.236	1.178	1.225	0.71	0.882
Shapiro-Wilk	0.837	0.885	0.855	0.875	0.788	0.885	0.908	0.902	0.898	0.875	0.915	0.903	0.872	0.896	0.915	0.89	0.985	0.987
P-value of Shapiro-Wilk	< .001	< .001	< .001	< .001	< .001	< .001	< .001	< .001	< .001	< .001	< .001	< .001	< .001	< .001	< .001	< .001	0.316	0.057
Minimum	1	1	1	1	1	1	1	1	1	1	1	1	1	1	1	1	1.25	1
Maximum	5	5	5	5	5	5	5	5	5	5	5	5	5	5	5	5	4.88	5

D) GENAI USAGE PATTERNS BY DEGREE LEVEL (BACHELOR'S = B. MASTER'S = M)																		
MEASURES OF ANALYSIS	*ITEMS FROM PART II OF THE SURVEY*																	
	11.		*12.*		*13.*		*14.*		*15.*		*16.*		*17.*		*18.*		*CI*	
Degree level	B	M	B	M	B	M	B	M	B	M	B	M	B	M	B	M	B	M
Valid	175	134	175	134	175	134	175	134	175	134	175	134	175	134	175	134	175	134
Missing	0	0	0	0	0	0	0	0	0	0	0	0	0	0	0	0	0	0
Median	4	4	4	4	4	4	3	3	2	2	3	3	3	3	3	3	3.25	3.13
Mean	3.549	3.463	3.669	3.672	3.697	3.53	3.126	3.127	2.491	2.53	2.783	2.776	3.097	2.724	2.977	2.918	3.176	3.095
Std. Deviation	1.086	1.142	0.961	1.024	1.127	1.174	1.182	1.312	1.169	1.369	1.114	1.29	1.197	1.241	1.169	1.269	0.757	0.928
Shapiro-Wilk	0.865	0.885	0.88	0.846	0.835	0.887	0.905	0.899	0.891	0.862	0.908	0.9	0.88	0.899	0.908	0.888	0.984	0.985
P-value of Shapiro-Wilk	< .001	< .001	< .001	< .001	< .001	< .001	< .001	< .001	< .001	< .001	< .001	< .001	< .001	< .001	< .001	< .001	0.038	0.147
Minimum	1	1	1	1	1	1	1	1	1	1	1	1	1	1	1	1	1	1
Maximum	5	5	5	5	5	5	5	5	5	5	5	5	5	5	5	5	4.88	5

Own study.
Legend: As in Table 2.4

TABLE 2.11 Spearman's correlation coefficients

A) GENAI USAGE PATTERNS BY AGE

≤ 20 YEARS

ITEMS	*11*	*12*	*13*	*14*	*15*	*16*	*17*	*18*	*CI*
11	NaN	NaN	0.59	NaN	NaN	NaN	NaN	NaN	0.64
12	NaN	NaN	NaN	NaN	NaN	NaN	0.60	NaN	0.60
13	0.59	NaN	NaN	NaN	NaN	NaN	NaN	0.59	0.59
14	NaN	NaN	NaN	NaN	0.54	0.78	0.55	0.53	0.75
15	NaN	NaN	NaN	0.54	NaN	0.69	NaN	NaN	0.53
16	NaN	NaN	NaN	0.78	0.69	NaN	NaN	0.68	0.75
17	NaN	0.60	NaN	0.55	NaN	NaN	NaN	NaN	0.65
18	NaN	NaN	0.59	0.53	NaN	0.68	NaN	NaN	0.85
CI	0.64	0.60	0.59	0.75	0.53	0.75	0.65	0.85	NaN

21–30 YEARS

ITEMS	*11*	*12*	*13*	*14*	*15*	*16*	*17*	*18*	*CI*
11	NaN	0.67	0.51	0.25	0.16	0.33	0.44	0.55	0.64
12	0.67	NaN	0.54	0.31	0.30	0.36	0.41	0.52	0.68
13	0.51	0.54	NaN	0.33	0.25	0.28	0.30	0.35	0.58
14	0.25	0.31	0.33	NaN	0.47	0.60	0.31	0.33	0.65
15	0.16	0.30	0.25	0.47	NaN	0.57	0.39	0.43	0.68
16	0.33	0.36	0.28	0.60	0.57	NaN	0.39	0.50	0.75
17	0.44	0.41	0.30	0.31	0.39	0.39	NaN	0.51	0.68
18	0.55	0.52	0.35	0.33	0.43	0.50	0.51	NaN	0.76
CI	0.64	0.68	0.58	0.65	0.68	0.75	0.68	0.76	NaN

31–40 YEARS

ITEMS	*11*	*12*	*13*	*14*	*15*	*16*	*17*	*18*	*CI*
11	NaN	0.72	0.66	0.53	NaN	0.61	0.58	0.56	0.79
12	0.72	NaN	0.61	0.54	NaN	0.49	0.44	0.53	0.74
13	0.66	0.61	NaN	0.44	0.52	0.55	0.54	0.57	0.78
14	0.53	0.54	0.44	NaN	NaN	0.64	0.51	0.48	0.70
15	NaN	NaN	0.52	NaN	NaN	0.57	0.55	0.50	0.60
16	0.61	0.49	0.55	0.64	0.57	NaN	0.79	0.81	0.87
17	0.58	0.44	0.54	0.51	0.55	0.79	NaN	0.85	0.83
18	0.56	0.53	0.57	0.48	0.50	0.81	0.85	NaN	0.85
CI	0.79	0.74	0.78	0.70	0.60	0.87	0.83	0.85	NaN

(Continued)

TABLE 2.11 (*Continued*) Spearman's correlation coefficients

				>40 YEARS					
ITEMS	*11*	*12*	*13*	*14*	*15*	*16*	*17*	*18*	*CI*
11	NaN	0.52	NaN	0.43	NaN	0.56	NaN	NaN	0.56
12	0.52	NaN	0.46	NaN	NaN	NaN	NaN	NaN	0.45
13	NaN	0.46	NaN	0.60	0.61	0.49	0.59	NaN	0.79
14	0.43	NaN	0.60	NaN	0.45	0.76	0.60	0.57	0.84
15	NaN	NaN	0.61	0.45	NaN	NaN	NaN	NaN	0.55
16	0.56	NaN	0.49	0.76	NaN	NaN	0.59	0.58	0.77
17	NaN	NaN	0.59	0.60	NaN	0.59	NaN	0.60	0.79
18	NaN	NaN	NaN	0.57	NaN	0.58	0.60	NaN	0.64
CI	0.56	0.45	0.79	0.84	0.55	0.77	0.79	0.64	NaN
			B) GENAI USAGE PATTERNS BY GENDER (WOMEN = W, MEN = M)						
				W					
ITEMS	*11*	*12*	*13*	*14*	*15*	*16*	*17*	*18*	*CI*
11	NaN	0.65	0.57	0.23	NaN	0.27	0.45	0.50	0.60
12	0.65	NaN	0.55	0.36	0.29	0.39	0.41	0.54	0.68
13	0.57	0.55	NaN	0.38	0.30	0.31	0.33	0.40	0.63
14	0.23	0.36	0.38	NaN	0.49	0.65	0.45	0.43	0.71
15	NaN	0.29	0.30	0.49	NaN	0.58	0.40	0.45	0.68
16	0.27	0.39	0.31	0.65	0.58	NaN	0.48	0.60	0.78
17	0.45	0.41	0.33	0.45	0.40	0.48	NaN	0.58	0.72
18	0.50	0.54	0.40	0.43	0.45	0.60	0.58	NaN	0.79
CI	0.60	0.68	0.63	0.71	0.68	0.78	0.72	0.79	NaN
				M					
ITEMS	*11*	*12*	*13*	*14*	*15*	*16*	*17*	*18*	*CI*
11	NaN	0.65	0.52	0.35	0.21	0.46	0.46	0.58	0.72
12	0.65	NaN	0.49	0.31	0.23	0.33	0.40	0.47	0.65
13	0.52	0.49	NaN	0.30	0.29	0.32	0.37	0.37	0.62
14	0.35	0.31	0.30	NaN	0.39	0.58	0.24	0.30	0.61
15	0.21	0.23	0.29	0.39	NaN	0.53	0.38	0.40	0.62
16	0.46	0.33	0.32	0.58	0.53	NaN	0.39	0.50	0.75
17	0.46	0.40	0.37	0.24	0.38	0.39	NaN	0.52	0.68
18	0.58	0.47	0.37	0.30	0.40	0.50	0.52	NaN	0.75
CI	0.72	0.65	0.62	0.61	0.62	0.75	0.68	0.75	NaN

(*Continued*)

TABLE 2.11 (*Continued*) Spearman's correlation coefficients

C) STUDENTS' AFFECTIVE-MOTIVATIONAL ATTITUDES BY FIELD OF STUDY (T = STEM, S = SOCIAL SCIENCES)

T

ITEMS	*11*	*12*	*13*	*14*	*15*	*16*	*17*	*18*	*CI*
11	NaN	0.54	0.41	NaN	NaN	0.22	0.55	0.56	0.59
12	0.54	NaN	0.42	NaN	NaN	NaN	0.39	0.42	0.51
13	0.41	0.42	NaN	0.34	0.26	0.25	0.28	0.41	0.63
14	NaN	NaN	0.34	NaN	0.43	0.54	0.26	0.30	0.66
15	NaN	NaN	0.26	0.43	NaN	0.41	NaN	0.28	0.55
16	0.22	NaN	0.25	0.54	0.41	NaN	0.30	0.37	0.65
17	0.55	0.39	0.28	0.26	NaN	0.30	NaN	0.46	0.63
18	0.56	0.42	0.41	0.30	0.28	0.37	0.46	NaN	0.74
CI	0.59	0.51	0.63	0.66	0.55	0.65	0.63	0.74	NaN

S

ITEMS	*11*	*12*	*13*	*14*	*15*	*16*	*17*	*18*	*CI*
11	NaN	0.69	0.60	0.34	0.24	0.41	0.41	0.54	0.68
12	0.69	NaN	0.55	0.41	0.33	0.45	0.42	0.53	0.72
13	0.60	0.55	NaN	0.34	0.31	0.34	0.37	0.38	0.63
14	0.34	0.41	0.34	NaN	0.44	0.65	0.40	0.40	0.68
15	0.24	0.33	0.31	0.44	NaN	0.62	0.49	0.49	0.69
16	0.41	0.45	0.34	0.65	0.62	NaN	0.51	0.63	0.81
17	0.41	0.42	0.37	0.40	0.49	0.51	NaN	0.60	0.73
18	0.54	0.53	0.38	0.40	0.49	0.63	0.60	NaN	0.79
CI	0.68	0.72	0.63	0.68	0.69	0.81	0.73	0.79	NaN

D) GENAI USAGE PATTERNS BY DEGREE LEVEL (B = BACHELOR'S, M = MASTER'S)

B

ITEMS	*11*	*12*	*13*	*14*	*15*	*16*	*17*	*18*	*CI*
11	NaN	0.61	0.49	0.25	NaN	0.28	0.49	0.59	0.65
12	0.61	NaN	0.46	0.29	0.15	0.31	0.44	0.50	0.64
13	0.49	0.46	NaN	0.28	0.22	0.24	0.33	0.42	0.62
14	0.25	0.29	0.28	NaN	0.29	0.54	0.30	0.28	0.59
15	NaN	0.15	0.22	0.29	NaN	0.46	0.28	0.34	0.55
16	0.28	0.31	0.24	0.54	0.46	NaN	0.38	0.44	0.69
17	0.49	0.44	0.33	0.30	0.28	0.38	NaN	0.48	0.70

(Continued)

TABLE 2.11 (*Continued*) Spearman's correlation coefficients

18	0.59	0.50	0.42	0.28	0.34	0.44	0.48	NaN	0.76
CI	0.65	0.64	0.62	0.59	0.55	0.69	0.70	0.76	NaN

M

ITEMS	*11*	*12*	*13*	*14*	*15*	*16*	*17*	*18*	*CI*
11	NaN	0.70	0.61	0.35	0.32	0.44	0.41	0.49	0.67
12	0.70	NaN	0.60	0.42	0.40	0.44	0.40	0.50	0.70
13	0.61	0.60	NaN	0.41	0.39	0.41	0.35	0.36	0.64
14	0.35	0.42	0.41	NaN	0.60	0.71	0.43	0.46	0.75
15	0.32	0.40	0.39	0.60	NaN	0.67	0.54	0.53	0.77
16	0.44	0.44	0.41	0.71	0.67	NaN	0.53	0.67	0.84
17	0.41	0.40	0.35	0.43	0.54	0.53	NaN	0.65	0.72
18	0.49	0.50	0.36	0.46	0.53	0.67	0.65	NaN	0.78
CI	0.67	0.70	0.64	0.75	0.77	0.84	0.72	0.78	NaN

Own study.
Legend: As in Table 2.5.

TABLE 2.12 Kruskal-Wallis test results: GenAI usage patterns and demographic characteristics

FACTOR	*STATISTIC (H)*	*DF*	*P*
Metric [Age]	not relevant	3	> 0.05
Personal details [Gender]	not relevant	1	> 0.05

Note: Tests are conducted separately for each variable, without accounting for multivariate effects.
Legend: As in Table 2.6.

clear, strong, or moderate differences in the frequency and methods of GenAI use depending on demographic and educational characteristics. At the same time, it is worth emphasizing that the lack of a moderate or strong correlation does not mean that there is no differentiation whatsoever. The Spearman's coefficient values obtained rather indicate a subtle, scattered nature of differences, which do not dominate the overall picture but are revealed at the level of individual aspects of GenAI use.

Next, as in step 1 of the study, additional calculations were performed using difference tests to verify hypothesis 2. First, the Kruskal-Wallis test was used, the results of which are presented in Table 2.12. The test did not reveal any significant differences between age groups and gender of students in terms of the frequency and methods of using GenAI. Due to the lack of statistical significance, no post hoc analyses were performed using Dunn's test.

Next, the Mann-Whitney U test was used. Based on this test, no significant differences were found in the frequency or methods of GenAI use

TABLE 2.13 Mann-Whitney U test results: GenAI usage patterns and student age

ITEMS RELATED TO GENAI USAGE PATTERNS	*U*	*P*
1. I regularly use GenAI in my studies and project preparation	Not relevant	> 0.05
2. I often use GenAI to search for and analyze information	Not relevant	> 0.05
3. I use GenAI to create notes or summaries of materials	Not relevant	> 0.05
4. I experiment with various GenAI tools (e.g., ChatGPT, Claude, Gemini)	Not relevant	> 0.05
5. I use GenAI to organize my studies (e.g., planning, reminders)	Not relevant	> 0.05
6. I explore new ways to use GenAI effectively	Not relevant	> 0.05
7. I use GenAI to solve problems in group projects	Not relevant	> 0.05
8. I implement GenAI in my daily learning tasks	Not relevant	> 0.05
Overall average for GenAI usage patterns (CI)	Not relevant	> 0.05

Note: Mann-Whitney U test.
Legend: As in Table 2.8.

depending on the demographic and educational characteristics of the students. Table 2.13 presents the results relating only to age, as the other results relating to gender, field of study, and degree level were the same. In each study (age, gender, field of study, and degree), the Mann-Whitney U test statistic was insignificant, and the probability was $p > 0.05$ (no basis for significant differences). Therefore, hypothesis 2 was not confirmed.

2.2.3 Step 3: verification of hypothesis 3

The course of the research was similar to steps 1 and 2. First, statistical analyses were performed to verify hypothesis 3, which assumed that attitudes toward GenAI are related to the intention to continue using it and recommending it to other students.

The first focus was on the intention to continue using GenAI, so item 19 was combined with items related to attitude components:

- Affective: 1–4, 6, 8, 10 (including enthusiasm, enjoyment, inspiration, influence on interest in learning),
- Behavioral: 11, 16, 18 (including regularity of use, exploring new ways of use),

- Cognitive: 21–24, 26–28, 30 (including belief that AI improves learning efficiency, facilitates academic tasks, supports competence development).

The results of the statistical analysis relating to intentions are presented in part a) of Table 2.14. Part b) of Table 2.14 presents the results of calculations relating to recommending GenAI to other students. To obtain these results, item 20 was combined with items relating to attitude components:

- Affective: 9 (positive attitude toward incorporating AI into the teaching process),
- Behavioral 17 (use of AI in solving problems in group projects),
- Cognitive 21–24, 27–28 (including the belief that AI improves learning effectiveness, facilitates academic tasks, and supports competence development).

The descriptive analysis for items 19 and 20, presented in Table 2.14, indicates that these variables were measured correctly, have a mean above the midpoint of the scale, are moderately differentiated, and cover the full range of the response scale. At the same time, the Shapiro-Wilk test showed a significant deviation from the normality of the distribution, which justified the use of non-parametric analysis methods. Therefore, Spearman's rank correlation analysis was performed. In accordance with the assumptions of hypothesis 3, the correlations of item 19 with the set of previously identified items describing affective, behavioral, and cognitive attitudes were checked first, as shown in Table 2.15.

In the case of the intention to continue using GenAI, Spearman's correlation analysis conducted for the entire sample (without taking into account demographic and educational characteristics) showed that all the relationships indicated in the hypothesis are statistically significant ($p < 0.05$), and some of them achieve a moderate strength of correlation with selected aspects of the ABC model components.

In particular, the intention to continue using GenAI (item 19) shows a moderate correlation with the following items:

1. Affective: 1: $\rho \approx 0.43$–0.53, 2: $\rho \approx 0.52$–0.61, 3: $\rho \approx 0.45$–0.57, 10: $\rho \approx 0.46$, which means that enthusiasm and enjoyment of using GenAI, a feeling of inspiration from its educational possibilities, and greater involvement in learning are conducive to declarations of continued use of GenAI,
2. Behavioral: 11: $\rho \approx 0.43$, 16: $\rho \approx 0.47$, 18: $\rho \approx 0.53$, which means that regular use of GenAI in learning, exploring new ways of using it, and implementing it into everyday learning tasks reinforce the

TABLE 2.14 Selected descriptive statistics results

	A) INTENTION AND STUDENT ATTITUDES																		
MEASURES OF ANALYSIS	*ITEMS FROM PART II OF THE SURVEY*																		
	1	*2*	*3*	*4*	*6*	*8*	*10*	*11*	*16*	*18*	*19*	*21*	*22*	*23*	*24*	*26*	*27*	*28*	*30*
Valid	309	309	309	309	309	309	309	309	309	309	309	309	309	309	309	309	309	309	309
Missing	0	0	0	0	0	0	0	0	0	0	0	0	0	0	0	0	0	0	0
Median	3	3	4	3	3	3	3	4	3	3	3	3	4	4	4	4	3	3	4
Mean	3.026	3.217	3.553	3.197	2.806	3.262	2.877	3.511	2.78	2.951	3.353	3.259	3.896	3.398	3.46	3.557	3.401	3.21	4.058
Std. Deviation	1.047	0.998	1.048	1.052	1.057	1.184	1.068	1.11	1.191	1.212	1.117	1.15	0.937	1.051	1.132	1.029	0.93	1.133	0.899
Shapiro-Wilk	0.902	0.897	0.877	0.907	0.91	0.904	0.914	0.875	0.908	0.901	0.903	0.894	0.831	0.899	0.899	0.888	0.887	0.903	0.827
P-value of Shapiro-Wilk	< .001	< .001	< .001	< .001	< .001	< .001	< .001	< .001	< .001	< .001	< .001	< .001	< .001	< .001	< .001	< .001	< .001	< .001	< .001
Minimum	1	1	1	1	1	1	1	1	1	1	1	1	1	1	1	1	1	1	1
Maximum	5	5	5	5	5	5	5	5	5	5	5	5	5	5	5	5	5	5	5

	B) RECOMMENDING STUDENT ATTITUDES								
	ITEMS FROM PART II OF THE SURVEY								
MEASURES OF ANALYSIS	*9*	*17*	*20*	*21*	*22*	*23*	*24*	*27*	*28*
Valid	309	309	309	309	309	309	309	309	309
Missing	0	0	0	0	0	0	0	0	0
Median	3	3	4	3	4	4	4	3	3
Mean	3.333	2.935	3.502	3.259	3.896	3.398	3.46	3.401	3.21
Std. Deviation	1.02	1.228	1.083	1.15	0.937	1.051	1.132	0.93	1.133
Shapiro-Wilk	0.891	0.893	0.896	0.894	0.831	0.899	0.899	0.887	0.903
P-value of Shapiro-Wilk	< .001	< .001	< .001	< .001	< .001	< .001	< .001	< .001	< .001
Minimum	1	1	1	1	1	1	1	1	1
Maximum	5	5	5	5	5	5	5	5	5

Own study.
Legend: As in Table 2.4.

TABLE 2.15 Spearman's correlation coefficients between the intention to continue using GenAI and attitudes toward this technology

ITEMS	*1*	*2*	*3*	*4*	*6*	*8*	*10*	*11*	*16*	*18*	*19*	*21*	*22*	*23*	*24*	*26*	*27*	*28*	*30*
1	NaN	0.68	0.53	0.50	0.46	0.42	0.39	0.40	0.39	0.46	0.43	0.37	0.35	0.40	0.37	0.37	0.43	0.40	0.23
2	0.68	NaN	0.60	0.59	0.55	0.40	0.48	0.50	0.42	0.52	0.52	0.41	0.41	0.43	0.42	0.44	0.47	0.35	0.32
3	0.53	0.60	NaN	0.55	0.47	0.43	0.46	0.48	0.33	0.42	0.45	0.39	0.45	0.46	0.42	0.45	0.45	0.38	0.38
4	0.50	0.59	0.55	NaN	0.57	0.36	0.56	0.31	0.34	0.41	0.33	0.43	0.31	0.37	0.31	0.38	0.41	0.32	0.22
6	0.46	0.55	0.47	0.57	NaN	0.38	0.65	0.36	0.40	0.38	0.37	0.56	0.28	0.44	0.31	0.40	0.44	0.53	0.23
8	0.42	0.40	0.43	0.36	0.38	NaN	0.40	0.32	0.58	0.38	0.43	0.35	0.25	0.39	0.36	0.33	0.38	0.32	0.27
10	0.39	0.48	0.46	0.56	0.65	0.40	NaN	0.37	0.37	0.47	0.39	0.54	0.26	0.43	0.34	0.42	0.43	0.39	0.22
11	0.40	0.50	0.48	0.31	0.36	0.32	0.37	NaN	0.36	0.54	0.38	0.41	0.64	0.44	0.45	0.42	0.44	0.32	0.36
16	0.39	0.42	0.33	0.34	0.40	0.58	0.37	0.36	NaN	0.55	0.35	0.38	0.28	0.41	0.34	0.34	0.37	0.37	0.25
18	0.46	0.52	0.42	0.41	0.38	0.38	0.47	0.54	0.55	NaN	0.45	0.43	0.48	0.43	0.41	0.38	0.48	0.38	0.35
19	0.43	0.52	0.45	0.33	0.37	0.43	0.39	0.38	0.35	0.45	NaN	0.49	0.43	0.53	0.56	0.47	0.44	0.38	0.42
21	0.37	0.41	0.39	0.43	0.56	0.35	0.54	0.41	0.38	0.43	0.49	NaN	0.39	0.52	0.39	0.51	0.43	0.50	0.27
22	0.35	0.41	0.45	0.31	0.28	0.25	0.26	0.64	0.28	0.48	0.43	0.39	NaN	0.53	0.47	0.45	0.52	0.40	0.47
23	0.40	0.43	0.46	0.37	0.44	0.39	0.43	0.44	0.41	0.43	0.53	0.52	0.53	NaN	0.54	0.59	0.56	0.48	0.44
24	0.37	0.42	0.42	0.31	0.31	0.36	0.34	0.45	0.34	0.41	0.56	0.39	0.47	0.54	NaN	0.48	0.44	0.40	0.55
26	0.37	0.44	0.45	0.38	0.40	0.33	0.42	0.42	0.34	0.38	0.47	0.51	0.45	0.59	0.48	NaN	0.52	0.52	0.41
27	0.43	0.47	0.45	0.41	0.44	0.38	0.43	0.44	0.37	0.48	0.44	0.43	0.52	0.56	0.44	0.52	NaN	0.49	0.44
28	0.40	0.35	0.38	0.32	0.53	0.32	0.39	0.32	0.37	0.38	0.38	0.50	0.40	0.48	0.40	0.52	0.49	NaN	0.30
30	0.23	0.32	0.38	0.22	0.23	0.27	0.22	0.36	0.25	0.35	0.42	0.27	0.47	0.44	0.55	0.41	0.44	0.30	NaN

Own study.
Legend: As in Table 2.5.

intention to continue using this technology, which is consistent with the habit construct in UTAUT2,

3. Cognitive: 21: $\rho \approx 0.53$, 22: $\rho \approx 0.49$, 23: $\rho \approx 0.58$, 24: $\rho \approx 0.60$, 28: $\rho \approx 0.51$, 30: $\rho \approx 0.46$, which means that students' belief that GenAI improves learning efficiency and facilitates academic tasks, as well as that it can support competence development and increase productivity, plays a key role in shaping the intention to continue using this technology.

The results confirm hypothesis 3 in the part concerning the intention to continue using GenAI, as they clearly indicate that all components of attitude have an impact on it. The most important are the cognitive component of the ABC model and the performance expectancy construct of UTAUT, followed by positive attitudes related to, among others, enjoyment and inspiration from GenAI. On the other hand, behaviors related to regular and practical use of GenAI play a supporting role in the readiness to continue using this technology.

An important element confirming hypothesis 3 in the part concerning the intention to continue using GenAI is the consistency of the direction of the obtained relationships. All significant correlations of item 19 with the other variables are positive, which means that more positive attitudes toward GenAI are consistently associated with a higher intention to continue using it. The correlations within the ABC components are high – between affective items: $\rho \approx 0.50$–0.69, between cognitive items: $\rho \approx 0.45$–0.63, and between behavioral items: $\rho \approx 0.40$–0.58.

To deepen the research, an additional analysis of the correlation between students' attitudes toward GenAI and their intention to continue using this technology was conducted, taking into account demographic and educational characteristics. Its results are presented in Table 2.16.

The results of the analysis indicate that the strength of the relationship between attitudes and intention to use GenAI varies with the age of students (Table 2.16 a). In younger age groups (≤20 years), correlations between intention to use and the affective component are weaker and less consistent, which may suggest that declarations of continued use are more situational in nature. In older age groups (especially >40 years), stronger correlations between intention and the cognitive component are observed, in particular with beliefs about the usefulness of GenAI for learning effectiveness and future work. This indicates that with age, the role of rational assessment of benefits increases, while the importance of emotional enthusiasm decreases. It should be emphasized that the differences in age mainly concern the strength of the relationships, not their direction or structure. This means that age acts as a factor modifying the intensity of the relationships but does not undermine

TABLE 2.16 Spearman's correlation coefficients – students' attitudes and their intention to continue using GenAI, taking into account demographic and educational characteristics

A) AGE ≤20 YEARS																			
ITEMS	*1*	*2*	*3*	*4*	*6*	*8*	*10*	*11*	*16*	*18*	*19*	*21*	*22*	*23*	*24*	*26*	*27*	*28*	*30*
1	NaN	NaN	NaN	NaN	NaN	NaN	NaN	NaN	NaN	0.50	NaN	NaN	NaN	NaN	NaN	NaN	NaN	NaN	NaN
2	NaN	NaN	NaN	0.65	NaN	NaN	NaN	0.70	NaN	0.53	0.53	NaN	NaN	NaN	NaN	NaN	NaN	NaN	NaN
3	NaN	NaN	NaN	NaN	NaN	NaN	NaN	0.61	NaN	NaN	0.75	NaN	NaN	NaN	NaN	NaN	NaN	0.56	NaN
4	NaN	0.65	NaN	NaN	NaN	NaN	NaN	NaN	NaN	NaN	NaN	NaN	NaN	NaN	NaN	NaN	0.58	NaN	NaN
6	NaN	NaN	NaN	NaN	NaN	NaN	0.63	NaN	0.66	NaN	NaN	0.62	NaN	NaN	NaN	NaN	NaN	0.49	NaN
8	NaN	NaN	NaN	NaN	NaN	NaN	0.56	NaN	0.78	NaN	0.65	NaN	NaN	0.52	NaN	NaN	NaN	0.69	NaN
10	NaN	NaN	NaN	NaN	0.63	0.56	NaN	NaN	0.66	NaN	NaN	0.64	NaN	NaN	NaN	0.62	NaN	0.66	NaN
11	NaN	0.70	0.61	NaN	NaN	NaN	NaN	NaN	NaN	NaN	0.67	NaN	0.51	NaN	0.55	NaN	NaN	NaN	NaN
16	NaN	NaN	NaN	NaN	0.66	0.78	0.66	NaN	NaN	0.68	NaN	0.50	NaN	0.50	NaN	NaN	NaN	0.68	NaN
18	0.50	0.53	NaN	NaN	NaN	NaN	NaN	NaN	0.68	NaN	NaN	NaN	NaN	NaN	NaN	NaN	NaN	NaN	NaN
19	NaN	0.53	0.75	NaN	NaN	0.65	NaN	0.67	NaN	NaN	NaN	NaN	NaN	NaN	NaN	NaN	NaN	NaN	NaN
21	NaN	NaN	NaN	NaN	0.62	NaN	0.64	NaN	0.50	NaN	NaN	NaN	NaN	0.57	NaN	NaN	NaN	0.57	NaN
22	NaN	NaN	NaN	NaN	NaN	NaN	NaN	0.51	NaN	NaN	NaN	NaN	NaN	NaN	NaN	0.52	0.51	NaN	NaN
23	NaN	NaN	NaN	NaN	NaN	0.52	NaN	NaN	0.50	NaN	NaN	0.57	NaN	NaN	NaN	NaN	NaN	0.61	NaN
24	NaN	NaN	NaN	NaN	NaN	NaN	NaN	0.55	NaN	NaN	NaN	NaN	NaN	NaN	NaN	NaN	0.55	NaN	0.81
26	NaN	NaN	NaN	NaN	NaN	NaN	0.62	NaN	NaN	NaN	NaN	NaN	0.52	NaN	NaN	NaN	NaN	0.61	0.49
27	NaN	NaN	NaN	0.58	NaN	NaN	NaN	NaN	NaN	NaN	NaN	NaN	0.51	NaN	0.55	NaN	NaN	NaN	0.63
28	NaN	NaN	0.56	NaN	0.49	0.69	0.66	NaN	0.68	NaN	NaN	0.57	NaN	0.61	NaN	0.61	NaN	NaN	NaN
30	NaN	NaN	NaN	NaN	NaN	NaN	NaN	NaN	NaN	NaN	NaN	NaN	NaN	NaN	0.81	0.49	0.63	NaN	NaN

(Continued)

TABLE 2.16 (*Continued*) Spearman's correlation coefficients – students' attitudes and their intention to continue using GenAI, taking into account demographic and educational characteristics

	21–30 YEARS																		
ITEMS	*1*	*2*	*3*	*4*	*6*	*8*	*10*	*11*	*16*	*18*	*19*	*21*	*22*	*23*	*24*	*26*	*27*	*28*	*30*
1	NaN	0.69	0.56	0.48	0.49	0.45	0.43	0.46	0.40	0.47	0.48	0.43	0.38	0.43	0.41	0.46	0.44	0.46	0.27
2	0.69	NaN	0.60	0.55	0.56	0.39	0.47	0.49	0.41	0.52	0.51	0.41	0.42	0.41	0.44	0.46	0.45	0.35	0.34
3	0.56	0.60	NaN	0.57	0.50	0.42	0.49	0.47	0.31	0.44	0.44	0.40	0.46	0.48	0.45	0.48	0.49	0.38	0.43
4	0.48	0.55	0.57	NaN	0.59	0.38	0.58	0.30	0.34	0.41	0.37	0.44	0.29	0.38	0.34	0.40	0.39	0.35	0.25
6	0.49	0.56	0.50	0.59	NaN	0.39	0.65	0.41	0.39	0.39	0.38	0.56	0.33	0.43	0.35	0.40	0.46	0.56	0.27
8	0.45	0.39	0.42	0.38	0.39	NaN	0.37	0.29	0.57	0.35	0.40	0.30	0.21	0.39	0.37	0.32	0.39	0.32	0.27
10	0.43	0.47	0.49	0.58	0.65	0.37	NaN	0.40	0.35	0.49	0.39	0.50	0.26	0.42	0.37	0.38	0.45	0.40	0.25
11	0.46	0.49	0.47	0.30	0.41	0.29	0.40	NaN	0.33	0.55	0.44	0.43	0.65	0.49	0.49	0.47	0.47	0.37	0.41
16	0.40	0.41	0.31	0.34	0.39	0.57	0.35	0.33	NaN	0.50	0.37	0.35	0.28	0.42	0.40	0.34	0.40	0.36	0.27
18	0.47	0.52	0.44	0.41	0.39	0.35	0.49	0.55	0.50	NaN	0.47	0.44	0.49	0.45	0.43	0.43	0.52	0.40	0.36
19	0.48	0.51	0.44	0.37	0.38	0.40	0.39	0.44	0.37	0.47	NaN	0.51	0.46	0.54	0.58	0.50	0.46	0.39	0.43
21	0.43	0.41	0.40	0.44	0.56	0.30	0.50	0.43	0.35	0.44	0.51	NaN	0.41	0.50	0.42	0.50	0.43	0.51	0.27
22	0.38	0.42	0.46	0.29	0.33	0.21	0.26	0.65	0.28	0.49	0.46	0.41	NaN	0.55	0.51	0.48	0.54	0.43	0.49
23	0.43	0.41	0.48	0.38	0.43	0.39	0.42	0.49	0.42	0.45	0.54	0.50	0.55	NaN	0.55	0.61	0.56	0.46	0.46
24	0.41	0.44	0.45	0.34	0.35	0.37	0.37	0.49	0.40	0.43	0.58	0.42	0.51	0.55	NaN	0.51	0.44	0.38	0.55
26	0.46	0.46	0.48	0.40	0.40	0.32	0.38	0.47	0.34	0.43	0.50	0.50	0.48	0.61	0.51	NaN	0.54	0.51	0.42
27	0.44	0.45	0.49	0.39	0.46	0.39	0.45	0.47	0.40	0.52	0.46	0.43	0.54	0.56	0.44	0.54	NaN	0.48	0.43
28	0.46	0.35	0.38	0.35	0.56	0.32	0.40	0.37	0.36	0.40	0.39	0.51	0.43	0.46	0.38	0.51	0.48	NaN	0.26
30	0.27	0.34	0.43	0.25	0.27	0.27	0.25	0.41	0.27	0.36	0.43	0.27	0.49	0.46	0.55	0.42	0.43	0.26	NaN

A) AGE 31–40 YEARS

ITEMS	*1*	*2*	*3*	*4*	*6*	*8*	*10*	*11*	*16*	*18*	*19*	*21*	*22*	*23*	*24*	*26*	*27*	*28*	*30*
1	NaN	0.68	0.57	0.68	NaN	0.42	NaN	0.35	0.41	0.43	0.39	0.35	0.50	0.35	NaN	NaN	0.41	NaN	NaN
2	0.68	NaN	0.59	0.74	0.51	0.46	0.51	0.60	0.49	0.51	0.56	0.61	0.47	0.63	NaN	0.39	0.69	0.46	0.38
3	0.57	0.59	NaN	0.68	NaN	0.45	NaN	0.58	0.39	0.34	0.36	0.33	0.52	NaN	NaN	NaN	0.53	NaN	NaN
4	0.68	0.74	0.68	NaN	0.55	NaN	0.50	0.46	0.40	0.40	NaN	0.44	NaN	0.40	NaN	NaN	0.58	NaN	NaN
6	NaN	0.51	NaN	0.55	NaN	NaN	0.67	NaN	NaN	0.33	NaN	0.67	NaN	0.47	NaN	0.39	0.55	0.41	NaN
8	0.42	0.46	0.45	NaN	NaN	NaN	0.51	0.53	0.59	0.52	0.56	0.50	0.36	NaN	0.42	0.40	0.43	NaN	0.36
10	NaN	0.51	NaN	0.50	0.67	0.51	NaN	0.38	NaN	0.32	0.34	0.65	NaN	0.46	NaN	0.48	0.42	NaN	NaN
11	0.35	0.60	0.58	0.46	NaN	0.53	0.38	NaN	0.61	0.56	NaN	0.36	0.63	0.41	NaN	0.48	0.50	0.39	NaN
16	0.41	0.49	0.39	0.40	NaN	0.59	NaN	0.61	NaN	0.81	0.38	0.39	0.50	0.35	NaN	NaN	0.43	0.45	0.37
18	0.43	0.51	0.34	0.40	0.33	0.52	0.32	0.56	0.81	NaN	0.47	0.41	0.63	0.48	0.38	NaN	0.42	0.45	0.46
19	0.39	0.56	0.36	NaN	NaN	0.56	0.34	NaN	0.38	0.47	NaN	0.61	0.45	0.61	0.56	0.36	0.40	NaN	0.60
21	0.35	0.61	0.33	0.44	0.67	0.50	0.65	0.36	0.39	0.41	0.61	NaN	NaN	0.65	NaN	0.68	0.52	0.45	0.38
22	0.50	0.47	0.52	NaN	NaN	0.36	NaN	0.63	0.50	0.63	0.45	NaN	NaN	0.48	0.36	NaN	0.43	0.45	0.42
23	0.35	0.63	NaN	0.40	0.47	NaN	0.46	0.41	0.35	0.48	0.61	0.65	0.48	NaN	0.54	0.60	0.70	0.57	0.50
24	NaN	NaN	NaN	NaN	NaN	0.42	NaN	NaN	NaN	0.38	0.56	NaN	0.36	0.54	NaN	NaN	0.36	0.51	0.46
26	NaN	0.39	NaN	NaN	0.39	0.40	0.48	0.48	NaN	NaN	0.36	0.68	NaN	0.60	NaN	NaN	0.63	0.50	NaN
27	0.41	0.69	0.53	0.58	0.55	0.43	0.42	0.50	0.43	0.42	0.40	0.52	0.43	0.70	0.36	0.63	NaN	0.67	0.45
28	NaN	0.46	NaN	NaN	0.41	NaN	NaN	0.39	0.45	0.45	NaN	0.45	0.45	0.57	0.51	0.50	0.67	NaN	0.44
30	NaN	0.38	NaN	NaN	NaN	0.36	NaN	NaN	0.37	0.46	0.60	0.38	0.42	0.50	0.46	NaN	0.45	0.44	NaN

(Continued)

TABLE 2.16 (*Continued*) Spearman's correlation coefficients – students' attitudes and their intention to continue using GenAI, taking into account demographic and educational characteristics

	>40 YEARS																		
ITEMS	*1*	*2*	*3*	*4*	*6*	*8*	*10*	*11*	*16*	*18*	*19*	*21*	*22*	*23*	*24*	*26*	*27*	*28*	*30*
1	NaN	0.92	0.70	0.64	0.71	NaN	0.50	0.46	NaN	NaN	0.45	NaN	NaN	NaN	NaN	NaN	0.52	NaN	NaN
2	0.92	NaN	0.71	0.69	0.69	NaN	0.55	0.55	NaN	0.45	0.51	NaN	NaN	NaN	0.49	NaN	0.60	NaN	NaN
3	0.70	0.71	NaN	0.72	NaN	0.47	NaN	0.58	NaN	NaN	0.51	NaN	NaN	NaN	0.58	NaN	0.43	0.48	0.44
4	0.64	0.69	0.72	NaN	NaN	0.45	NaN	0.47	NaN	NaN	0.48	NaN	0.57	0.57	NaN	NaN	NaN	NaN	NaN
6	0.71	0.69	NaN	NaN	NaN	NaN	0.62	0.44	0.56	0.48	0.44	0.50	NaN	NaN	NaN	0.47	0.54	0.49	NaN
8	NaN	NaN	0.47	0.45	NaN	NaN	0.53	NaN	0.46	NaN	0.55	0.49	0.49	0.44	0.64	NaN	NaN	0.47	NaN
10	0.50	0.55	NaN	NaN	0.62	0.53	NaN	NaN	NaN	0.52	NaN	0.62	0.63	0.73	0.62	0.55	0.58	0.47	NaN
11	0.46	0.55	0.58	0.47	0.44	NaN	NaN	NaN	0.56	NaN	NaN	NaN	0.50	0.49	0.57	NaN	NaN	0.52	NaN
16	NaN	NaN	NaN	NaN	0.56	0.46	NaN	0.56	NaN	0.58	NaN	NaN	NaN	NaN	NaN	0.43	NaN	0.45	NaN
18	NaN	0.45	NaN	NaN	0.48	NaN	0.52	NaN	0.58	NaN	NaN	NaN	NaN	NaN	0.50	NaN	NaN	0.50	NaN
19	0.45	0.51	0.51	0.48	0.44	0.55	NaN	NaN	NaN	NaN	NaN	NaN	NaN	NaN	NaN	0.59	0.46	NaN	NaN
21	NaN	NaN	NaN	NaN	0.50	0.49	0.62	NaN	NaN	NaN	NaN	NaN	0.71	0.56	0.54	0.50	0.61	0.72	NaN
22	NaN	NaN	NaN	0.57	NaN	0.49	0.63	0.50	NaN	NaN	NaN	0.71	NaN	0.86	0.62	0.55	0.56	0.53	NaN
23	NaN	NaN	NaN	0.57	NaN	0.44	0.73	0.49	NaN	NaN	NaN	0.56	0.86	NaN	0.62	0.59	0.61	0.55	NaN
24	NaN	0.49	0.58	NaN	NaN	0.64	0.62	0.57	NaN	0.50	NaN	0.54	0.62	0.62	NaN	0.64	0.55	0.77	0.65
26	NaN	NaN	NaN	NaN	0.47	NaN	0.55	NaN	0.43	NaN	0.59	0.50	0.55	0.59	0.64	NaN	NaN	0.62	0.67
27	0.52	0.60	0.43	NaN	0.54	NaN	0.58	NaN	NaN	NaN	0.46	0.61	0.56	0.61	0.55	NaN	NaN	0.65	NaN
28	NaN	NaN	0.48	NaN	0.49	0.47	0.47	0.52	0.45	0.50	NaN	0.72	0.53	0.55	0.77	0.62	0.65	NaN	0.70
30	NaN	NaN	0.44	NaN	NaN	NaN	NaN	NaN	NaN	NaN	NaN	NaN	NaN	NaN	0.65	0.67	NaN	0.70	NaN

B) GENDER (WOMEN = W, MEN = M)

	W																	
ITEMS	*1*	*2*	*3*	*4*	*6*	*8*	*10*	*11*	*16*	*18*	*19*	*21*	*22*	*23*	*24*	*26*	*27*	*28*	*30*
1	NaN	0.63	0.54	0.42	0.42	0.42	0.43	0.35	0.39	0.44	0.49	0.46	0.36	0.50	0.42	0.47	0.50	0.44	0.29
2	0.63	NaN	0.64	0.57	0.54	0.41	0.51	0.48	0.42	0.51	0.55	0.47	0.46	0.44	0.45	0.47	0.51	0.42	0.34
3	0.54	0.64	NaN	0.53	0.42	0.46	0.51	0.51	0.36	0.50	0.55	0.43	0.53	0.51	0.49	0.61	0.50	0.45	0.47
4	0.42	0.57	0.53	NaN	0.55	0.40	0.63	0.26	0.34	0.39	0.37	0.44	0.40	0.35	0.29	0.41	0.40	0.37	0.25
6	0.42	0.54	0.42	0.55	NaN	0.40	0.64	0.36	0.42	0.44	0.37	0.57	0.36	0.45	0.30	0.41	0.53	0.58	0.23
8	0.42	0.41	0.46	0.40	0.40	NaN	0.40	0.27	0.63	0.45	0.52	0.39	0.29	0.43	0.39	0.38	0.39	0.35	0.33
10	0.43	0.51	0.51	0.63	0.64	0.40	NaN	0.37	0.41	0.52	0.45	0.55	0.37	0.49	0.38	0.46	0.46	0.46	0.22
11	0.35	0.48	0.51	0.26	0.36	0.27	0.37	NaN	0.27	0.50	0.36	0.42	0.62	0.36	0.42	0.43	0.42	0.40	0.38
16	0.39	0.42	0.36	0.34	0.42	0.63	0.41	0.27	NaN	0.60	0.40	0.43	0.29	0.42	0.36	0.34	0.43	0.44	0.30
18	0.44	0.51	0.50	0.39	0.44	0.45	0.52	0.50	0.60	NaN	0.48	0.48	0.53	0.48	0.48	0.45	0.50	0.48	0.38
19	0.49	0.55	0.55	0.37	0.37	0.52	0.45	0.36	0.40	0.48	NaN	0.53	0.42	0.49	0.59	0.45	0.40	0.41	0.40
21	0.46	0.47	0.43	0.44	0.57	0.39	0.55	0.42	0.43	0.48	0.53	NaN	0.45	0.52	0.40	0.58	0.51	0.58	0.27
22	0.36	0.46	0.53	0.40	0.36	0.29	0.37	0.62	0.29	0.53	0.42	0.45	NaN	0.48	0.44	0.49	0.58	0.43	0.52
23	0.50	0.44	0.51	0.35	0.45	0.43	0.49	0.36	0.42	0.48	0.49	0.52	0.48	NaN	0.50	0.54	0.59	0.51	0.44
24	0.42	0.45	0.49	0.29	0.30	0.39	0.38	0.42	0.36	0.48	0.59	0.40	0.44	0.50	NaN	0.45	0.42	0.40	0.55
26	0.47	0.47	0.61	0.41	0.41	0.38	0.46	0.43	0.34	0.45	0.45	0.58	0.49	0.54	0.45	NaN	0.60	0.58	0.40
27	0.50	0.51	0.50	0.40	0.53	0.39	0.46	0.42	0.43	0.50	0.40	0.51	0.58	0.59	0.42	0.60	NaN	0.58	0.46
28	0.44	0.42	0.45	0.37	0.58	0.35	0.46	0.40	0.44	0.48	0.41	0.58	0.43	0.51	0.40	0.58	0.58	NaN	0.33
30	0.29	0.34	0.47	0.25	0.23	0.33	0.22	0.38	0.30	0.38	0.40	0.27	0.52	0.44	0.55	0.40	0.46	0.33	NaN

(Continued)

TABLE 2.16 (*Continued*) Spearman's correlation coefficients – students' attitudes and their intention to continue using GenAI, taking into account demographic and educational characteristics

	M																		
ITEMS	*1*	*2*	*3*	*4*	*6*	*8*	*10*	*11*	*16*	*18*	*19*	*21*	*22*	*23*	*24*	*26*	*27*	*28*	*30*
1	NaN	0.72	0.52	0.58	0.51	0.37	0.37	0.44	0.36	0.48	0.34	0.28	0.31	0.27	0.32	0.26	0.33	0.31	NaN
2	0.72	NaN	0.56	0.59	0.57	0.38	0.46	0.53	0.41	0.52	0.49	0.35	0.35	0.41	0.40	0.41	0.42	0.27	0.30
3	0.52	0.56	NaN	0.58	0.52	0.40	0.42	0.46	0.29	0.34	0.34	0.36	0.35	0.40	0.34	0.28	0.40	0.29	0.28
4	0.58	0.59	0.58	NaN	0.57	0.32	0.49	0.36	0.33	0.42	0.28	0.41	0.21	0.39	0.34	0.35	0.40	0.25	0.18
6	0.51	0.57	0.52	0.57	NaN	0.37	0.67	0.35	0.38	0.32	0.37	0.56	0.20	0.43	0.33	0.40	0.35	0.48	0.23
8	0.37	0.38	0.40	0.32	0.37	NaN	0.44	0.37	0.51	0.31	0.32	0.33	0.19	0.32	0.34	0.27	0.36	0.27	0.19
10	0.37	0.46	0.42	0.49	0.67	0.44	NaN	0.37	0.35	0.42	0.33	0.53	NaN	0.39	0.29	0.38	0.41	0.33	0.22
11	0.44	0.53	0.46	0.36	0.35	0.37	0.37	NaN	0.46	0.58	0.42	0.38	0.66	0.52	0.46	0.41	0.46	0.25	0.35
16	0.36	0.41	0.29	0.33	0.38	0.51	0.35	0.46	NaN	0.50	0.29	0.32	0.27	0.39	0.31	0.35	0.29	0.28	0.18
18	0.48	0.52	0.34	0.42	0.32	0.31	0.42	0.58	0.50	NaN	0.41	0.37	0.42	0.38	0.33	0.30	0.46	0.27	0.32
19	0.34	0.49	0.34	0.28	0.37	0.32	0.33	0.42	0.29	0.41	NaN	0.47	0.43	0.56	0.52	0.49	0.47	0.34	0.44
21	0.28	0.35	0.36	0.41	0.56	0.33	0.53	0.38	0.32	0.37	0.47	NaN	0.34	0.53	0.36	0.44	0.34	0.43	0.28
22	0.31	0.35	0.35	0.21	0.20	0.19	NaN	0.66	0.27	0.42	0.43	0.34	NaN	0.57	0.51	0.40	0.44	0.35	0.41
23	0.27	0.41	0.40	0.39	0.43	0.32	0.39	0.52	0.39	0.38	0.56	0.53	0.57	NaN	0.59	0.64	0.50	0.44	0.44
24	0.32	0.40	0.34	0.34	0.33	0.34	0.29	0.46	0.31	0.33	0.52	0.36	0.51	0.59	NaN	0.50	0.46	0.40	0.55
26	0.26	0.41	0.28	0.35	0.40	0.27	0.38	0.41	0.35	0.30	0.49	0.44	0.40	0.64	0.50	NaN	0.42	0.45	0.43
27	0.33	0.42	0.40	0.40	0.35	0.36	0.41	0.46	0.29	0.46	0.47	0.34	0.44	0.50	0.46	0.42	NaN	0.37	0.42
28	0.31	0.27	0.29	0.25	0.48	0.27	0.33	0.25	0.28	0.27	0.34	0.43	0.35	0.44	0.40	0.45	0.37	NaN	0.26
30	NaN	0.30	0.28	0.18	0.23	0.19	0.22	0.35	0.18	0.32	0.44	0.28	0.41	0.44	0.55	0.43	0.42	0.26	NaN

C) FIELD OF STUDY (STEM = T, SOCIAL SCIENCES = S)

	T																		
ITEMS	*1*	*2*	*3*	*4*	*6*	*8*	*10*	*11*	*16*	*18*	*19*	*21*	*22*	*23*	*24*	*26*	*27*	*28*	*30*
1	NaN	0.65	0.42	0.41	0.43	NaN	0.36	0.40	NaN	0.43	0.20	0.29	0.35	0.29	0.20	0.21	0.36	0.38	NaN
2	0.65	NaN	0.50	0.40	0.37	0.25	0.29	0.42	NaN	0.42	0.34	0.21	0.41	0.28	0.34	0.25	0.36	NaN	0.24
3	0.42	0.50	NaN	0.38	0.38	0.26	0.32	0.35	NaN	0.33	NaN	0.27	0.39	0.28	0.26	0.26	0.39	0.29	0.21
4	0.41	0.40	0.38	NaN	0.49	0.24	0.62	NaN	NaN	0.30	NaN	0.37	NaN	0.30	0.29	0.27	0.33	0.24	NaN
6	0.43	0.37	0.38	0.49	NaN	0.26	0.64	0.25	NaN	0.24	NaN	0.48	NaN	0.35	0.22	0.28	0.43	0.50	NaN
8	NaN	0.25	0.26	0.24	0.26	NaN	0.28	0.22	0.54	0.29	0.21	NaN	NaN	0.28	NaN	NaN	NaN	NaN	NaN
10	0.36	0.29	0.32	0.62	0.64	0.28	NaN	0.20	NaN	0.26	0.23	0.53	NaN	0.32	0.24	0.36	0.41	0.32	NaN
11	0.40	0.42	0.35	NaN	0.25	0.22	0.20	NaN	0.22	0.56	0.31	0.23	0.58	0.41	0.36	0.38	0.44	0.30	0.23
16	NaN	NaN	NaN	NaN	NaN	0.54	NaN	0.22	NaN	0.37	NaN	NaN	NaN	0.29	0.20	NaN	0.20	NaN	NaN
18	0.43	0.42	0.33	0.30	0.24	0.29	0.26	0.56	0.37	NaN	0.27	0.25	0.37	0.36	0.30	0.21	0.38	0.26	0.24
19	0.20	0.34	NaN	NaN	NaN	0.21	0.23	0.31	NaN	0.27	NaN	0.38	0.34	0.43	0.46	0.20	NaN	NaN	0.37
21	0.29	0.21	0.27	0.37	0.48	NaN	0.53	0.23	NaN	0.25	0.38	NaN	0.29	0.50	0.26	0.38	0.36	0.40	NaN
22	0.35	0.41	0.39	NaN	NaN	NaN	NaN	0.58	NaN	0.37	0.34	0.29	NaN	0.49	0.36	0.44	0.47	0.34	0.32
23	0.29	0.28	0.28	0.30	0.35	0.28	0.32	0.41	0.29	0.36	0.43	0.50	0.49	NaN	0.50	0.50	0.50	0.39	0.34
24	0.20	0.34	0.26	0.29	0.22	NaN	0.24	0.36	0.20	0.30	0.46	0.26	0.36	0.50	NaN	0.35	0.29	NaN	0.50
26	0.21	0.25	0.26	0.27	0.28	NaN	0.36	0.38	NaN	0.21	0.20	0.38	0.44	0.50	0.35	NaN	0.43	0.33	0.25
27	0.36	0.36	0.39	0.33	0.43	NaN	0.41	0.44	0.20	0.38	NaN	0.36	0.47	0.50	0.29	0.43	NaN	0.44	0.31
28	0.38	NaN	0.29	0.24	0.50	NaN	0.32	0.30	NaN	0.26	NaN	0.40	0.34	0.39	NaN	0.33	0.44	NaN	NaN
30	NaN	0.24	0.21	NaN	NaN	NaN	NaN	0.23	NaN	0.24	0.37	NaN	0.32	0.34	0.50	0.25	0.31	NaN	NaN

(Continued)

TABLE 2.16 (*Continued*) Spearman's correlation coefficients – students' attitudes and their intention to continue using GenAI, taking into account demographic and educational characteristics

	S																		
ITEMS	*1*	*2*	*3*	*4*	*6*	*8*	*10*	*11*	*16*	*18*	*19*	*21*	*22*	*23*	*24*	*26*	*27*	*28*	*30*
1	NaN	0.69	0.57	0.54	0.48	0.50	0.41	0.40	0.53	0.47	0.53	0.40	0.36	0.44	0.44	0.44	0.46	0.41	0.30
2	0.69	NaN	0.64	0.66	0.63	0.46	0.56	0.53	0.55	0.56	0.61	0.49	0.41	0.49	0.46	0.52	0.52	0.44	0.35
3	0.57	0.64	NaN	0.63	0.52	0.50	0.52	0.54	0.45	0.46	0.57	0.44	0.48	0.53	0.48	0.53	0.48	0.42	0.45
4	0.54	0.66	0.63	NaN	0.61	0.42	0.53	0.37	0.46	0.46	0.41	0.46	0.38	0.41	0.32	0.44	0.44	0.35	0.26
6	0.48	0.63	0.52	0.61	NaN	0.44	0.66	0.41	0.51	0.45	0.47	0.60	0.34	0.49	0.35	0.46	0.45	0.55	0.27
8	0.50	0.46	0.50	0.42	0.44	NaN	0.46	0.36	0.60	0.42	0.53	0.42	0.33	0.44	0.44	0.41	0.45	0.43	0.33
10	0.41	0.56	0.52	0.53	0.66	0.46	NaN	0.44	0.51	0.57	0.46	0.54	0.31	0.48	0.39	0.44	0.44	0.42	0.27
11	0.40	0.53	0.54	0.37	0.41	0.36	0.44	NaN	0.41	0.54	0.43	0.49	0.66	0.45	0.48	0.44	0.44	0.34	0.41
16	0.53	0.55	0.45	0.46	0.51	0.60	0.51	0.41	NaN	0.63	0.47	0.48	0.34	0.46	0.40	0.43	0.44	0.46	0.33
18	0.47	0.56	0.46	0.46	0.45	0.42	0.57	0.54	0.63	NaN	0.53	0.51	0.53	0.46	0.46	0.46	0.53	0.43	0.39
19	0.53	0.61	0.57	0.41	0.47	0.53	0.46	0.43	0.47	0.53	NaN	0.53	0.49	0.58	0.60	0.60	0.54	0.51	0.46
21	0.40	0.49	0.44	0.46	0.60	0.42	0.54	0.49	0.48	0.51	0.53	NaN	0.45	0.53	0.44	0.56	0.46	0.54	0.32
22	0.36	0.41	0.48	0.38	0.34	0.33	0.31	0.66	0.34	0.53	0.49	0.45	NaN	0.55	0.53	0.46	0.54	0.43	0.53
23	0.44	0.49	0.53	0.41	0.49	0.44	0.48	0.45	0.46	0.46	0.58	0.53	0.55	NaN	0.55	0.63	0.58	0.53	0.49
24	0.44	0.46	0.48	0.32	0.35	0.44	0.39	0.48	0.40	0.46	0.60	0.44	0.53	0.55	NaN	0.53	0.51	0.49	0.57
26	0.44	0.52	0.53	0.44	0.46	0.41	0.44	0.44	0.43	0.46	0.60	0.56	0.46	0.63	0.53	NaN	0.56	0.61	0.48
27	0.46	0.52	0.48	0.44	0.45	0.45	0.44	0.44	0.44	0.53	0.54	0.46	0.54	0.58	0.51	0.56	NaN	0.51	0.50
28	0.41	0.44	0.42	0.35	0.55	0.43	0.42	0.34	0.46	0.43	0.51	0.54	0.43	0.53	0.49	0.61	0.51	NaN	0.38
30	0.30	0.35	0.45	0.26	0.27	0.33	0.27	0.41	0.33	0.39	0.46	0.32	0.53	0.49	0.57	0.48	0.50	0.38	NaN

D) DEGREE LEVEL (BACHELOR'S = B, MASTER'S=M)

	B																		
ITEMS	*1*	*2*	*3*	*4*	*6*	*8*	*10*	*11*	*16*	*18*	*19*	*21*	*22*	*23*	*24*	*26*	*27*	*28*	*30*
1	NaN	0.65	0.44	0.43	0.34	0.31	0.27	0.39	0.25	0.44	0.34	0.24	0.32	0.27	0.35	0.33	0.37	0.31	0.20
2	0.65	NaN	0.54	0.51	0.46	0.37	0.33	0.47	0.32	0.51	0.51	0.31	0.40	0.35	0.45	0.37	0.41	0.25	0.31
3	0.44	0.54	NaN	0.40	0.40	0.29	0.36	0.46	0.16	0.35	0.37	0.30	0.40	0.38	0.37	0.38	0.34	0.32	0.36
4	0.43	0.51	0.40	NaN	0.50	0.29	0.47	0.22	0.19	0.34	0.25	0.37	0.20	0.31	0.33	0.31	0.31	0.27	NaN
6	0.34	0.46	0.40	0.50	NaN	0.33	0.62	0.30	0.30	0.36	0.27	0.54	0.22	0.39	0.26	0.34	0.38	0.53	0.16
8	0.31	0.37	0.29	0.29	0.33	NaN	0.36	0.27	0.56	0.33	0.37	0.25	0.24	0.31	0.30	0.28	0.31	0.20	0.24
10	0.27	0.33	0.36	0.47	0.62	0.36	NaN	0.28	0.22	0.34	0.29	0.52	0.18	0.36	0.30	0.40	0.34	0.40	0.17
11	0.39	0.47	0.46	0.22	0.30	0.27	0.28	NaN	0.28	0.59	0.43	0.31	0.65	0.43	0.50	0.44	0.45	0.35	0.35
16	0.25	0.32	0.16	0.19	0.30	0.56	0.22	0.28	NaN	0.44	0.26	0.27	0.21	0.32	0.28	0.33	0.28	0.30	0.17
18	0.44	0.51	0.35	0.34	0.36	0.33	0.34	0.59	0.44	NaN	0.39	0.35	0.45	0.39	0.44	0.39	0.45	0.37	0.29
19	0.34	0.51	0.37	0.25	0.27	0.37	0.29	0.43	0.26	0.39	NaN	0.39	0.44	0.49	0.51	0.36	0.36	0.25	0.41
21	0.24	0.31	0.30	0.37	0.54	0.25	0.52	0.31	0.27	0.35	0.39	NaN	0.33	0.43	0.31	0.41	0.37	0.46	0.15
22	0.32	0.40	0.40	0.20	0.22	0.24	0.18	0.65	0.21	0.45	0.44	0.33	NaN	0.56	0.49	0.48	0.54	0.36	0.43
23	0.27	0.35	0.38	0.31	0.39	0.31	0.36	0.43	0.32	0.39	0.49	0.43	0.56	NaN	0.49	0.57	0.52	0.46	0.42
24	0.35	0.45	0.37	0.33	0.26	0.30	0.30	0.50	0.28	0.44	0.51	0.31	0.49	0.49	NaN	0.50	0.42	0.33	0.52
26	0.33	0.37	0.38	0.31	0.34	0.28	0.40	0.44	0.33	0.39	0.36	0.41	0.48	0.57	0.50	NaN	0.45	0.47	0.34
27	0.37	0.41	0.34	0.31	0.38	0.31	0.34	0.45	0.28	0.45	0.36	0.37	0.54	0.52	0.42	0.45	NaN	0.43	0.39
28	0.31	0.25	0.32	0.27	0.53	0.20	0.40	0.35	0.30	0.37	0.25	0.46	0.36	0.46	0.33	0.47	0.43	NaN	0.23
30	0.20	0.31	0.36	NaN	0.16	0.24	0.17	0.35	0.17	0.29	0.41	0.15	0.43	0.42	0.52	0.34	0.39	0.23	NaN

(Continued)

TABLE 2.16 (*Continued*) Spearman's correlation coefficients – students' attitudes and their intention to continue using GenAI, taking into account demographic and educational characteristics

	M																		
ITEMS	*1*	*2*	*3*	*4*	*6*	*8*	*10*	*11*	*16*	*18*	*19*	*21*	*22*	*23*	*24*	*26*	*27*	*28*	*30*
1	NaN	0.71	0.63	0.58	0.60	0.54	0.53	0.41	0.53	0.48	0.53	0.51	0.39	0.53	0.39	0.42	0.49	0.50	0.27
2	0.71	NaN	0.67	0.67	0.67	0.44	0.65	0.54	0.52	0.52	0.56	0.53	0.44	0.53	0.40	0.51	0.54	0.47	0.35
3	0.63	0.67	NaN	0.73	0.55	0.59	0.59	0.52	0.51	0.52	0.54	0.50	0.52	0.54	0.47	0.53	0.58	0.45	0.41
4	0.58	0.67	0.73	NaN	0.66	0.45	0.66	0.41	0.52	0.49	0.43	0.50	0.45	0.45	0.30	0.46	0.51	0.38	0.33
6	0.60	0.67	0.55	0.66	NaN	0.43	0.70	0.44	0.53	0.42	0.47	0.60	0.37	0.52	0.38	0.48	0.52	0.53	0.33
8	0.54	0.44	0.59	0.45	0.43	NaN	0.46	0.38	0.61	0.44	0.49	0.45	0.27	0.48	0.42	0.38	0.45	0.45	0.30
10	0.53	0.65	0.59	0.66	0.70	0.46	NaN	0.47	0.55	0.63	0.51	0.57	0.36	0.52	0.39	0.44	0.55	0.38	0.29
11	0.41	0.54	0.52	0.41	0.44	0.38	0.47	NaN	0.44	0.49	0.37	0.54	0.63	0.47	0.40	0.41	0.43	0.31	0.39
16	0.53	0.52	0.51	0.52	0.53	0.61	0.55	0.44	NaN	0.67	0.48	0.51	0.37	0.50	0.40	0.35	0.47	0.45	0.35
18	0.48	0.52	0.52	0.49	0.42	0.44	0.63	0.49	0.67	NaN	0.54	0.53	0.52	0.49	0.39	0.38	0.52	0.39	0.43
19	0.53	0.56	0.54	0.43	0.47	0.49	0.51	0.37	0.48	0.54	NaN	0.60	0.44	0.58	0.60	0.60	0.53	0.51	0.46
21	0.51	0.53	0.50	0.50	0.60	0.45	0.57	0.54	0.51	0.53	0.60	NaN	0.48	0.63	0.48	0.62	0.50	0.52	0.44
22	0.39	0.44	0.52	0.45	0.37	0.27	0.36	0.63	0.37	0.52	0.44	0.48	NaN	0.49	0.47	0.42	0.49	0.46	0.53
23	0.53	0.53	0.54	0.45	0.52	0.48	0.52	0.47	0.50	0.49	0.58	0.63	0.49	NaN	0.60	0.61	0.60	0.51	0.47
24	0.39	0.40	0.47	0.30	0.38	0.42	0.39	0.40	0.40	0.39	0.60	0.48	0.47	0.60	NaN	0.46	0.46	0.48	0.60
26	0.42	0.51	0.53	0.46	0.48	0.38	0.44	0.41	0.35	0.38	0.60	0.62	0.42	0.61	0.46	NaN	0.60	0.57	0.50
27	0.49	0.54	0.58	0.51	0.52	0.45	0.55	0.43	0.47	0.52	0.53	0.50	0.49	0.60	0.46	0.60	NaN	0.55	0.51
28	0.50	0.47	0.45	0.38	0.53	0.45	0.38	0.31	0.45	0.39	0.51	0.52	0.46	0.51	0.48	0.57	0.55	NaN	0.40
30	0.27	0.35	0.41	0.33	0.33	0.30	0.29	0.39	0.35	0.43	0.46	0.44	0.53	0.47	0.60	0.50	0.51	0.40	NaN

Own study.

Legend: As in Table 2.5.

the existence of a common, stable mechanism for shaping intentions to use GenAI in the studied population of students, regardless of their age.

With regard to gender (Table 2.16 b), the strength of the correlation also varies. In women, correlations were more often moderate, while in men, weak and moderate correlations prevailed, although they were still statistically significant. No strong correlations or negative correlations were found, which indicates a consistent but moderate relationship between the intention to use GenAI and the attitudes of female and male students. In men, slightly stronger correlations were found primarily in the cognitive component of attitude, in particular, beliefs about the usefulness of GenAI for future work and competence development, which indicates the dominant role of performance expectancy (UTAUT) in shaping the intention to use GenAI in this group. In contrast, among women, slightly stronger correlations were found for both the affective component, especially enjoyment, inspiration, and enthusiasm associated with using GenAI, and the cognitive component, which includes the assessment of GenAI in terms of educational and creative usefulness. This may mean that in men, the intention to use GenAI is more pragmatic and instrumental, while in women it is more balanced, emotional, and cognitive in nature. As in the case of age, the differences indicated do not change the overall pattern of dependence, which confirms the universal nature of the mechanisms shaping the intention to use GenAI regardless of gender.

With regard to field of study (Table 2.16 c), differences in the strength and structure of correlations can be observed. Among STEM students, the correlations are mainly weak to moderate ($\rho \approx 0.20$–0.46), while among social science students, they are more often moderate ($\rho \approx 0.50$–0.60). In addition, clear differences in the structure of correlations can be observed. In the group of STEM students, the intention to continue using GenAI is most strongly correlated with the cognitive component, especially with beliefs about the educational and professional usefulness of technology. Correlations with the affective and behavioral components are weaker or moderate. In contrast, among social science students, the intention to use shows quite strong and numerous correlations with both the affective and cognitive and behavioral components, indicating a more holistic attitude. This means that for social science students, emotions, user experience, and cognitive beliefs jointly shape the intention to use GenAI, while for STEM students, pragmatic and user-related factors dominate. The differences indicated do not undermine the previously indicated nature of the mechanisms shaping the intention to use GenAI but confirm it – the direction of the relationship is the same. All significant correlations with the intention to continue using GenAI are positive and relate to the same basic components of attitude.

In the case of recommending GenAI to other students (item 20), Spearman's correlation analysis conducted for the entire sample (without

TABLE 2.17 Spearman's correlation coefficients between students' attitudes and their recommendation of GenAI

ITEMS	*9*	*17*	*20*	*21*	*22*	*23*	*24*	*26*	*27*	*28*
9	NaN	0.39	0.50	0.44	0.46	0.50	0.37	0.45	0.48	0.40
17	0.39	NaN	0.43	0.32	0.38	0.38	0.28	0.38	0.38	0.30
20	0.50	0.43	NaN	0.57	0.49	0.51	0.52	0.46	0.48	0.43
21	0.44	0.32	0.57	NaN	0.39	0.52	0.39	0.51	0.43	0.50
22	0.46	0.38	0.49	0.39	NaN	0.53	0.47	0.45	0.52	0.40
23	0.50	0.38	0.51	0.52	0.53	NaN	0.54	0.59	0.56	0.48
24	0.37	0.28	0.52	0.39	0.47	0.54	NaN	0.48	0.44	0.40
26	0.45	0.38	0.46	0.51	0.45	0.59	0.48	NaN	0.52	0.52
27	0.48	0.38	0.48	0.43	0.52	0.56	0.44	0.52	NaN	0.49
28	0.40	0.30	0.43	0.50	0.40	0.48	0.40	0.52	0.49	NaN

Own study.
Legend: As in Table 2.5.

taking into account demographic and educational characteristics) showed consistent, moderate positive correlations with most of the other items describing attitudes toward GenAI ($\rho \approx 0.43$–0.57), as shown in Table 2.17. This means that the willingness to recommend GenAI is not an incidental reaction, but results from a consistent set of attitudes.

The highest correlation coefficients for item 20 relate to the cognitive attitude component, which clearly fits into the performance expectancy construct (UTAUT). This applies in particular to items: 21: $\rho \approx 0.57$, 23: $\rho \approx 0.51$, 24: $\rho \approx 0.52$, 26: $\rho \approx 0.46$, 28: $\rho \approx 0.46$, which means that recommending GenAI to other students is associated with the belief that this technology improves learning efficiency, supports the development of competencies, is essential in future work, supports creativity, and increases productivity. Therefore, recommending GenAI to others is primarily a normative action based on a rational assessment of its benefits.

Item 20 also correlates moderately with positive attitudes toward GenAI (especially A from the ABC model and hedonic motivation (UTAUT2), in particular with items 9: $\rho \approx 0.50$, 22: $\rho \approx 0.49$. These relationships indicate that a positive attitude toward the inclusion of GenAI in teaching and a positive assessment of the experience of facilitating task performance when using GenAI reinforce the tendency to recommend this technology to others, although they play a supporting rather than a dominant role.

The smallest but moderate correlations of item 20 were found with behavioral items, including item 17: $\rho \approx 0.43$, 27: $\rho \approx 0.48$. This means that practical experience in using GenAI in group projects and observable benefits related to the provision of valuable information by GenAI encourage the recommendation of this technology, but are not sufficient on their own without a cognitive assessment of its usefulness.

Referring the results of the correlation analysis to hypothesis 3, it can be concluded that it has been confirmed. The willingness to recommend GenAI (item 20) shows significant, weak to moderate positive correlations with key components of the attitude toward GenAI, covering all ABC components. The strongest correlations relate to the cognitive component, i.e., beliefs about the usefulness of GenAI for learning effectiveness, competence development, and future work, which is consistent with UTAUT/UTAUT2, where it is treated as a manifestation of social internalization of beliefs about the usefulness of GenAI.

To deepen the research, an additional analysis of the correlation between students' attitudes and their willingness to recommend GenAI was conducted, taking into account their demographic and educational characteristics. The results of the analysis are presented in Table 2.18.

The analysis shows that in all age groups, the correlations for item 20 are clearly positive (Table 2.18 a). This means that regardless of age, the more positive the students' emotions, the stronger their beliefs about the usefulness of GenAI, and the richer their experience of using it, the greater their willingness to recommend it to other students. It should also be noted that the strength of the relationship between students' attitudes toward GenAI and their recommendation of it clearly increases with the age of the students. In the youngest group (≤ 20 years), the relationships are few and moderate ($\rho \approx 0.49–0.57$), in the 21–30 age group they are numerous and moderate ($\rho \approx 0.43–0.61$), in the 31–40 age group, they are moderate to strong ($\rho \approx 0.56–0.70$), while in the >40 age group, they are the strongest ($\rho \approx 0.58–0.86$). This indicates a systematic strengthening of the relationship between attitudes and GenAI recommendation with life and educational experience. In addition, the structure of the correlation changes with age. Among the youngest students, GenAI recommendation is based on single, fragmentary premises, mainly cognitive and social. In the 21–30 age group, a balanced arrangement of ABC components is observed, while in older groups, the cognitive component – performance expectancy – begins to dominate, supported by the affective component – habit. The affective component plays only a supporting role in all groups. The results obtained are consistent with the assumptions of the UTAUT/UTAUT2 model.

With regard to gender (Table 2.18 b), in both men and women, all significant correlations between attitudes toward GenAI and willingness to recommend it are positive. This means that, regardless of gender, more positive emotions, stronger beliefs about usefulness, and greater experience in using GenAI are associated with a greater willingness to recommend it to

TABLE 2.18 Spearman's correlation coefficients – students' attitudes toward GenAI and their willingness to recommend it, taking into account their demographic and educational characteristics

A) AGE

≤ 20 YEARS

ITEMS	*9*	*17*	*20*	*21*	*22*	*23*	*24*	*26*	*27*	*28*
9	NaN	NaN	NaN	0.55	NaN	NaN	NaN	NaN	NaN	NaN
17	NaN	NaN	0.64	NaN	0.60	NaN	NaN	NaN	0.52	NaN
20	NaN	0.64	NaN	NaN	NaN	NaN	NaN	NaN	0.49	NaN
21	0.55	NaN	NaN	NaN	NaN	0.57	NaN	NaN	NaN	0.57
22	NaN	0.60	NaN	NaN	NaN	NaN	NaN	0.52	0.51	NaN
23	NaN	NaN	NaN	0.57	NaN	NaN	NaN	NaN	NaN	0.61
24	NaN	NaN	NaN	NaN	NaN	NaN	NaN	NaN	0.55	NaN
26	NaN	NaN	NaN	NaN	0.52	NaN	NaN	NaN	NaN	0.61
27	NaN	0.52	0.49	NaN	0.51	NaN	0.55	NaN	NaN	NaN
28	NaN	NaN	NaN	0.57	NaN	0.61	NaN	0.61	NaN	NaN

21–30 YEARS

ITEMS	*9*	*17*	*20*	*21*	*22*	*23*	*24*	*26*	*27*	*28*
9	NaN	0.40	0.50	0.41	0.46	0.53	0.40	0.47	0.51	0.42
17	0.40	NaN	0.38	0.32	0.33	0.39	0.28	0.41	0.41	0.34
20	0.50	0.38	NaN	0.59	0.48	0.52	0.54	0.48	0.47	0.43
21	0.41	0.32	0.59	NaN	0.41	0.50	0.42	0.50	0.43	0.51
22	0.46	0.33	0.48	0.41	NaN	0.55	0.51	0.48	0.54	0.43
23	0.53	0.39	0.52	0.50	0.55	NaN	0.55	0.61	0.56	0.46
24	0.40	0.28	0.54	0.42	0.51	0.55	NaN	0.51	0.44	0.38
26	0.47	0.41	0.48	0.50	0.48	0.61	0.51	NaN	0.54	0.51
27	0.51	0.41	0.47	0.43	0.54	0.56	0.44	0.54	NaN	0.48
28	0.42	0.34	0.43	0.51	0.43	0.46	0.38	0.51	0.48	NaN

31–40 YEARS

ITEMS	*9*	*17*	*20*	*21*	*22*	*23*	*24*	*26*	*27*	*28*
9	NaN	0.39	0.58	0.47	0.51	0.40	NaN	0.38	0.46	0.40
17	0.39	NaN	0.61	0.32	0.59	0.39	NaN	NaN	0.35	0.33
20	0.58	0.61	NaN	0.61	0.56	0.56	0.44	NaN	0.61	0.44
21	0.47	0.32	0.61	NaN	NaN	0.65	NaN	0.68	0.52	0.45
22	0.51	0.59	0.56	NaN	NaN	0.48	0.36	NaN	0.43	0.45
23	0.40	0.39	0.56	0.65	0.48	NaN	0.54	0.60	0.70	0.57
24	NaN	NaN	0.44	NaN	0.36	0.54	NaN	NaN	0.36	0.51

(Continued)

TABLE 2.18 (*Continued*) Spearman's correlation coefficients – students' attitudes toward GenAI and their willingness to recommend it, taking into account their demographic and educational characteristics

26	0.38	NaN	NaN	0.68	NaN	0.60	NaN	NaN	0.63	0.50
27	0.46	0.35	0.61	0.52	0.43	0.70	0.36	0.63	NaN	0.67
28	0.40	0.33	0.44	0.45	0.45	0.57	0.51	0.50	0.67	NaN
					>40 YEARS					
ITEMS	*9*	*17*	*20*	*21*	*22*	*23*	*24*	*26*	*27*	*28*
9	NaN	NaN	0.58	0.62	0.50	0.48	0.68	0.45	0.47	0.62
17	NaN	NaN	0.52	NaN	0.43	0.49	0.43	0.59	NaN	0.43
20	0.58	0.52	NaN	0.78	0.70	0.54	0.59	0.58	0.54	0.54
21	0.62	NaN	0.78	NaN	0.71	0.56	0.54	0.50	0.61	0.72
22	0.50	0.43	0.70	0.71	NaN	0.86	0.62	0.55	0.56	0.53
23	0.48	0.49	0.54	0.56	0.86	NaN	0.62	0.59	0.61	0.55
24	0.68	0.43	0.59	0.54	0.62	0.62	NaN	0.64	0.55	0.77
26	0.45	0.59	0.58	0.50	0.55	0.59	0.64	NaN	NaN	0.62
27	0.47	NaN	0.54	0.61	0.56	0.61	0.55	NaN	NaN	0.65
28	0.62	0.43	0.54	0.72	0.53	0.55	0.77	0.62	0.65	NaN
					B) GENAI USAGE PATTERNS BY GENDER (WOMEN = W, MEN = M)					
					W					
ITEMS	*9*	*17*	*20*	*21*	*22*	*23*	*24*	*26*	*27*	*28*
9	NaN	0.42	0.53	0.48	0.51	0.51	0.42	0.50	0.50	0.41
17	0.42	NaN	0.36	0.42	0.34	0.41	0.31	0.40	0.40	0.38
20	0.53	0.36	NaN	0.56	0.52	0.49	0.50	0.48	0.49	0.41
21	0.48	0.42	0.56	NaN	0.45	0.52	0.40	0.58	0.51	0.58
22	0.51	0.34	0.52	0.45	NaN	0.48	0.44	0.49	0.58	0.43
23	0.51	0.41	0.49	0.52	0.48	NaN	0.50	0.54	0.59	0.51
24	0.42	0.31	0.50	0.40	0.44	0.50	NaN	0.45	0.42	0.40
26	0.50	0.40	0.48	0.58	0.49	0.54	0.45	NaN	0.60	0.58
27	0.50	0.40	0.49	0.51	0.58	0.59	0.42	0.60	NaN	0.58
28	0.41	0.38	0.41	0.58	0.43	0.51	0.40	0.58	0.58	NaN
					M					
ITEMS	*9*	*17*	*20*	*21*	*22*	*23*	*24*	*26*	*27*	*28*
9	NaN	0.34	0.45	0.39	0.39	0.49	0.32	0.39	0.46	0.39
17	0.34	NaN	0.49	0.23	0.39	0.34	0.24	0.33	0.34	0.20
20	0.45	0.49	NaN	0.59	0.46	0.52	0.53	0.43	0.47	0.44

(Continued)

TABLE 2.18 (*Continued*) Spearman's correlation coefficients – students' attitudes toward GenAI and their willingness to recommend it, taking into account their demographic and educational characteristics

21	0.39	0.23	0.59	NaN	0.34	0.53	0.36	0.44	0.34	0.43
22	0.39	0.39	0.46	0.34	NaN	0.57	0.51	0.40	0.44	0.35
23	0.49	0.34	0.52	0.53	0.57	NaN	0.59	0.64	0.50	0.44
24	0.32	0.24	0.53	0.36	0.51	0.59	NaN	0.50	0.46	0.40
26	0.39	0.33	0.43	0.44	0.40	0.64	0.50	NaN	0.42	0.45
27	0.46	0.34	0.47	0.34	0.44	0.50	0.46	0.42	NaN	0.37
28	0.39	0.20	0.44	0.43	0.35	0.44	0.40	0.45	0.37	NaN

C) STUDENTS' AFFECTIVE-MOTIVATIONAL ATTITUDES BY FIELD OF STUDY (T = STEM; S = SOCIAL SCIENCES)

T

ITEMS	*9*	*17*	*20*	*21*	*22*	*23*	*24*	*26*	*27*	*28*
9	NaN	0.40	0.39	0.32	0.41	0.39	0.23	0.36	0.42	0.41
17	0.40	NaN	0.42	0.31	0.48	0.36	0.26	0.33	0.41	0.40
20	0.39	0.42	NaN	0.46	0.37	0.42	0.42	0.21	0.44	0.32
21	0.32	0.31	0.46	NaN	0.29	0.50	0.26	0.38	0.36	0.40
22	0.41	0.48	0.37	0.29	NaN	0.49	0.36	0.44	0.47	0.34
23	0.39	0.36	0.42	0.50	0.49	NaN	0.50	0.50	0.50	0.39
24	0.23	0.26	0.42	0.26	0.36	0.50	NaN	0.35	0.29	NaN
26	0.36	0.33	0.21	0.38	0.44	0.50	0.35	NaN	0.43	0.33
27	0.42	0.41	0.44	0.36	0.47	0.50	0.29	0.43	NaN	0.44
28	0.41	0.40	0.32	0.40	0.34	0.39	NaN	0.33	0.44	NaN

S

ITEMS	*9*	*17*	*20*	*21*	*22*	*23*	*24*	*26*	*27*	*28*
9	NaN	0.37	0.53	0.48	0.47	0.54	0.43	0.48	0.51	0.40
17	0.58	0.41	0.48	0.54	0.31	0.48	0.39	0.44	0.44	0.42
20	0.37	NaN	0.43	0.35	0.31	0.39	0.29	0.39	0.37	0.26
21	0.53	0.43	NaN	0.62	0.54	0.55	0.56	0.56	0.50	0.47
22	0.48	0.35	0.62	NaN	0.45	0.53	0.44	0.56	0.46	0.54
23	0.47	0.31	0.54	0.45	NaN	0.55	0.53	0.46	0.54	0.43
24	0.54	0.39	0.55	0.53	0.55	NaN	0.55	0.63	0.58	0.53
26	0.43	0.29	0.56	0.44	0.53	0.55	NaN	0.53	0.51	0.49
27	0.48	0.39	0.56	0.56	0.46	0.63	0.53	NaN	0.56	0.61
28	0.51	0.37	0.50	0.46	0.54	0.58	0.51	0.56	NaN	0.51

(Continued)

TABLE 2.18 (*Continued*) Spearman's correlation coefficients – students' attitudes toward GenAI and their willingness to recommend it, taking into account their demographic and educational characteristics

D) GENAI USAGE PATTERNS BY DEGREE LEVEL (B = BACHELOR'S, M = MASTER'S)

					B					
ITEMS	*9*	*17*	*20*	*21*	*22*	*23*	*24*	*26*	*27*	*28*
9	NaN	0.38	0.38	0.38	0.45	0.45	0.36	0.46	0.45	0.41
17	0.38	NaN	0.39	0.24	0.45	0.33	0.33	0.43	0.39	0.35
20	0.38	0.39	NaN	0.51	0.47	0.45	0.52	0.37	0.44	0.39
21	0.38	0.24	0.51	NaN	0.33	0.43	0.31	0.41	0.37	0.46
22	0.45	0.45	0.47	0.33	NaN	0.56	0.49	0.48	0.54	0.36
23	0.45	0.33	0.45	0.43	0.56	NaN	0.49	0.57	0.52	0.46
24	0.36	0.33	0.52	0.31	0.49	0.49	NaN	0.50	0.42	0.33
26	0.46	0.43	0.37	0.41	0.48	0.57	0.50	NaN	0.45	0.47
27	0.45	0.39	0.44	0.37	0.54	0.52	0.42	0.45	NaN	0.43
28	0.41	0.35	0.39	0.46	0.36	0.46	0.33	0.47	0.43	NaN
					M					
ITEMS	*9*	*17*	*20*	*21*	*22*	*23*	*24*	*26*	*27*	*28*
9	NaN	0.42	0.62	0.51	0.47	0.55	0.39	0.43	0.53	0.41
17	0.42	NaN	0.48	0.48	0.30	0.47	0.26	0.32	0.39	0.30
20	0.62	0.48	NaN	0.66	0.53	0.59	0.53	0.55	0.53	0.49
21	0.51	0.48	0.66	NaN	0.48	0.63	0.48	0.62	0.50	0.52
22	0.47	0.30	0.53	0.48	NaN	0.49	0.47	0.42	0.49	0.46
23	0.55	0.47	0.59	0.63	0.49	NaN	0.60	0.61	0.60	0.51
24	0.39	0.26	0.53	0.48	0.47	0.60	NaN	0.46	0.46	0.48
26	0.43	0.32	0.55	0.62	0.42	0.61	0.46	NaN	0.60	0.57
27	0.53	0.39	0.53	0.50	0.49	0.60	0.46	0.60	NaN	0.55
28	0.41	0.30	0.49	0.52	0.46	0.51	0.48	0.57	0.55	NaN

Own study.
Legend: As in Table 2.5.

other students. No negative correlations or reversals of the relationship are observed. However, depending on gender, the strength of the correlation between attitudes toward GenAI and willingness to recommend it differs, while maintaining a positive direction in both groups. In men, moderate correlations prevail ($\rho \approx 0.43$–0.59), concentrated mainly around the UTAUT performance expectancy construct, which indicates that recommending

GenAI in this group is primarily the result of a rational assessment of its educational and professional usefulness. In women, on the other hand, stronger and more dispersed correlations ($\rho \approx 0.48$–0.60) are observed, covering not only performance expectancy but also hedonic motivation and habit, which suggests a more multidimensional mechanism of technology acceptance, consistent with the extended UTAUT2 model. As a result, gender does not change the mechanism of forming the intention to recommend GenAI itself, but modifies the relative weight of individual UTAUT/UTAUT2 constructs, strengthening the role of emotions and user experience in women.

With regard to the field of study (Table 2.18 c), among both STEM and social science students, all significant correlations between attitudes toward GenAI and willingness to recommend it are positive. This means that regardless of the educational profile, an increase in positive emotions, user experience, and beliefs about the usefulness of GenAI is associated with a greater willingness to recommend it to other students. No negative correlations or reversals of the relationship are observed. However, there are differences in the strength of the relationship between attitudes toward GenAI and willingness to recommend it, depending on the field of study. In the STEM group, weak to moderate relationships ($\rho \approx 0.21$–0.50) predominate, with the highest values rarely exceeding $\rho \approx 0.50$. This means that attitudes toward GenAI influence the recommendation of this technology, but this influence is limited and selective. In the social sciences group, the correlations are stronger and more homogeneous, mostly moderate ($\rho \approx 0.43$–0.63), and in several cases approaching the threshold of strong correlations. This indicates that among social science students, attitudes toward GenAI are more strongly integrated with the willingness to recommend it.

Qualitative differences in the structure of the relationship should also be noted. Among STEM students, the structure of the relationship is hierarchical and narrow. The strongest correlations concern the cognitive component of attitude, in particular, beliefs about the usefulness of GenAI for learning effectiveness, supporting competence development, and the practical value of information generated by AI. The affective and behavioral components show weaker and less consistent links, suggesting that emotions and habits are not the main mechanisms for recommending GenAI in this group. This structure corresponds to the classic UTAUT model, in which performance expectancy is the dominant predictor of intention. In the group of social science students, a dense and multidimensional structure is observed, in which GenAI recommendation is strongly linked to the cognitive component (educational, professional, and creative utility), behavioral (habit, integration of AI with practice), and affective (positive attitude, acceptance of GenAI). These relationships reinforce each other, creating a coherent system in which none of the ABC components play a purely auxiliary role. This pattern is consistent with UTAUT2, where, in addition to performance expectancy, hedonic motivation and habit play an important role.

With regard to the level of study (Table 2.18 d), among both Bachelor's and Master's students, all significant correlations between attitudes toward GenAI and willingness to recommend it are positive. This means that, regardless of the stage of education, stronger beliefs about the usefulness of GenAI, greater experience in its use, and a more positive emotional attitude are associated with a greater willingness to recommend this technology to other students. No negative correlations or changes in the sign of the relationship are observed. However, depending on the level of study, the strength of the relationship between attitudes toward GenAI and willingness to recommend it clearly varies. Among Bachelor's students, moderate correlations ($\rho \approx 0.33$–0.57) predominate, indicating a stable but low level of association between attitudes and the intention to recommend. At the Master's level, stronger and more homogeneous correlations ($\rho \approx 0.48$–0.66) are observed, which indicates greater consistency of attitudes and their stronger translation into intentional behavior. The increase in the strength of the relationship with the level of study suggests that educational experience strengthens the mechanisms of GenAI acceptance. In addition, a clear differentiation is also visible in the structure of the relationship. In the Bachelor's group, a selective structure dominates, in which the cognitive component of attitude and performance expectancy plays a key role, supported by selected elements of the behavioral component and habit, while the affective component plays a secondary role. This arrangement corresponds to the classic UTAUT model, which assumes the primacy of rational assessment of the usefulness of technology. In the Master's group, the structure of dependencies is integrated and multidimensional – recommending GenAI is strongly linked to the cognitive, behavioral, and affective components. The role of habit and hedonic motivation is strengthened, which is consistent with the assumptions of UTAUT2 and indicates a more mature mechanism of technology acceptance based on experience.

In summary, additional correlation analyses broken down by age, gender, field of study, and degree show that the willingness to recommend GenAI to other students is positively associated with attitudes toward this technology in all groups. Demographic and educational factors differentiate the strength and structure of these relationships, but do not change their direction or basic mechanism. Regardless of the group, recommending GenAI is most strongly associated with the cognitive component of attitude, corresponding to the construct of performance expectancy, with the increasing importance of habit and user experience in older and more educationally advanced groups. The results obtained do not undermine hypothesis 3, but confirm it, pointing to the universal nature of the mechanisms shaping the propensity to recommend

GenAI, with the simultaneous role of demographic and educational variables as moderators of the strength and configuration of the relationships.

Since hypothesis 3 does not concern differences between groups, but rather relationships between variables, no additional intergroup tests (such as the Mann-Whitney U test or the Kruskal-Wallis test) were performed. The use of these tests would not contribute significant information to the verification of hypothesis 3.

2.2.4 Step 4: verification of hypothesis 4

The research process was similar to the previous steps. First, statistical analyses were performed to verify the hypothesis that students perceive GenAI as a tool that supports learning effectiveness and competence development while being aware of its limitations.

The analysis compares items relating to specific benefits of using GenAI in terms of student learning and competence development, i.e., 21–24, 26–28, and 30, with items relating to awareness of the limitations of GenAI, i.e., 25 and 29. This approach made it possible to check whether a positive assessment of the usefulness of GenAI coexists with a critical and reflective approach to this technology. The results of the statistical analysis are presented in Table 2.19.

TABLE 2.19 Selected descriptive statistics – benefits of using GenAI and awareness of its limitations

MEASURES OF ANALYSIS	*SYNTHETIC INDICES DERIVED FROM PART II OF THE SURVEY (SI)*			
	21	*26–28*	*30*	*25 AND 29*
Valid	309	309	309	309
Missing	0	0	0	0
Median	3.5	3.33	4	4.5
Mean	3.503	3.389	4.058	4.129
Std. Deviation	0.84	0.854	0.899	0.758
Shapiro-Wilk	0.963	0.967	0.827	0.868
P-value of Shapiro-Wilk	< .001	< .001	< .001	< .001
Minimum	1	1	1	1
Maximum	5	5	5	5

Own study.
Legend: As in Table 2.4.

It should be noted that the analysis includes average synthetic indicators (SI) from items 21–24, 26–28, 30, 25, and 29, which is justified theoretically and methodologically because of the following:

- Items 21–24 form a coherent block relating to learning effectiveness and competence development (performance expectancy),
- Items 26–28 refer to productivity, creativity, and the value of information,
- Item 30 concerns the perception of the role of GenAI in education in the future,
- Items 25 and 29 describe awareness of the limitations and conditions for the safe use of GenAI.

Aggregation into averages allows us to limit the random variability of individual responses, capture the general trend of attitudes rather than reactions to individual statements, and maintain consistency with the UTAUT/UTAUT2 approach.

The results of the analysis show that the mean values for the synthetic indicators are clearly above the neutral point of the scale (3), as for items SI 21–24 Mean (M) is 3.5, Median (Me) 3.5; for items SI 26–28 M=3.39, Me = 3.33; and for item 30 M=4.06, Me=4. This means that students rather agree or strongly agree with the statements about the positive impact of GenAI on learning and competence development. The particularly high M for item 30 indicates a strong belief in the growing role of GenAI in education, which reinforces the cognitive component of the attitude. At the same time, the results for SI 25 and 29 are the highest: M = 4.13, Me = 4.5. This shows that students are highly aware of the errors of GenAI, the need for critical evaluation of generated content, and the principles of safe use of AI tools. This means that the positive assessment of GenAI is not uncritical.

The results obtained clearly confirm hypothesis 4. Students perceive GenAI as a tool that supports learning effectiveness, competence development, productivity, and creativity while at the same time demonstrating a high awareness of its limitations and potential risks. This pattern of responses indicates a mature, reflective attitude toward GenAI, consistent with the assumptions of technology acceptance models (UTAUT/UTAUT2), in which high performance expectancy coexists with a rational assessment of the conditions and limitations of technology use.

It should be noted that the Shapiro-Wilk test results showed significant deviations from the normal distribution for all variables ($p < .001$), which does not undermine the interpretation of means and medians as measures of central tendency with a large sample size ($N = 309$), but justifies the use of non-parametric statistics. Therefore, Spearman's correlation analysis was performed, the results of which are presented in Table 2.20.

TABLE 2.20 Spearman's correlation coefficients benefits of using GenAI and awareness of its limitations

SYNTHETIC INDICES DERIVED FROM PART II OF THE SURVEY	*21–24*	*26*	*30*	*25 AND 29*
21	NaN	0.75	0.53	0.39
26–28	0.75	NaN	0.44	0.38
30	0.53	0.44	NaN	0.48
25–29	0.39	0.38	0.48	NaN

Own study.
Legend: As in Table 2.5.

Based on these, it can be concluded that statistically significant positive correlations were obtained between all synthetic average indicators relating to the benefits of GenAI (SI 21–24, 26–28, 30) and the indicator relating to awareness of its limitations (25 and 29). Although the strength of these correlations was weak to moderate, their direction was consistent and unambiguous. This means that students who are more aware of the benefits of using GenAI are also more likely to declare awareness of its limitations. It follows that a positive assessment of GenAI is not associated with uncritical acceptance of the technology, but coexists with a reflective and responsible approach to its use.

Additional correlation analyses were performed, taking into account the demographic and educational characteristics of the students. The results are presented in Table 2.21.

With regard to age (Table 2.21 a), it can be seen that among the youngest students ≤20 years of age, there are moderate positive correlations between the various dimensions of perceived GenAI benefits. The relationship between learning effectiveness and competence development (SI 21–24) and productivity and creativity (SI 26–28) is clear ($\rho = 0.68$), as is their relationship with the perceived role of GenAI in education (30; $\rho = 0.49–0.54$). Awareness of the limitations of GenAI (SI 25 and 29) correlates only with the area of productivity and creativity ($\rho = 0.55$), while it does not show a direct relationship with learning effectiveness or the overall vision of the role of GenAI. This indicates a fragmented, still inconsistent structure of attitudes, in which benefits and limitations are not fully integrated.

Among students aged 21–30, the relationships take on a more consistent and orderly structure. Correlations between benefit indicators are strong (SI 21–24 ↔ 26–28: $\rho = 0.75$) or moderate (SI 21–24 ↔ 30: $\rho = 0.52$). Importantly, awareness of GenAI limitations (SI 25 and 29) shows positive correlations with all areas of benefits ($\rho = 0.35–0.48$). This means that in this group,

TABLE 2.21 Spearman's correlation coefficients – benefits of using GenAI and awareness of its limitations among students, taking into account their demographic and educational characteristics

		A) AGE		
		≤ 20 YEARS		
SI	*21–24*	*26–28*	*30*	*25 AND 29*
21–24	NaN	0.68	0.54	NaN
26–28	0.68	NaN	0.49	0.55
30	0.54	0.49	NaN	NaN
25 and 29	NaN	0.55	NaN	NaN
		21–30 YEARS		
SI	*21–24*	*26–28*	*30*	*25 AND 29*
21–24	NaN	0.75	0.52	0.40
26–28	0.75	NaN	0.43	0.35
30	0.52	0.43	NaN	0.48
25 and 29	0.40	0.35	0.48	NaN
		31–40 YEARS		
SI	*21–24*	*26–28*	*30*	*25 AND 29*
21–24	NaN	0.72	0.62	0.49
26–28	0.72	NaN	0.40	0.53
30	0.62	0.40	NaN	0.49
25 and 29	0.49	0.53	0.49	NaN
		>40 YEARS		
SI	*21–24*	*26–28*	*30*	*25 AND 29*
21–24	NaN	0.84	0.53	NaN
26–28	0.84	NaN	0.67	0.57
30	0.53	0.67	NaN	0.58
25 and 29	NaN	0.57	0.58	NaN
		B) GENAI USAGE PATTERNS BY GENDER (WOMEN = W, MEN = M)		
		W		
SI	*21–24*	*26–28*	*30*	*25 AND 29*
21–24	NaN	0.76	0.54	0.40
26–28	0.76	NaN	0.45	0.36
30	0.54	0.45	NaN	0.58
25 and 29	0.40	0.36	0.58	NaN

(Continued)

TABLE 2.21 (*Continued*) Spearman's correlation coefficients – benefits of using GenAI and awareness of its limitations among students, taking into account their demographic and educational characteristics

		M		
SI	*21–24*	*26–28*	*30*	*25 AND 29*
21–24	NaN	0.74	0.52	0.39
26–28	0.74	NaN	0.43	0.42
30	0.52	0.43	NaN	0.35
25 and 29	0.39	0.42	0.35	NaN
C) STUDENTS' AFFECTIVE-MOTIVATIONAL ATTITUDES BY FIELD OF STUDY (T = STEM, S = SOCIAL SCIENCES)				
		T		
SI	*21–24*	*26–28*	*30*	*25 AND 29*
21–24	NaN	0.67	0.45	0.27
26–28	0.67	NaN	0.27	0.30
30	0.45	0.27	NaN	0.25
25 and 29	0.27	0.30	0.25	NaN
		S		
SI	*21–24*	*26–28*	*30*	*25 AND 29*
21–24	NaN	0.79	0.56	0.44
26–28	0.79	NaN	0.52	0.41
30	0.56	0.52	NaN	0.56
25 and 29	0.44	0.41	0.56	NaN
D) GENAI USAGE PATTERNS BY DEGREE LEVEL (B = BACHELOR'S, M = MASTER'S)				
		B		
SI	*21–24*	*26–28*	*30*	*25 AND 29*
21–24	NaN	0.74	0.47	0.33
26–28	0.74	NaN	0.37	0.30
30	0.47	0.37	NaN	0.37
25 and 29	0.33	0.30	0.37	NaN
		M		
SI	*21–24*	*26–28*	*30*	*25 AND 29*
21–24	NaN	0.76	0.61	0.47
26–28	0.76	NaN	0.54	0.47
30	0.61	0.54	NaN	0.61
25 and 29	0.47	0.47	0.61	NaN

Own study.
Legend: As in Table 2.5.

a positive assessment of GenAI coexists with reflectiveness and a critical approach, rather than uncritical acceptance of technology. The structure of attitudes becomes cognitively integrated.

In students aged 31–40, a further strengthening of the strength of correlations and their greater homogeneity is observed. The relationship between learning effectiveness and productivity ($\rho = 0.72$) and between these areas and the role of GenAI in education ($\rho = 0.62$) is clearly moderate to strong. Awareness of the limitations of GenAI correlates moderately with all benefit indicators ($\rho \approx 0.49$–0.53), indicating a mature, reflective attitude in which benefits and limitations are treated as complementary elements of technology assessment.

In the oldest age group, students >40 years old, the strongest integration of perceived GenAI benefits is evident. The correlation between learning effectiveness and productivity and creativity is very high ($\rho = 0.84$), and their relationship with the perceived role of GenAI in education is quite strong ($\rho = 0.53$–0.67). Awareness of the limitations of GenAI shows moderate positive correlations with productivity ($\rho = 0.57$) and with the vision of the role of GenAI in education ($\rho = 0.58$), although it is not directly related to the assessment of learning effectiveness. This indicates a strong perception of benefits while maintaining a critical awareness of limitations.

In summary, it can be concluded that with age, both the strength and consistency of the relationship between the perceived benefits of GenAI increase, and the relationship between benefits and awareness of limitations becomes more stable and reflective. In younger groups, attitudes are more selective, while in older groups they are integrated and mature. These results support the hypothesis that students can simultaneously perceive the educational and competence benefits of GenAI and be aware of its limitations, with the degree of integration increasing with age.

With regard to gender (Table 2.21 b), it can be seen that in the male group there are moderate positive correlations between all the indicators analyzed. The relationship between perceived learning effectiveness and competence development (SI 21–24) and productivity and creativity (SI 26–28) is strong ($\rho = 0.74$), indicating a consistent perception of the various dimensions of the benefits of using GenAI. Both of these areas are also moderately related to the perceived role of GenAI in education (30; $\rho = 0.43$–0.52). At the same time, awareness of the limitations of GenAI (SI 25–29) shows moderate positive correlations with both effectiveness and competence ($\rho = 0.39$) and productivity and creativity ($\rho = 0.42$), while its relationship with the overall vision of the role of GenAI in education is weaker ($\rho = 0.35$). This means that in men, the perception of the benefits of GenAI coexists with reflectiveness, but awareness of limitations is more pragmatic and selective, more strongly associated with immediate practical effects than with a long-term vision of technology.

In the group of women, the correlation structure is more diverse and, in some cases, stronger. As with men, there is a strong correlation between learning effectiveness and competence development (SI 21–24) and productivity and creativity (SI 26–28) ($\rho = 0.76$), which confirms the consistency of the perceived benefits. The correlations between these indicators and the role of GenAI in education (30) are moderate ($\rho = 0.45$–0.54). However, the key difference is the relationship with awareness of the limitations of GenAI (SI: 25–29). In the group of women, this indicator correlates moderately with the perceived role of GenAI in education ($\rho = 0.58$), while its relationships with other areas of benefits are weaker ($\rho = 0.36$–0.40). This means that among women, critical awareness of the limitations of GenAI is strongly integrated with reflection on its long-term significance for education and not only with the current assessment of its practical benefits.

In summary, for both women and men, the perceived benefits of GenAI form a coherent, positively linked system of beliefs, while differences emerge in the way awareness of limitations is integrated. In men, awareness of limitations is moderately and pragmatically linked to immediate benefits, while in women it is more reflective and strategic in nature, strongly linked to the assessment of the role of GenAI in education. These results do not undermine the hypothesis, but rather reinforce it, indicating the existence of a mature, non-uncritical attitude toward GenAI regardless of gender, with simultaneous differences in the structure of this attitude.

With regard to the field of study (Table 2.21 c), it can be observed that in the group of technical students, there are moderate positive correlations between the individual dimensions of the perceived benefits of GenAI. The strongest relationship is between learning effectiveness and competence development (SI 21–24) and productivity and creativity (SI 26–28), where $\rho = 0.67$, indicating a consistent but moderate perception of educational benefits. The relationships between these indicators and the perceived role of GenAI in education (30) are weaker ($\rho = 0.27$–0.45). In contrast, the relationships between awareness of the limitations of GenAI (SI 25 and 29) and the benefit indicators are weak ($\rho = 0.25$–0.30), which means that STEM students' reflection on the limitations of the technology is relatively poorly integrated with their assessment of its educational usefulness. The structure of attitudes is selective, focusing mainly on the practical aspects of GenAI use.

Among social science students, the correlations are clearly stronger and more homogeneous. The correlation between learning effectiveness and competence development (SI 21–24) and productivity and creativity (SI 26–28) is strong ($\rho = 0.79$), indicating an integrated perception of different areas of benefit. Both of these dimensions are also moderately related to the perceived role of GenAI in education (30; $\rho = 0.52$–0.56). In contrast, awareness of the limitations of GenAI (SI 25 and 29) shows moderate positive correlations with all benefit indicators (ρ = 0.41–0.56). This means that in this group, a positive assessment of GenAI coexists with high reflectiveness and a critical approach. The structure of attitudes is consistent and integrated, combining the perception of benefits with an awareness of the limitations of technology.

In summary, the field of study clearly differentiates both the strength and structure of the relationship between the perceived benefits of GenAI and awareness of its limitations. In the STEM group, attitudes are more instrumental and fragmented, while among social science students they are more integrated and reflective. These results reinforce the hypothesis, indicating that students can simultaneously perceive the benefits of GenAI and be aware of its limitations, with the degree of this integration depending on the educational profile.

With regard to the level of study (Table 2.21 d), it can be observed that in the group of Bachelor's students there are moderate positive correlations between the individual dimensions of the perceived benefits of GenAI. The strongest relationship is between learning effectiveness and competence development (SI 21–24) and productivity and creativity (SI 26–28) (ρ = 0.74), indicating a consistent, strongly integrated perception of educational benefits. The relationships between these indicators and the perceived role of GenAI in education (30) are weaker (ρ = 0.37–0.47). In turn, the relationships between awareness of GenAI limitations (SI 25–29) and benefit indicators are weak (ρ = 0.30–0.37). This means that among first-cycle students, critical awareness of the limitations of technology coexists with the perception of benefits but is not yet integrated into the overall assessment of the role of GenAI in education. The structure of attitudes is selective and pragmatic.

Among Master's students, the correlations are clearly stronger and more homogeneous. The correlation between learning effectiveness and competence development (SI 21–24) and productivity and creativity (SI 26–28) is high (ρ = 0.76), indicating a strongly integrated perception of benefits. Both of these dimensions are also moderately related to the perceived role of GenAI in education (30; ρ = 0.54–0.61). However, it is worth emphasizing the differences in awareness of the limitations of GenAI (SI 25–29), which in this group moderately correlates with all benefit indicators (ρ = 0.47–0.61), including the strongest correlation with the overall assessment of the role of GenAI in education (ρ = 0.61). This means that among second-cycle students, a positive assessment of GenAI is strongly linked to reflection on its limitations, which indicates a mature, integrated attitude toward technology.

In summary, the level of study significantly differentiates both the strength and structure of the relationship between the perceived benefits of GenAI and awareness of its limitations. Bachelor's students have more instrumental and fragmented attitudes, while Master's students have more integrated and reflective attitudes. These results support the hypothesis that students can simultaneously recognize the benefits of using GenAI and be aware of its limitations, with the degree of integration increasing with educational experience.

2.3 SUMMARY AND DIRECTION FOR FURTHER RESEARCH

In summarizing the presented research, it is worth referring to the adopted hypotheses.

Hypothesis 1 assumed that students' affective-motivational attitudes toward GenAI are determined by their demographic and educational characteristics. To verify this, the research focused on analyzing the affective-motivational component of attitudes toward GenAI, corresponding to the affective component in the ABC model and the constructs of hedonic motivation, effort expectancy, and, partially, performance expectancy in UTAUT/UTAUT2. Statistical analyses showed that the age of students significantly differentiates affective-motivational attitudes, which was confirmed by the Kruskal-Wallis test. Post hoc analyses using Dunn's test revealed that the most pronounced differences occur between students ≤20 years of age and the >40 age group, with older students showing more positive affective-motivational attitudes toward GenAI. At the same time, no significant differences were found in terms of gender, field of study, or degree level, both at the synthetic index level and for most individual items. This means that although age plays a role in differentiating the intensity of emotional and motivational responses, the overall pattern of attitudes toward GenAI remains relatively stable in other groups. In light of UTAUT2, these results suggest that hedonic motivation and comfort in using GenAI increase with life experience, which may be associated with greater cognitive autonomy and a realistic approach to technology. Based on the research results, it can be concluded that hypothesis 1 was only partially confirmed.

Hypothesis 2 assumed that students differ in the frequency and methods of using GenAI, depending on demographic and educational characteristics. Its verification therefore required analyses relating to the behavioral component of attitudes toward GenAI, corresponding to the behavioral component in the ABC model and the constructs of habit, performance expectancy, and, partially, social influence in UTAUT2. The results of the analyses clearly indicate that students do not differ significantly in the frequency or methods of using GenAI depending on age, gender, field of study, or level of study. Both the Kruskal-Wallis and Mann-Whitney U tests did not show statistically significant differences, including for the synthetic GenAI usage patterns index. Correlation analyses did indicate minor, scattered relationships, but their strength was weak and unsystematic. This means that GenAI usage behaviors are universal and uniform, independent of the demographic and educational characteristics studied. In the context of UTAUT2, these results can be interpreted as the effect of the normalization of GenAI technology in the academic environment, where the availability of tools, similar facilitating conditions, and environmental pressure lead to similar usage patterns. Based on the research results obtained, it can be concluded that hypothesis 2 was not confirmed.

Hypothesis 3 assumed that attitudes toward GenAI are related to the intention to continue using it and recommending it to other students. Its verification therefore required examining the relationships between the components of the ABC model of attitudes (affective, behavioral, and cognitive) and the intention to continue using GenAI and the willingness to recommend it. Spearman's correlation analyses showed moderate and positive relationships between intention and recommendation and all attitude components, with the strongest correlations being for the cognitive component. In particular, performance expectancy was most strongly associated with the willingness to recommend GenAI, which is consistent with the key assumption of UTAUT and UTAUT2, according to which the belief in the usefulness of technology is the main predictor of intention. At the same time, in older age groups and at higher levels of study, the importance of habit and user experience increased, indicating a shift from declarative motivation to practice-based motivation. Analyses broken down by age, gender, field of study, and degree level showed that these factors modify the strength and configuration of the relationships but do not change their direction or basic mechanism. Based on the research results, it can be concluded that hypothesis 3 has been clearly and fully confirmed.

Hypothesis 4 assumed that students perceive GenAI as a tool that supports learning effectiveness and competence development, while being aware of its limitations. To verify this, the research focused on identifying the relationship between the perceived benefits of GenAI (including learning effectiveness, competence development, productivity, creativity) and awareness of its limitations and conditions for safe use. The research was based on synthetic indicators relating to benefits and limitations, which ensured consistency with UTAUT/UTAUT2 and reduced random variability.

The results of descriptive statistics and Spearman's correlation analysis allowed us to conclude that hypothesis 4 is true. Furthermore, it was found that the relationships between the perceived benefits of using GenAI and awareness of its limitations are present in all demographic and educational groups, indicating their stable and consistent nature. With increasing age, students show a stronger positive correlation, especially between perceived learning effectiveness and awareness of the limitations of GenAI, suggesting growing reflectiveness and cognitive maturity. Gender differences are quantitative rather than qualitative – women show slightly stronger correlations, but their direction and structure remain the same as for men. In turn, educational characteristics, such as field of study and degree level, mainly modify the intensity of the correlations, with social science students and master's degree students more often revealing stronger links between the perceived benefits of GenAI and critical awareness of its limitations. In light of the UTAUT/UTAUT2 model, the results confirm the role of demographic and educational characteristics as moderators of the strength of the relationship, rather than its direction, in line with the assumptions of this theory. The stronger correlations observed among older students, Master's degree students, and social science students may indicate the greater importance of performance expectancy and facilitating conditions in shaping reflective and conscious use of GenAI. At the same time, the fact that these relationships remain positive in all groups suggests the universal nature of the technology acceptance mechanism, in which perceived benefits coexist with critical assessment of limitations rather than contradicting them. The results of additional analyses taking into account the demographic and educational characteristics of students do not undermine but reinforce the positive verification of hypothesis 4.

The results of the study should be referred to the currently important theory of connectivism (Jung, 2019), which views student learning as a process occurring in networks involving people, digital tools, and information resources. According to this approach, knowledge is not only internalized by the individual but dispersed in dynamic connection systems, and the learner's key competence becomes the ability to identify, integrate, and critically evaluate sources of information. In this context, GenAI can be understood as another node in the student's cognitive network, whose usefulness depends on the quality of interaction and the ability to reflectively use the generated content.

Research results indicating a strong relationship between the perceived benefits of using GenAI and the simultaneous awareness of its limitations empirically support the assumptions of connectivism. Students do not treat GenAI as an indisputable epistemic authority but as a tool requiring critical verification, which corresponds to the connectivist understanding of learning as a process of continuous assessment of the credibility of nodes and connections in the knowledge network. This attitude can be interpreted as a manifestation of mature network learning, in which technology serves as a cognitive support rather than a substitute for thinking.

Additionally, the relationships between attitudes toward GenAI and the intention to continue using it and recommending it to other students can be understood as a mechanism for the diffusion of innovation in the educational environment. From a connectivism perspective, recommending a tool means expanding the learning network and pointing out valuable cognitive nodes to other participants in the educational system. In this sense, the research results complement the UTAUT/UTAUT2 model with the dimension of learning theory, showing that the acceptance of technology and the intention to use it are embedded in the broader context of networked educational practices.

It would be worthwhile to conduct further research in this area to better understand the mechanisms of integrating AI-generated content with other sources of knowledge and the competence of critical information evaluation. It would also be interesting to operationalize connectivist competencies and link them to UTAUT/UTAUT2 constructs, which would contribute to the development of a coherent model explaining both technology acceptance and learning quality in GenAI-based environments.

3 Critical thinking competences and the use of generative AI

The rapid development of generative artificial intelligence (GenAI) has quickly changed the practice of learning and performing cognitive tasks in higher education. Students are increasingly using GenAI tools to support them in analyzing information, formulating arguments, and generating alternative solutions. On the one hand, this helps them to increase their work efficiency, gives them quick access to information, and supports the learning process through explanations, examples, and content structuring. On the other hand, however, there are growing concerns that access to instant answers generated by GenAI may lead to cognitive offloading, overreliance on the tool, and, as a consequence, a weakening of independent, reflective thinking and a decline in critical thinking (CT) skills.

Existing research on the impact of GenAI on critical and reflective thinking skills provides valuable but inconclusive findings. Some studies indicate that the appropriate use of ChatGPT can support the development of cognitive skills, including elements of critical and reflective thinking, especially when the tool is used as a guide, advisor, and when it supports analysis, the generation of counterarguments, or the verification of hypotheses. An example is experimental research with a pretest and posttest design and a control group, which reported changes in critical and reflective thinking during a teaching intervention using ChatGPT (Essel et al., 2024). At the same time, there is growing evidence to suggest the opposite. It is believed that GenAI may increase cognitive comfort and the feeling

DOI: 10.1201/9781003795926-3

of providing ready-made answers but does not necessarily translate into correctness and quality of reasoning. In such cases, a mechanism known in the literature as automation bias is observed, which is a specific type of overreliance, defined as a tendency to place excessive trust in the recommendations of automated systems, even if they are incomplete or incorrect (Romeo & Conti, 2025). In the context of education, this means a potential increase in the certainty of answers without a parallel increase in accuracy, which directly affects the reflectiveness and intellectual autonomy of the person using GenAI. Research shows that, in particular, more frequent use of GenAI tools may be associated with lower declared or observed CT skills (Gerlich, 2025).

Systematic reviews (Guo et al., 2026) emphasize that although the literature on ChatGPT and CT is growing rapidly, there is a certain cognitive gap in the research. This is because most of the publications in this field to date have described the results of short-term studies, which usually compared two conditions: the use of GenAI and the non-use of GenAI. In contrast, studies comparing three conditions analyzed single tasks or a short series of activities, which limits the possibility of drawing conclusions about long-term effects.

In response to this gap, a 3-month experiment was conducted among a group of 54 project management students. The choice of this group was not accidental, as CT skills are particularly important in teaching and in the practice of project management (especially investment projects). Uncritical acceptance of GenAI recommendations (e.g., "the project is profitable because the NPV is positive, so it can be implemented") can lead to erroneous conclusions and decisions in practice, which has negative consequences, including financial losses, for which one is legally responsible (Bijańska & Wodarski, 2024b).

The study assumes that it is currently necessary to maintain a balance in the educational process between technological support in the form of AI and the intellectual autonomy of students, understood as their ability to independently formulate and justify conclusions, critically evaluate data and premises, and consciously make decisions about the degree of trust in GenAI and their own reasoning. In educational practice, this autonomy does not have to mean a complete abandonment of technology, but it does require students to maintain an active cognitive process. The point is that they should be aware of the need to verify results, question assumptions, check the correctness and completeness of arguments, and reflect on possible errors in AI. In this view, it is therefore crucial not only whether students use GenAI but also whether they use it in a way that maintains their responsibility for reasoning, inference, and decision-making.

Three experimental conditions were introduced in the study: no use of GenAI, limited use of GenAI (limit), and full access to GenAI. Furthermore, the study was long term in nature. As mentioned, it lasted three months and included weekly meetings, which made it possible to observe changes in CT skills in the course of learning and the implementation of a real investment project. Furthermore, in addition to assessing the correctness and quality of solutions, the study operationalized reflectivity through metacognitive measures based on response confidence calibration.

3.1 RESEARCH OBJECTIVE AND HYPOTHESES

In light of the considerations presented in the introduction, the main objective of the study was to answer the following questions:

- Does the use of GenAI in a long-term teaching project strengthen or weaken students' reflective thinking?
- Does limiting the use of GenAI (setting a limit) allow for a beneficial balance between technological support and students' intellectual autonomy?

These questions are important both theoretically, as they test the mechanisms of cognitive offloading and automation bias in a learning environment, and practically, as they will provide grounds for designing rules for the use of AI in education. Consequently, the results of this research may contribute to the discussion on how to minimize the risk of over-reliance on GenAI while exploiting the potential of this technology as a source of structuring, alternative generation, and analytical support.

The study tested three hypotheses relating to the conditions of the experiment, in which it was assumed that:

1. In a condition without access to AI, students will demonstrate high reflectivity (good calibration of certainty and low overestimation), but the increase in CT skills during the intervention will be relatively small.
2. In the condition of limited access to GenAI, students will achieve the most beneficial balance between technological support and intellectual autonomy, which will translate into the greatest increase in CT skills while strengthening reflectivity.

3. With full access to GenAI, there will be an increase in overestimation and a deterioration in confidence calibration, which will mean a weakening of reflectivity and intellectual autonomy, even if the competency score increases moderately.

3.2 RESEARCH METHODOLOGY

3.2.1 Theoretical foundations

The theoretical basis for research on the relationship between CT skills and the use of AI in academic teaching is provided by considerations regarding the mechanisms of AI's impact on students' CT skills, metacognition, and reflectivity.

The research was based on two particularly important mechanisms of GenAI's impact on the cognitive process and learning, which have already been mentioned. These are cognitive offloading (Chirayath et al., 2025) and automation bias (Romeo & Conti, 2025). Cognitive offloading means transferring part of the cognitive effort to GenAI, which can lead to reduced engagement in independent reasoning, error analysis, and argumentation. As a result, users perform fewer cognitive operations "internally" and more often accept ready-made answers or structures generated by the tool, which can weaken independent thinking. Automation bias, on the other hand, describes the tendency to rely excessively on the recommendations of automated systems and to reduce the level of monitoring their correctness, which leads to a loss of cognitive vigilance (complacency). The classic view of this phenomenon indicates that automation can result in both errors resulting from uncritical acceptance of the system's suggestions and a lowering of the standard of information verification (lower quality control). In the context of GenAI, this mechanism can manifest itself in the form of increased confidence in the answer without an increase in its accuracy, i.e., in the form of overconfidence.

It can therefore be concluded that GenAI mechanisms influence CT skills, which are understood as the ability to analyze arguments and assumptions (CT1), evaluate the quality of evidence and sources (CT2), draw conclusions and detect cognitive errors (CT3), and think probabilistically and make decisions under conditions of risk (CT4) (Butler et al., 2012). In the context of student collaboration with GenAI, it is important to note that CT may be weakened if some of the key analytical operations are taken over by this technology and the student ceases to actively verify the premises and consequences of reasoning (cognitive offloading mechanism).

In the studies described in this chapter, CT skills were operationalized based on the scores of task tests, which were assessed independently by two experts and then averaged. The following basic indicators were used:

- Mean test score (Butler et al., 2012), which in educational research is also referred to as the group mean score, hereinafter referred to as "Score" or "Score_mean",
- Standard deviation of test scores (Field, 2013), hereinafter referred to as "Score_sd",
- Change score (Dimitrov & Rumrill, 2003), hereinafter referred to as "Δ" or "Δ Score (POST–PRE)".

The Score_mean indicator is the average level of performance on the CT competency task test (referred to as T-CT) in a given measurement (initial, final, intermediate, referred to as PRE, POST, MID, as described in Section 3.2.2). Assuming that the student's result is the sum of the scores for *m* tasks, the following is calculated:

1. The average score for the task, assessed by two experts:

$$\text{Score}_{ij} = \frac{P_{ij}^{(1)} + P_{ij}^{(2)}}{2},$$

2. The student's total score in the test:

$$\text{Score}_i = \sum_{j=1}^{m} \text{Score}_{ij},$$

3. The average score in the group (in a given measurement):

$$\text{Score\_mean} = \frac{1}{N}\sum_{i=1}^{N} \text{Score}_i,$$

where N is the number of students in the group (in a given experimental condition).

The Score_{sd} indicator is the standard deviation of the T-CT test results in the group, i.e., a measure of the dispersion of CT skills. It is calculated using the following formula:

$$\text{Score}_{\text{sd}} = \sqrt{\frac{1}{N-1}\sum_{i=1}^{N} (\text{Score}_i - \text{Score}_{\text{mean}})^2}.$$

In an educational context, this indicator allows us to assess whether a given condition (e.g., GenAI limit) promotes a more uniform increase in competence or rather deepens the differences between students.

The Δ Score (POST–PRE) indicator represents the change in the level of CT skills during the teaching intervention, i.e., the difference between the final measurement (POST) and the initial measurement (PRE). It is a key indicator for assessing the effect of the experiment in a pretest-posttest system, as it shows whether CT skills have increased as a result of the teaching process. Formula:

1. At the student level:

$$\Delta\text{Score}_i = \text{Score}_{i,\text{POST}} - \text{Score}_{i,\text{PRE}},$$

2. For the average change in the group:

$$\Delta\text{Score}_i = \frac{1}{N}\sum_{i=1}^{N} \Delta\text{Score}.$$

Metacognition and reflectiveness (CT5) are an individual's ability to monitor the quality of their own conclusions and control the decision-making process. In the study, this was operationalized as the accuracy of monitoring one's own responses, understood as the consistency between subjectively declared certainty and the objective correctness of the solution. For each task, students provided a confidence statement on a scale of 0–100%, which was converted to a probabilistic scale of 0–1. For student i and task j, confidence was defined as:

$$p_{ij} = \frac{\text{confidence}_{ij}}{100}.$$

The correctness of the task solution was coded binarily as $C_{ij} \in \{0,1\}$, where the value 1 meant a fully correct answer (obtaining the maximum score for the task). In order to determine correctness, the average rating of two independent experts was used:

$$\text{Score}_{ij} = \frac{P_{ij}^{(1)} + P_{ij}^{(2)}}{2}.$$

On this basis, the mean confidence rating, abbreviated as "Conf" or "Conf_mean", and the mean accuracy, abbreviated as "Acc" or "Acc_{mean}", were calculated (Fleming & Lau, 2014):

$$\text{Conf\_mean}_i = \frac{1}{m}\sum_{j=1}^{m} p_{ij},$$

$$\text{Acc}_{\text{mean}_i} = \frac{1}{m}\sum_{j=1}^{m} C_{ij}.$$

here m is the number of tasks in the test.

Next, appropriate indicators were used, in accordance with the classification of metacognitive monitoring measures (Fleming & Lau, 2014; Schraw, 2009). The Brier score, used to assess the quality of probabilistic forecasts (the lower the value, the better the calibration), referred to hereafter as "Brier" or "Brier_mean" was adopted as the basic measure of calibration error:

$$\text{Brier\_mean}_i = \frac{1}{m}\sum_{j=1}^{m} (p_{ij} - C_{ij})^2.$$

In addition, a directional measure of overestimation, calibration bias, was determined, understood as the difference between the average declared confidence and the average accuracy (overconfidence bias). This indicator was referred to in the rest of the text as "BIAS" or "BIAS_mean":

$$\text{BIAS\_mean}_i = \text{Conf\_mean}_i - \text{Acc\_mean}_i.$$

Positive values of the BIAS indicator indicate overestimation (overconfidence relative to correctness), while negative values indicate underestimation. In order to assess the ability to distinguish between situations in which the student is correct and situations in which they make a mistake, the confidence discrimination Δ indicator was used, expressed as the difference between the average confidence for correct and incorrect answers:

$$\Delta_i = \overline{p}_{i,C=1} - \overline{p}_{i,C=0}$$

where

$$\overline{p}_{i,C=1} = \frac{1}{n_1}\sum_{j:C_{ij}=1} p_{ij},$$

$$\overline{p}_{i,C=0} = \frac{1}{n_0}\sum_{j:C_{ij}=0} p_{ij},$$

a n_1 and n_0 denote the number of correct and incorrect answers, respectively.

The effect of the teaching intervention was assessed by comparing the PRE and POST measurement results (Dimitrov & Rumrill, 2003). For each change scores X indicator, the change over time was calculated:

$$\Delta X_{\text{POST-PRE}} = X_{\text{POST}} - X_{\text{PRE}}.$$

3.2.2 Course of the study

The research was conducted in three stages, which included preparing the experiment, then conducting it, and finally performing calculations and drawing conclusions.

3.2.2.1 Preparation of the experiment

Before the experiment began, a 12-week teaching cycle was planned, including lectures and project work, during which students were to develop an investment project plan enabling the production of a new product. It was assumed that the scope of the project work would include, in sequence:

- Presentation of the project team composition and definition of its roles,
- Identification and analysis of stakeholders and development of a communication plan,
- Developing a risk register,
- Preparation of a work breakdown structure (WBS),
- Developing a schedule for project preparation, implementation, and operation,
- Allocating resources to activities,
- Developing a project budget,
- Assessing the financial effectiveness of the project (NPV, IRR, payback period),
- Analysis and assessment of project implementation and operation scenarios in conditions different from those assumed,
- Assessment of the risk of not achieving the expected financial results,
- Determination of the size of the management budget.

At the preparatory stage, the study design was defined as a teaching experiment with three conditions differing in the level of permissible use of GenAI during the implementation of project works. The following groups (conditions) were distinguished:

1. No access to GenAI,
2. Limited use of GenAI (limit), i.e., a maximum of three times during a single class,
3. Unrestricted use of GenAI.

It was assumed that the group without access to GenAI would be the control condition, which would allow for the estimation of the natural increase in competence resulting from the implementation of classes and project work, regardless of technological support, as well as to distinguishing the effect of GenAI intervention from the effect of teaching itself.

The independent variable was operationalized as the level of exposure to GenAI during project work, while maintaining a consistent teaching program, uniform lecture materials, and identical project requirements. In order to limit the influence of confounding variables, it was decided that CT competence measurements (task tests described later) would be performed under controlled conditions, without the possibility of using GenAI and the Internet, which would allow the results to be interpreted as a change in competence rather than a difference in current performance supported by these tools.

Before the study began, an information brochure was prepared, presenting the objectives of the study, the method of data processing, and the principles of voluntary participation, as well as information that participation in the study and the results of the measurements would not affect the final grade for the course. A method of assigning students to three research groups was also adopted, assuming their highest possible comparability in terms of basic demographic characteristics. The sample structure included two age groups (20–30 years and 31–40 years) and both genders, so the assignment to groups was planned with control of the distribution of these characteristics (stratification) to minimize the risk of overrepresentation of a particular category in one of the groups. The allocation was based on a random procedure within the strata, which allowed for a balance between conditions and increased the internal validity of the conclusions.

In addition, a set of tools for measuring CT and reflective thinking skills was adopted, consisting of 30-minute task-based tests:

- T-CT-PRE (pretest): for preliminary measurement, to be conducted before the first project classes,
- T-CT-POST (posttest): for final assessment, which should be conducted after the last project class as well as 15-minute task tests,
- T-CT-MID1: for the first intermediate measurement, which should be carried out in the fifth week of the teaching cycle,
- T-CT-MID2: for the second intermediate measurement, which should be conducted in the ninth week of the teaching cycle.

The T-CT-PRE and T-CT-POST tests are presented in Table 3.1. They included ten tasks related to specific components of CT skills (analyze arguments and assumptions (CT1), evaluate the quality of evidence and sources (CT2), draw conclusions and detect cognitive errors (CT3), think probabilistically and make decisions under conditions of risk (CT4), as well as metacognition and reflectivity (CT5)). The T-CT-PRE version was constructed independently of specialist financial knowledge, while T-CT-POST included tasks related to investment project planning, with particular emphasis on assessing its financial effectiveness, scenario analysis, and risk assessment, including for determining the managerial budget.

The scope of indirect measurements T-CT-MID1 and T-CT-MID2 is presented in Table 3.2. They were in a shortened form (five tasks each) and were related to the stages of project implementation. T-CT-MID1 concerned a critical analysis of the completeness and consistency of the WBS and scope planning, while T-CT-MID2 included tasks related to the interpretation of financial performance assessment results, scenario analysis, and decision-making under conditions of financial risk.

It was agreed that, if necessary, the content of the tasks would be explained before the tests were taken.

In all tests, for each task, students will provide a subjective assessment of certainty (0–100%) in addition to their answers. The consistency between certainty and the correctness of the answers will be analyzed using the indicators described in Section 4.2.1. It was assumed that the tests would be assessed by two independent professors. The assessment scale for each task will be 1–4 points, and the assessment will take into account both the correctness of the answers and the quality of the short justifications where they were required. In order to increase the consistency of assessments, it was planned to assess anonymized works on the basis of an adopted identification code, without information about group affiliation, which limited the risk of bias in the assessment. In addition, it was planned to verify the consistency of assessments between assessors.

Since the key condition for interpreting the results was the actual difference in the level of GenAI use between groups, it was assumed that a procedure for monitoring compliance with the experimental conditions would be implemented. It was assumed that after each project class, students would fill out a short log (micro-log), the content of which is presented in Table 3.3.

It was assumed that in the group without GenAI and in the limited group, the microgram would be a tool for controlling the limit. In group G1 (without GenAI), an indication of 1, and in G2 (limited use), an indication of 4+ would mean that the limit had been exceeded. Students who exceeded the limit would be excluded from the experiment. To reduce the risk of declarative errors, the possibility of an ad hoc random audit was provided for in selected weeks, consisting of the presentation of usage history (e.g., a list of prompts) by randomly selected individuals, which allowed for an assessment of the degree of compliance with the conditions.

TABLE 3.1 Test templates for preliminary and final measurement of critical thinking (CT) skills

A) INITIAL MEASUREMENT: T-CT-PRE

CT COMPONENT	*NO TASK*	*CONTENT TASK*	*PLACE ANSWER*	*CONFIDENCE 0–100%*	*POINTS …/4*
CT1	1.	The manager says: "We should carry out this project because we have extensive experience in similar projects". Indicate the conclusion. Indicate one explicit premise.			
	2.	The report states: "If we increase the number of people working on the project, it will definitely be completed faster". What is suspicious or uncertain about this sentence? Give one condition that would have to be met for the sentence to be true.			
CT2	3.	The team wants to estimate the demand for a new product. It has two sources of information: – 5 comments on a forum, – a research company report (description of the method and data). Select the most reliable source and briefly justify your choice.			
	4.	The project costs include purchase of machinery, materials, energy, and salaries. Identify two additional important cost elements that are not listed here but could affect the outcome of the project.			

CT3	5.	After making changes to its offer, the company saw a 12% increase in sales. The manager says, "This is definitely the result of these changes, so let's always do this". Is this a reliable conclusion? Give 2 other possible explanations for the increase in sales.
	6.	The team is very focused on the success of the project and ignores critical comments. a) What is this error in thinking called (or describe it in your own words)? b) What can be done to limit this kind of thinking in the project?
CT4	7.	There are two options for implementing the project. Option A: 60% chance of a profit of PLN 500,000, 40% chance of a loss of PLN -200,000; Option B: 90% chance of a profit of PLN 250,000, 10% chance of a loss of PLN -150,000. Calculate the expected value (average result) for options A and B. Justify which option you choose (2 sentences).
CT4	8.	The profitability of the project depends on the selling price and the number of customers, but you are not sure about this. List two questions that need to be answered before you make a decision. Give one simple way to assess this (e.g., "what if...").

(Continued)

TABLE 3.1 (*Continued*) Test templates for preliminary and final measurement of critical thinking (CT) skills

CT COMPONENT	NO TASK	CONTENT TASK	PLACE ANSWER	CONFIDENCE 0–100%	POINTS .../4
A) INITIAL MEASUREMENT: T-CT-PRE					
CT5	9.	Write 2–3 sentences to the statement: "What could cause my assessment of the project to be wrong?" Give at least 2 reasons how this can be checked.			
	10.	You have a ready recommendation: "Implement the project". What two things will you check before you believe it? What two warning signs could indicate that this recommendation is wrong?			
B) FINAL MEASUREMENT: T-CT-POST					
CT1	1.	The final report states: "The project should be implemented because the average expected NPV is positive". Indicate: One key assumption for the argument to be true, One piece of information that is necessary for this argument to be complete.			
	2.	Argument: "Since we have taken the pessimistic scenario into account, the financial risk of the project is already under control". Identify the gap in reasoning. Add a condition/piece of information that would strengthen the argument.			

CT2	3.	To estimate the costs and revenues of the project, you have: – One supplier offer with no expiration date, – Three current offers with parameters and delivery terms, – "average costs" found on the Internet without a source. Choose the most reliable basis and justify your choice (two sentences).
	4.	The NPV and IRR analysis took into account CAPEX and revenues but omitted: machine maintenance costs, training, the impact of delays on cash flows, and quality maintenance costs. Indicate two consequences of these omissions for the NPV and IRR results.
CT3	5.	The manager says: "In the base case scenario, the NPV is positive, so the project is likely to be successful". Assess the correctness of this conclusion. Provide two arguments that need to be verified in order to accept this reasoning.
CT3	6.	The team makes the following statement: "This is a good project because the previous investment was very successful". What cognitive error may be present here? What analytical procedure will you implement to reduce the risk of erroneous conclusions?

(Continued)

TABLE 3.1 (*Continued*) Test templates for preliminary and final measurement of critical thinking (CT) skills

B) FINAL MEASUREMENT: T-CT-POST

CT COMPONENT	*NO TASK*	*CONTENT TASK*	*PLACE ANSWER*	*CONFIDENCE 0–100%*	*POINTS …/4*
CT4	7.	The following scenarios exist for the investment project: base case: NPV = +PLN 200.000 (p = 0.6), pessimistic: NPV = –PLN 150.000 (p = 0.3), optimistic: NPV = +PLN 450.000 (p = 0.1). Make a decision: *implement/do not implement/implement conditionally*, and then justify it in 1–2 sentences, referring to the risk. Indicate one "stop-go" condition and one element that should be included in the management budget (management reserve) to mitigate the risk.			
	8.	The sensitivity analysis determined that if the sales price falls by 8% or the sales volume falls by 12%, the investment project becomes unprofitable (NPV < 0). Provide: Two measures to reduce the risk of project unprofitability, One "stop-go" indicator that is worth monitoring during the project implementation.			
CT5	9.	Write 2–3 sentences: "What are the 2 most important weaknesses of my financial performance and project risk analysis, and how can I check or mitigate them?"			
	10.	You are wondering whether to set a management budget (reserve) for the project. List two factors that justify its existence. Give two rules that will allow it to be activated.			

Own study.

TABLE 3.2 Test patterns for indirect measurement of critical thinking (CT) skills

A) FIRST INDIRECT MEASUREMENT IN WEEK 5: T-CT-MID1

CT COMPONENT	*NO TASK*	*CONTENT TASK*	*PLACE ANSWER*	*CONFIDENCE 0–100%*	*POINTS …/4*
CT1	1.	Your WBS includes the following justification: "The WBS is complete because it covers all the main stages of the project". Identify the flaw in this reasoning. Provide one condition/piece of information that would actually strengthen this statement.			
CT2	2	To assess whether the WBS is complete and realistic, you can rely on: • Comparison with three similar projects (historical data), • General examples from the Internet. Choose the best basis and justify your choice (1–2 sentences).			
CT3	3.	The manager says: "Since each work package has a designated person responsible for it, the schedule will definitely not be delayed". Assess the correctness of the statement. Give two reasons why this conclusion may be incorrect.			
CT4	4.	Identify two risks typical for the WBS/schedule planning stage and suggest one action to mitigate each of them.			
CT5	5.	*Write 2–3 sentences:* "*Which element of my WBS plan is the weakest and how can I know that I am wrong?*" (give at least one way to check).			

(*Continued*)

TABLE 3.2 (*Continued*) Test patterns for indirect measurement of critical thinking (CT) skills

B) SECOND INDIRECT MEASUREMENT IN WEEK 9: T-CT-MID2

CT COMPONENT	*NO TASK*	*CONTENT TASK*	*PLACE ANSWER*	*CONFIDENCE 0–100%*	*POINTS …/4*
CT1	1.	The plan states, "The project should be implemented because the NPV is positive". Identify one key assumption hidden in this statement. Provide one piece of information without which this recommendation is incomplete.			
CT2	2.	There are two financial analyses: • Only NPV and IRR results without assumptions, • NPV and IRR results with assumptions (including costs, price, etc.) and data sources. Which is more reliable and why?			
CT3	3.	The manager concludes: "Since IRR is greater than the discount rate, the project is safe and the risk is low". Assess the correctness of this conclusion. Give two arguments as to why this conclusion may be wrong.			
CT4	4.	In the base case scenario, NPV > 0, but in the pessimistic scenario, NPV < 0. Give your recommendation (implement/do not implement/implement conditionally) and indicate the basis for your recommendation (1–2 sentences).			
CT5	5.	Write 2–3 sentences: "What do I need to check before accepting the conclusions from NPV/IRR?" Indicate at least two verification elements.			

Own study.

TABLE 3.3 Information collected in the microblog

Student ID:
Date of class:
Have you used GenAI for project work since the last class? (Yes / No)
If yes: how many times? (0 / 1 / 2 / 3 / 4+)
What activities did you use GenAI for?
• generating ideas
• analysis/inference
• checking for errors/criticism
• summarizing/editing
• calculations/spreadsheets
• other.

Own study.

3.2.2.2 Conducting the experiment

The experiment was conducted on 54 students of project management, in accordance with the assumptions adopted in point 1. The students agreed to participate in the experiment and accepted its assumptions. Among other things, they accepted that the experimental conditions would apply throughout the entire period of the project part and their own work on developing an investment project plan and that competence measurements would be carried out in controlled conditions without access to GenAI and the Internet. In addition, they agreed that their assignment to the experimental conditions would be based on a stratified random sampling method, taking into account gender (women, men) and age group (20–30, 31–40), in order to ensure the highest possible comparability of the groups in terms of demographic characteristics.

The experiment began with the assignment of students to three experimental conditions: G1: no access to GenAI, G2: access limit to GenAI, and G3: full access to GenAI, as shown in Table 3.4. In each stratum, the distribution between conditions was as equal as possible (differences of no more than 1 person), which allowed for balanced sample sizes across the entire sample (18 people in each condition).

The students were then anonymized (assigned IDs from S01 to S54). They then completed the initial T-CT-PRE test, after which they carried out project work in accordance with their scope, without changing their group assignments, and after each class they completed a micro-test on their phones. In the event of absence, they did the same as part of their own work (e.g., at home). During the experiment, an ad hoc random audit was used, which never detected any limit being exceeded. In weeks 5 and 9, they completed the T-CT-MID1 and T-CT-MID2 intermediate tests, and in the last class, after completing the project plan, the T-CT-POST final test.

TABLE 3.4 Characteristics of groups in the experiment

STRATUM			*EXPERIMENTAL CONDITIONS*		
AGE (YEARS)	*GENDER*	*NUMBER OF STUDENTS*	*NO ACCESS TO GENAI*	*ACCESS LIMIT TO GENAI*	*FULL ACCESS TO GENAI*
20–30	Women	13	5	4	4
	Men	16	5	6	5
31–40	Women	11	4	3	4
	Men	14	4	5	5
Total		54	18	18	18

Own study.

3.2.2.3 Calculations and conclusions

The calculations were based on data collected at the level of individual test tasks, i.e., for each student and each measurement (tests: PRE, MID1, MID2, POST). For each task, the following were entered: the score awarded independently by two assessors (Professor 1 and Professor 2), the maximum number of points possible for a given task (four points), and the level of confidence in the answer declared by the student (in %). These data were then combined with information about the experimental condition (no GenAI, limit, full access) and demographic characteristics (age and gender) to enable comparative analyses. In the first step, the data format was standardized: it was ensured that all point values were in the range of 0–4 and confidence values in the range of 0–100%. Next, the average score for each task was calculated as the mean of Professor 1's and Professor 2's scores. This minimized the impact of individual differences in assessment and provided a more stable measure of response quality.

In addition, to enable the analysis of reflectivity and calibration, each task was described by two additional variables. The first was the subjective probability of the answer being correct (p). The student's declared confidence was converted to a scale of 0–1 by dividing the percentage by 100. The resulting variable p was interpreted as the student's subjective judgment that their answer was correct. The second variable, used to calculate the Brier score and accuracy, was the correctness indicator C (if the student scored the maximum 4/4 points, $C = 1$; if they scored less, $C = 0$). This approach allowed us to measure confidence in relation to the complete correctness of the answer. As a result, the calibration assessment applied to situations where the student actually met the criterion of "correct answer" rather than "partially correct".

Next, a partial Brier score was calculated for each task to measure the discrepancy between subjective certainty and objective correctness.

The Brier score has a significant advantage in the context of the experiment, as it allows us to detect situations in which GenAI potentially reinforces the "appearance of correctness" and increases confidence, but does not improve the actual quality of the answer.

The next step was to aggregate the indicators at the level of the entire test for a given student and a given measurement (PRE, MID1, MID2, POST). For this purpose, the Score, Conf, Acc, Brier, and BIAS indicators were calculated. In addition, the Δ discrimination index was calculated, answering the question: Can the student distinguish between situations in which they are right and those in which they are wrong? After calculating the indicators at the test level, an analysis of changes over time was performed. The most important measure was the change between the initial and final measurements: $\Delta X = X_{POST} - X_{PRE}$. It was calculated for indicators such as Score, Brier, BIAS, and **Δ.**

The final stage in the calculations was to compare the obtained indicators between the three experimental groups: without access to GenAI, with limited access to GenAI, and with full access to GenAI.

First, the POST mean values were compared, followed by the mean values of the changes between PRE and POST (growth dynamics). Next, analogous comparisons were made taking into account demographic characteristics, by dividing the participants into age subgroups of 20–30 and 31–40 as well as into women and men. Demographic analyses were treated as supplementary only due to the small number of people in the subgroups.

The entire calculation procedure was adopted in order to separate the two levels of assessment – CT skills and reflectivity, metacognition. Due to the extensive nature of the results, the publication does not present the complete database for statistical analysis, nor the complete set of calculations leading to the conclusions formulated below.

Table 3.5 presents the average values of competence and reflectivity indicators at four measurement points: PRE, MID1, MID2, and POST for the entire sample. The sample shows an overall increase in task performance

TABLE 3.5 Descriptive statistics of competence and reflectivity indicators for the entire group in all measurements

TEST	*SCORE_ MEAN*	*RESULT_ SD*	*CONF_ MEAN*	*ACC_ MEAN*	*BRIER_ MEAN*	*BIAS_ MEAN*	*DELTA_ MEAN*
T-CT-MID1	13.13889	1.603112	0.65863	0.051852	0.425956	0.606778	0.142847
T-CT-MID2	13.57407	1.846484	0.676296	0.077778	0.427591	0.598519	0.184167
T-CT-POST	27.88889	2.661158	0.656963	0.098148	0.42879	0.558815	0.21528
T-CT-PRE	23.66667	2.36324	0.626315	0.018519	0.411055	0.607796	0.182577

Own study.

during the experiment (the T-CT score increases between PRE and POST), indicating the development of CT competence during the course. Over time, the average declared confidence also changes, indicating a growing (or variable) sense of control over the tasks. Calibration indicators (Brier and BIAS) show that an increase in confidence alone does not always mean an improvement in reflectiveness, as consistency between confidence and correctness is key. The Δ value (the difference in confidence between correct and incorrect answers) allows to assess students' ability to distinguish between "I know" and "I don't know" situations. These results provide a baseline for further comparative analysis between experimental conditions, showing the overall direction of change across the sample.

An analysis of changes in competence and reflectivity indicators between the pretest and posttest, presented in Table 3.6, confirms that the experiment has a measurable effect on the level of CT competence across the entire group. At the same time, calibration indicators show that reflectivity may develop differently than competence. In particular, it is possible that students improve their scores but begin to overestimate their own answers. In the context of GenAI, this is important because this technology can support the generation of solutions, but at the same time reinforce a sense of "apparent correctness". The overall result of the entire sample is informative, and in order to draw conclusions about the impact of GenAI on CT, it is necessary to break down the data into experimental conditions. For this reason, comparative analyses between groups are crucial.

A comparison of the final measurement results (posttest) suggests that the final level of competence and reflectiveness may vary depending on how GenAI is used, as shown in Table 3.7.

In a situation where the group did not have access to GenAI, the lowest level of competence can be observed, accompanied by stable reflectivity, caution, and cognitive control. In contrast, the group that was given full access to GenAI showed very high confidence with low accuracy (increased Brier and BIAS), which translated into strong overestimation and significantly poorer calibration, interpreted as a decrease in reflectivity. However, in a

TABLE 3.6 Change in competence and reflectivity indicators between pretest and posttest

	Δ POST-PRE					
STAT	*SCORE*	*BRIER*	*BIAS*	*CONF*	*ACC*	*Δ*
mean	4.222222	0.017735	−0.04898	0.030648	0.07963	−0.02969
std	3.64933	0.143766	0.14655	0.091703	0.120345	0.086946

Own study.

TABLE 3.7 Competence and reflectivity indicators in the final measurement – in the posttest

		POSTTEST					
CONDITION	*N*	*SCORE*	*BRIER*	*BIAS*	*CONF*	*ACC*	*Δ*
No access to GenAI	18	25.72222	0.208039	0.407111	0.468222	0.061111	0.289375
GenAI access limit	18	30.63889	0.230631	0.375611	0.558944	0.183333	0.274995
Full access to GenAI	18	27.30556	0.847702	0.893722	0.943722	0.05	0.010694

Own study.

condition where students' access to GenAI was limited, the highest level of competence can be observed, while maintaining relatively good calibration of confidence. This allows us to conclude that with limited GenAI support, there is an increase in students' ability to think independently, consciously, and critically, i.e., to formulate conclusions based on their own reasoning rather than on ready-made GenAI answers. In other words, in this condition, a strengthening of intellectual autonomy and reflective thinking can be observed, which leads to the conclusion that it is important to maintain a balance between GenAI support and intellectual autonomy.

In summary, the analysis of the posttest indicators shows that the mere availability of GenAI is not unequivocally beneficial or harmful, as what matters is how the use of this technology is regulated.

From the point of view of answering the research questions, namely:

- Does the use of GenAI in a long-term teaching project strengthen or weaken students' reflective thinking?
- Does the condition of limited use of GenAI (limit) allow for a beneficial balance between technological support and students' intellectual autonomy?

the results presented in Table 3.8 and Figure 3.1 are of the utmost importance.

These results indicate that when students have full access to GenAI, there is an increase in overestimation and a deterioration in confidence calibration, which means a weakening of reflectivity and intellectual autonomy. It is worth mentioning that this effect occurred despite explaining this phenomenon in lectures, with examples of when GenAI was wrong (Bijańska & Wodarski, 2024a). In a situation where students worked without access to GenAI, their reflectiveness may be good even without this technology, but the development of competences is slower. In contrast, the group of students who worked with

TABLE 3.8 Summary of changes in competence and reflectivity indicators between the initial and final measurements (Post-Pre)

		Δ					
CONDITION	*N*	*SCORE*	*BRIER*	*BIAS*	*CONF*	*ACC*	*Δ*
No access to GenAI	18	1.25	−0.06925	−0.09317	−0.05428	0.038889	
GenAI access limit	18	6.94444	−0.07262	−0.15156	0.015111	0.166667	−0.04736
Full access to GenAI	18	4.472222	0.195 079	0.097778	0.131111	0.0333	0.023333

Own study.

Note: Δ was not calculated for the No GenAI condition because in this group, some of the tests did not contain fully correct answers, which makes it impossible to determine the difference in confidence between correct and incorrect answers.

limited access to GenAI showed the strongest improvement in reflectiveness with a simultaneous increase in competence, which supports the previously formulated conclusion that controlled use of GenAI is beneficial, rather than its complete exclusion or unlimited access. The results obtained confirm all the research hypotheses.

An additional analysis was also conducted at the individual level, from which it can be concluded that students differ significantly in terms of competence and reflectivity development. Some students achieved a high increase in their scores and, at the same time, improved calibration, which indicates a mature learning style. Others achieved an increase in their scores but showed an increase in overestimation, which may indicate growing confidence without full understanding. Individual data are particularly important in the context of working with GenAI, as they show that the use of the tool depends on the user's strategy. Due to the extensive nature of the results, they are not presented in the publication.

An analysis of CT and reflective thinking competency indicators was also conducted, taking into account the gender and age of students. The PRE-POST analysis showed that limited access to GenAI leads to the greatest increase in competence, while improving confidence calibration and reducing overestimation, especially in the group of women aged 31–40. On the other hand, full access to GenAI is associated with a deterioration in reflectivity (increase in Brier and BIAS) in all subgroups, most strongly in the group of young men, which may indicate a weakening of intellectual autonomy due to growing confidence that is inadequate to correctness. The variation in results by age and gender may be due to different self-regulation and cognitive control strategies when using a generative tool. For example,

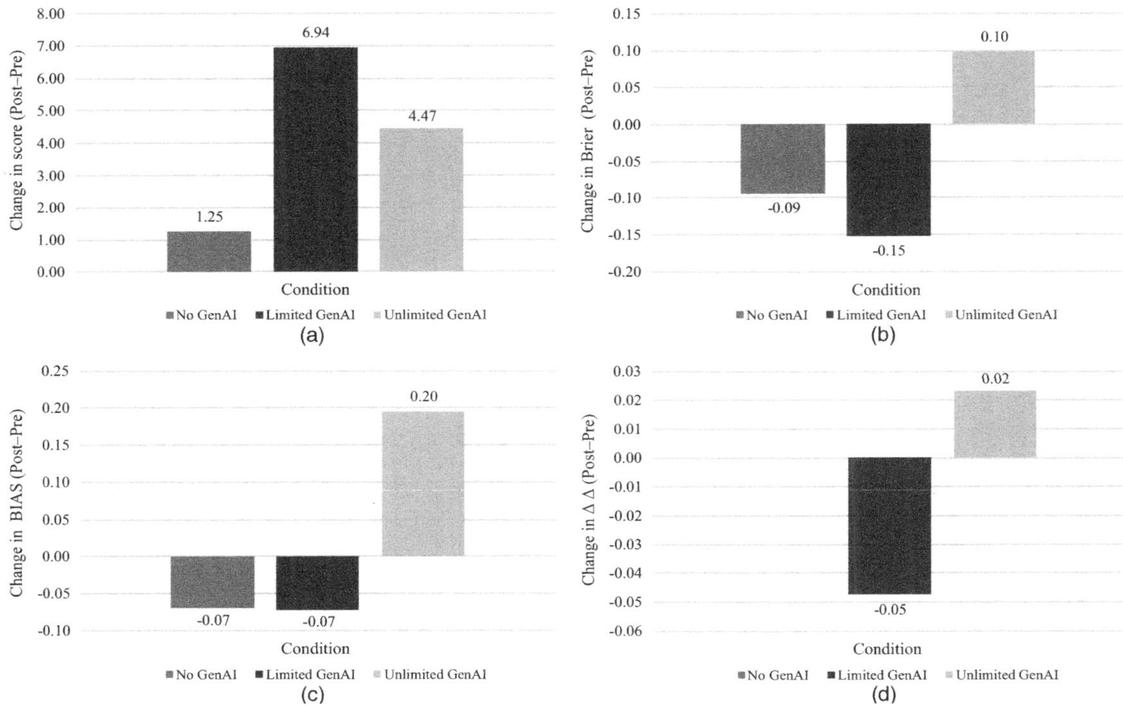

FIGURE 3.1 Changes in competence and reflectivity indicators between the initial and final measurements (Post-Pre) in three experimental conditions

Own study.

women aged 31–40 may have more established learning strategies and a greater tendency to critically monitor their own conclusions, so even without GenAI they may show improved calibration (decrease in Brier/BIAS). At the same time, with full access to GenAI, men may place greater "trust in the tool" as expert support, leading to overconfidence and overestimation, especially when the answers sound professional. In the case of limited access to GenAI, the results are most favorable, as this technology helps at critical points, but the need for independent reasoning forces active processing, which enhances reflectiveness and maintains intellectual autonomy. It should be emphasized that with such small subgroup sizes based on demographic characteristics (n = 3–6), the above observations are not statistically significant. However, they support the conclusion that it is not the use of GenAI itself that determines changes in reflectivity, but the degree of restrictions that maintain a balance between technological support and intellectual autonomy.

3.3 SUMMARY AND DIRECTION FOR FURTHER RESEARCH

Contemporary research on the educational use of GenAI emphasizes that the impact of the tool is neither clearly negative nor positive but depends on the manner and frequency of use. Studies analyzing GenAI dependence have indicated that frequent reliance on the tool is associated with lower levels of CT. In turn, research on metacognition emphasizes the importance of calibrating trust and confidence as a condition for the optimal integration of GenAI suggestions into the decision-making process. Consequently, it is reasonable to treat reflectivity (in the sense of confidence calibration) as a key mechanism mediating between GenAI use and the quality of independent thinking. The results of this study confirm these conclusions. They show that, under conditions of full, unlimited access to GenAI, students experienced an increase in overestimation and a deterioration in confidence calibration, which means a weakening of their reflectivity and intellectual autonomy. In contrast, when students worked without access to GenAI, their reflectivity was good even without this technology, but their competence development was slower. In contrast, the group of students who worked with limited access to AI showed the strongest improvement in reflectivity with a simultaneous increase in competence, indicating that controlled use of AI is beneficial, rather than its complete exclusion or unlimited access. The results obtained confirm all the research hypotheses. However, it should be emphasized that research on the impact of GenAI on CT skills and reflectivity should be further explored.

Further research should focus on the long-term effects of using GenAI, and it is worth considering not only quantitative limits but also, for example, limits depending on the stage of work or type of task. In addition, it would be interesting to gain a deeper understanding of mediating mechanisms, such as cognitive offloading and automation bias, as well as moderating factors that determine whether GenAI supports or weakens reflectivity. It would also be interesting to investigate how long CT skills and reflectivity persist after GenAI support is withdrawn. It would also be worthwhile to deepen research on students' intellectual autonomy, which was only in the background in this study.

4 Attitudes, perceptions, and self-regulated learning in the use of AI in psychology education

The rapid integration of artificial intelligence (AI) tools, particularly generative systems such as ChatGPT, is transforming higher education. These technologies are increasingly used for studying, writing, and problem-solving across disciplines, including Psychology. As AI becomes more embedded in academic life, questions arise regarding its pedagogical impact, ethical implications, and effects on students' learning processes.

For psychology education, the emergence of AI is particularly significant. Psychology students are future professionals expected to understand human cognition, ethical responsibility, and technological mediation in human behavior. Understanding how they perceive and use AI during their training may illuminate broader shifts in how knowledge, reasoning, and self-regulation operate in digital learning environments (Kasneci et al., 2023).

This chapter presents the results of a study exploring attitudes, perceptions, and self-regulated learning (SRL) strategies associated with the use of ChatGPT among undergraduate psychology students. The study combines theoretical models of technology acceptance (TAM and UTAUT) with constructs from SRL theory (Zimmerman, 2000, 2002).

 DOI: 10.1201/9781003795926-4

4.1 THEORETICAL FRAMEWORK

4.1.1 AI in higher education

AI has emerged as one of the most influential technological developments in higher education in recent decades. The proliferation of generative AI systems, particularly large language models capable of producing coherent, contextually relevant text, has accelerated the integration of AI into students' everyday academic practices. Unlike earlier educational technologies, generative AI is not limited to information retrieval or administrative support; instead, it actively participates in cognitive tasks such as explanation, synthesis, summarization, and content generation (Kasneci et al., 2023).

In higher education, AI has been framed as a powerful tool for enhancing learning efficiency, personalization, and accessibility. AI-based systems can provide immediate feedback, adaptive support, and scaffolding for complex tasks, thereby potentially improving students' comprehension and academic performance (Zhai, 2022). In the case of psychology students, whose training often involves abstract theoretical constructs, methodological reasoning, and applied case analysis, AI tools may serve as valuable aids for understanding difficult concepts and organizing information. Empirical findings increasingly show that students primarily use AI to support learning-related activities such as writing assignments, summarizing content, and clarifying unfamiliar material, rather than for purely technical or computational purposes (Rudolph et al., 2023).

However, the educational integration of AI also introduces significant pedagogical challenges. One central concern is the risk of surface learning, whereby students rely on AI-generated outputs without engaging in deeper cognitive processing. The ease with which AI produces plausible explanations and academic-style text may encourage passive consumption rather than active knowledge construction (Risko & Gilbert, 2016). This concern is especially relevant in psychology education, where learning outcomes emphasize critical thinking, epistemic vigilance, and reflective practice. The tension between efficiency and depth of learning has become a defining feature of current debates on AI in higher education (Selwyn, 2019).

Recent empirical evidence suggests that students' perceptions of AI are often ambivalent, combining recognition of its usefulness with awareness of potential negative consequences (Floridi & Chiriatti, 2020). Students may value AI as a learning aid while simultaneously expressing concern about its impact on their thinking skills and autonomy. This ambivalence reflects broader societal discourses surrounding AI, in which technological optimism coexists with ethical anxiety (Kasneci et al., 2023). Understanding how students conceptualize AI's role in their academic learning is therefore essential for developing pedagogical approaches that harness AI's benefits while mitigating its risks.

4.1.2 Technology acceptance and attitude models

To understand students' engagement with AI, it is essential to consider theoretical models of technology acceptance and attitudes. The technology acceptance model (TAM) posits that individuals' intention to use a technology is primarily determined by perceived usefulness and perceived ease of use (Davis, 1989). These perceptions shape attitudes toward the technology, which in turn influence actual usage behavior. TAM has been widely applied in educational contexts and remains a robust framework for explaining students' adoption of digital tools.

Extensions of TAM, such as the Unified Theory of Acceptance and Use of Technology (UTAUT), incorporate additional factors, including social influence and facilitating conditions (Venkatesh et al., 2003). In higher education, social norms, peer practices, and institutional expectations can strongly shape students' use of AI. When AI tools become normalized within academic contexts, adoption may occur rapidly, even in the absence of explicit pedagogical guidance.

Empirical studies consistently demonstrate that students perceive AI tools as highly usable and useful, which explains their widespread adoption (Davis, 1989; Rudolph et al., 2023). However, acceptance models alone are insufficient to capture the complexity of students' attitudes toward AI. Unlike earlier educational technologies, AI systems raise epistemic and ethical questions that extend beyond instrumental considerations (Bender et al., 2021; Floridi & Chiriatti, 2020).

Recent research suggests that students' attitudes toward AI are multidimensional, encompassing not only perceived benefits but also perceived risks and moral evaluations (Kasneci et al., 2023). Concerns about dependency, loss of skill development, misinformation, and academic integrity may coexist with positive evaluations of efficiency and convenience (Cotton et al., 2024; Risko & Gilbert, 2016). This pattern reflects the emergence of critical acceptance, in which users adopt technology while remaining aware of its limitations and potential harms (Floridi & Chiriatti, 2020;

Selwyn, 2019). Such critical acceptance is particularly relevant in psychology education, where reflective judgment and skepticism are core disciplinary values.

4.1.3 Ethical and professional considerations

Ethical and professional considerations constitute a central dimension of AI use in psychology education. AI systems are not neutral tools; in the contrary, they are embedded with values, assumptions, and biases derived from their training data and design (Bender et al., 2021). Consequently, their use raises ethical issues related to responsibility, transparency, authorship, and fairness. For psychology students, who are future professionals bound by ethical codes, engagement with AI involves not only academic but also professional identity formation.

One of the most pressing ethical concerns is academic integrity. The use of AI to generate written assignments challenges traditional notions of authorship and originality (Bretag, 2013). While AI-assisted writing may support learning, it can also blur the boundary between legitimate assistance and misconduct particularly when institutional guidelines are unclear (Perkins et al., 2024). Students' perceptions of these issues are often conflicted, reflecting uncertainty about institutional expectations and ethical norms. Empirical evidence indicates that many students recognize ethical risks but continue to use AI due to perceived necessity or competitive pressure (Kasneci et al., 2023; McCabe et al., 2012).

Beyond academic integrity, AI use raises broader ethical questions related to critical thinking and moral agency. Psychology education emphasizes ethical decision-making, reflexivity, and accountability (American Psychological Association, 2017). If AI tools are used uncritically, they may undermine students' engagement in ethical reasoning by outsourcing judgment to automated systems (Borenstein & Howard, 2021). Conversely, AI can also serve as a catalyst for ethical reflection, prompting students to consider issues such as bias, data privacy, and societal impact (Floridi et al., 2018).

Students' perceptions of AI's impact on ethical self-reflection often reflect this duality. Some students perceive AI as enhancing ethical awareness by exposing them to diverse perspectives or ethical dilemmas, while others view it as diminishing responsibility by distancing them from the consequences of their academic actions (Bearman et al., 2024). This ambivalence underscores the need for explicit ethical education regarding AI use in psychology programs, moving beyond compliance-based approaches toward reflective and values-oriented frameworks (Akgun & Greenhow, 2022; Rest et al., 1999).

4.1.4 SRL and metacognition

SRL provides a critical theoretical lens for understanding how students interact with AI in educational contexts. SRL refers to learners' active control over cognitive, motivational, and metacognitive processes, including goal setting, strategy use, monitoring, and self-evaluation (Panadero, 2017; Zimmerman & Schunk, 2011). Metacognition, in particular, involves awareness and regulation of one's own thinking processes and plays a central role in deep learning and transfer (Dulonsky & Metcalfe, 2009; Flavell, 1979).

From an SRL perspective, AI can function either as a supportive scaffold or as a substitute for self-regulation. When used strategically, AI may help students plan tasks, generate alternative explanations, and monitor understanding. For example, AI-generated feedback can prompt reflection and revision, supporting metacognitive regulation (Kasneci et al., 2023; Nicol & Macfarlane-Dick, 2006). However, when used passively, AI may reduce the need for self-monitoring and critical evaluation, leading to diminished engagement in metacognitive processes (Azevedo & Taub, 2020).

The concept of cognitive offloading is particularly relevant in this context. Cognitive offloading occurs when individuals rely on external tools to perform cognitive tasks, thereby reducing internal cognitive effort (Risko & Gilbert, 2016). While offloading can increase efficiency, excessive reliance may impair skill development and self-regulation (Barr et al., 2015). Psychology students' perceptions that AI may weaken critical thinking can be interpreted through this lens.

Empirical findings indicate that students often display high levels of SRL while simultaneously using AI extensively. This apparent paradox suggests that self-regulation and AI use are not mutually exclusive. Rather, the educational impact of AI depends on how it is integrated into students' regulatory processes (Winne & Hadwin, 2008). The lack of strong associations between SRL and AI attitudes observed in recent studies suggests that acceptance of AI may occur independently of self-regulatory competence (Bearman et al., 2024; Teo, 2011). Nevertheless, evidence that students with stronger cognitive strategies perceive fewer risks associated with AI implies that self-regulation may buffer against negative perceptions and misuse (Broadbent & Poon, 2015).

Integrating AI into psychology education therefore requires pedagogical approaches that explicitly support metacognitive awareness and self-regulation. Rather than treating AI as an external tool, educators can frame it as an object of reflection, encouraging students to evaluate when, how, and why AI should be used. Such approaches align with contemporary views of SRL as contextually situated and socially mediated (Hadwin et al., 2017; Panadero, 2017).

In sum, the theoretical framework described above integrates perspectives from AI in higher education, TAMs, ethical and professional psychology, and SRL. Together, these perspectives provide a comprehensive foundation for understanding psychology students' attitudes, perceptions, and learning processes in relation to AI use, and they highlight the need for reflective, ethically grounded, and self-regulated approaches to AI integration in psychology education (Floridi et al., 2018; Zimmerman, 2002).

4.2 OBJECTIVES

The general objective of this study was to analyze attitudes, perceptions, and SRL in the use of AI among psychology students.

The specific objectives were the following:

1. To describe psychology students' attitudes toward AI, including perceived usefulness, perceived ease of use, perceived risks, and ethical and societal evaluations.
2. To examine the prevalence and purposes of AI use in psychology studies.
3. To analyze students' perceptions of AI's impact on learning, critical thinking, and ethical self-reflection.
4. To assess levels of SRL, including motivation, cognitive strategies, and metacognitive self-regulation.
5. To explore relationships between attitudes toward AI and SRL variables.
6. To examine potential differences by sex and age in AI attitudes, perceptions, and SRL.

4.3 METHODOLOGY

4.3.1 Design

A cross-sectional, descriptive–correlational design was employed. Data were collected at a single time point using self-report questionnaires. Quantitative data were obtained through structured and validated questionnaires, and qualitative data were collected through open-ended questions about students' experiences and reflections. This design was appropriate for exploring relationships among attitudes toward AI, perceptions of its impact, and SRL variables in a natural educational.

4.3.2 Participants

The sample consisted of 46 undergraduate psychology students enrolled at a Spanish university. Participants ranged in age from 18 to 27 years (M = 20.24, SD = 1.93). The sample was predominantly female (84.8%), reflecting the gender distribution typically observed in psychology programs. Participation was voluntary, and informed consent was obtained from all students.

4.3.3 Instruments

1. The *AI Attitude Scale* (AIAS-4) (Grassini, 2023) is a 5-item 10-point Likert-scale instrument based on TAM and UTAUT, which measures perceived usefulness on humanity and on work, potential societal impact, behavior intention (perceived ease of use), perceived risks, and overall evaluation of AI's impact on humanity (ethics and responsibility).
2. The *Self-Regulation Learning Scale* (ESAA-2) (Fernández-de-Castro et al., 2024), a 40-item 5-point Likert-scale, which includes three subscales: (a) motivation and attitudes toward learning, (b) cognitive strategies, and (c) self-assessment and metacognitive self-regulation.

Additionally, open-ended questions assessed whether students used AI in their studies, the purposes of use (e.g., assignments, summaries), and perceived effects of AI on learning, critical thinking, and ethical self-reflection. These variables were analyzed descriptively and through categorical comparisons.

4.3.4 Procedure

The study was conducted in May 2025. After ethical approval by the Faculty Research Committee, the questionnaire was administered during the regular academic activities. Questionnaires were administered anonymously, and confidentiality was guaranteed. The study followed ethical guidelines for research with human participants.

4.3.5 Data analysis

Quantitative data were analyzed using SPSS 29. For descriptive statistics, mean and standard deviations were used in the case of quantitative variables and frequencies and percentages, for qualitative variables. Pearson correlations were conducted to examine relationships among attitudes toward AI and SRL variables; linear regression analyses were performed; and Mann-Whitney U tests were used to compare the AI attitudes and the self-regulation variables between groups of sex and age. Chi-square tests were used to compare the qualitative variables by sex and groups of age.

4.4 RESULTS

Participants age ranged from 18 to 27 years ($\bar{X}$ = 20.24, SD = 1.93). The sample was predominantly female (84.8%), with 15.2% identifying as male. Most students were born and currently resided in the province of Córdoba, Spain, which shows a geographically homogeneous sample.

Regarding attitudes toward AI, students reported moderately positive perceptions. Perceived usefulness of AI for improving quality of life showed a mean of 6.39 (SD = 1.90), and perceived usefulness for improving work or academic performance yielded a mean of 6.00 (SD = 2.36). Behavioral intention, operationalized as perceived ease of use, showed a comparatively higher mean score ($\bar{X}$ = 7.61, SD = 2.08), suggesting that students generally experience AI tools as accessible and easy to use. Perceived risks associated with technology received intermediate scores ($\bar{X}$ = 5.91, SD = 2.48), indicating the coexistence of perceived benefits and concerns. The overall evaluation of the global impact of AI on humanity, including ethical and responsibility considerations, was also situated at a moderate level ($\bar{X}$ = 6.20; SD = 1.81). The total score for attitudes toward AI showed a mean of 32.11 (SD = 6.81), reflecting generally favorable but not uncritical attitudes.

With respect to SRL, the ESAA-2 total score showed relatively high values ($\bar{X}$ = 155.50, SD = 16.61), indicating adequate levels of self-regulatory competence among participants. The subscale motivation and attitudes toward learning showed a mean of 42.48 (SD = 4.84); the subscale cognitive strategies yielded a mean of 63.15 (SD = 7.25); and the subscale self-assessment and metacognitive self-regulation showed a mean of 49.87 (SD = 6.69). These data indicate that students report good motivational, cognitive, and metacognitive resources for regulating their learning processes.

4.5 USE OF AI IN PSYCHOLOGY EDUCATION

The use of AI was highly prevalent. A total of 93.5% of students reported using AI tools (e.g., ChatGPT or similar applications) in their psychology studies, whereas only 6.5% indicated non-use. Regarding the types of use reported, Figure 4.1 represents the percentages of different uses of AI used specifically in students of psychology:

Students were also asked how they perceived AI to influence their way of studying and learning psychology. The most frequent category was facilitation of comprehension of difficult concepts and deeper understanding (45.7%), followed by support for summarizing, organizing material, and studying more efficiently (37.0%). A smaller proportion of participants highlighted assisted creativity for generating ideas in written assignments (13.0%), while only 4.3% primarily emphasized perceived risks or negative effects.

Concerning the perceived impact of AI on critical thinking, 58.7% reported that AI worsens it, 17.4% believed it improves critical thinking, 13.0% expressed a dual effect (both improvement and deterioration, depending on the situation of use), and 10.9% described a neutral effect (neither

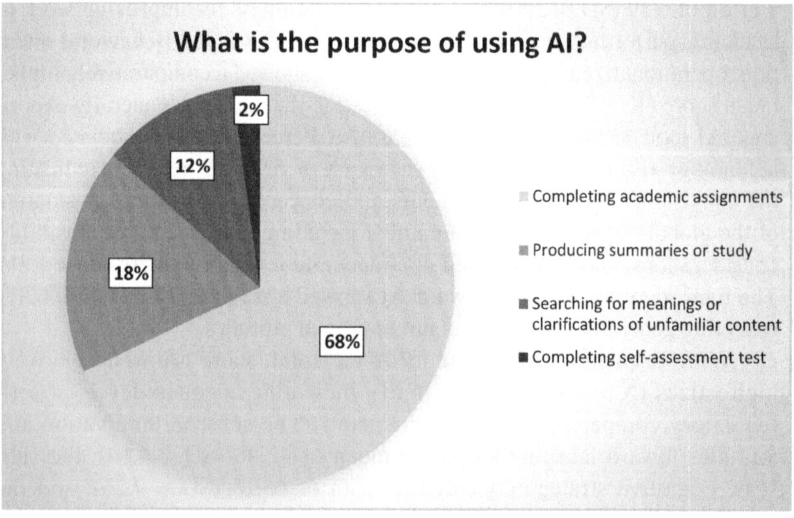

FIGURE 4.1 Frequency diagram of the different uses of AI in students of psychology

improvement nor worsening). With regard to the ethical self-reflection, 34.8% perceived worsening, 30.4% perceived improvement, 23.9% reported neutrality, and 10.9% described a dual effect.

4.6 CORRELATIONAL ANALYSES

The perceived usefulness of AI for improving quality of life correlated positively with perceived usefulness for improving work ($r = .649$, $p < .001$). Both indicators of perceived usefulness correlated significantly with behavioral intention/perceived ease of use ($r = .320$, $p = .030$; $r = .630$, $p < .001$, respectively). These variables also correlated significantly with the overall evaluation of AI's societal and ethical impact ($r = .487$, $p < .001$; $r = .422$, $p = .003$).

Perceived risks associated with technology did not correlate significantly with most of the AI attitude components, indicating that perceived risks may constitute a relatively independent dimension from perceived benefits. Notably, there were no significant correlations between AI attitudes and the dimensions of SRL (motivation, cognitive strategies, and metacognitive self-regulation). This suggests that students' self-regulatory learning competencies are largely independent of their attitudes toward AI usage.

Within the SRL domain, significant correlations were observed between motivation and cognitive strategies ($r = .656$, $p < .001$), motivation and metacognitive self-regulation ($r = .572$, $p < .001$), and cognitive strategies and metacognitive self-regulation ($r = .744$, $p < .001$). These correlations reflect internal coherence of the SRL construct.

4.7 REGRESSION ANALYSES

Multiple regression analyses were conducted using the three SRL dimensions as predictors and the AI-related criteria measured in this study as dependent variables. For behavioral intention/perceived ease of use, the regression model was not significant ($F(3,42) = 0.513$, $p = .675$), explaining only 3.5% of variance ($R^2 = .035$); as well as in the case of perceived risks associated with technology, in which the model was not significant ($F(3,42) = 2.145$, $p = .109$), with $R^2 = .133$. In contrast, within this model, cognitive strategies emerged as a significant negative predictor ($B = -0.199$, $p = .018$), indicating that students who reported a higher use of cognitive learning strategies tended to report lower levels of perceived technological risks. For the overall evaluation of AI's societal impact and total attitudes toward AI, regression models were not significant.

4.8 GROUP COMPARISONS BY GENDER AND AGE

Mann-Whitney U tests revealed no significant sex differences in any of the AI attitude or SRL variables ($p > .05$). Males and females presented similar rank distributions, despite the unequal group size (39 women and 7 men). Regarding age, participants were divided into two groups (18–20 vs. 21–27 years). Significant age differences emerged in self-assessment and metacognitive self-regulation, with older students (21–23 years) scoring higher ($U = 159.50$, $p = .037$). There were trends toward higher scores in cognitive strategies and total SRL among older students, although these did not reach statistical significance. Also, no significant differences were observed for the rest of AI-related qualitative variables by sex or age.

In summary, results indicate (a) widespread AI use in psychology education, (b) moderately positive attitudes coexisting with awareness of risks, (c) relatively high levels of SRL, (d) limited predictive associations between SRL and AI attitudes, and (e) scarce differences by sex and age, except for metacognitive regulation.

4.9 DISCUSSION

The present study examined attitudes, perceptions, and SRL in the context of AI use among psychology students. The findings provide an informative snapshot of how emerging AI technologies are being incorporated into university learning and how students experience their benefits and challenges.

4.9.1 Prevalence and patterns of AI use

The extremely high prevalence of AI use (over 90%) confirms that AI tools have rapidly integrated into higher education practices. This result is consistent with recent research documenting widespread student adoption of generative AI tools (Kasneci et al., 2023; Rudolph et al., 2023). The most frequent uses – writing assignments, summarizing content, and clarifying unfamiliar concepts – align with descriptions of AI as a cognitive support for text production, knowledge organization, and comprehension enhancement (Zhai, 2022). However, the heavy reliance on AI for assignment production raises concerns regarding authorship, originality, and academic integrity (Cotton et al., 2024).

4.9.2 Ambivalent attitudes toward AI

The coexistence of positive attitudes and perceived risks supports the notion of ambivalence toward AI. Students recognize AI's usefulness for improving quality of life and academic performance and perceive it as easy to use, which is consistent with the TAM, where perceived usefulness and ease of use predict behavioral intention (Davis, 1989; Venkatesh & Davis, 2000). Significant correlations between these variables observed in the present study reinforce TAM and suggest that psychological students' acceptance of AI tools follows similar cognitive mechanisms to other forms of educational technology.

At the same time, students express concerns about potential risks, including deterioration of critical thinking and ethical implications. This dual perception reflects broader societal debates about AI's unintended consequences, such as algorithmic bias, overreliance on automated outputs, misinformation, and erosion of academic skills (Bender et al., 2021; Floridi & Chiriatti, 2020; Lund et al., 2023).

4.9.3 Critical thinking and ethical reflection

One of the most striking findings is that a majority of students believe AI worsens critical thinking. This perception is consistent with the concept of cognitive offloading, in which individuals rely on external tools to perform cognitive operations that they would otherwise carry out internally (Risko & Gilbert, 2016). Generative AI provides ready-made explanations and text constructions, potentially reducing the need to actively reason, synthesize, and evaluate information. Psychology students may be especially sensitive to this risk due to their disciplinary focus on cognitive processes, reasoning, and scientific evaluation.

Perceptions regarding ethical self-reflection were mixed, with similar proportions reporting improvement and deterioration. On the one hand, AI technologies introduce ethical dilemmas – plagiarism, privacy, transparency, and responsible use – which may stimulate ethical reflection (Jobin et al., 2019). On the other hand, automatic generation of content may distance students from personal responsibility for their own academic production, potentially weakening ethical awareness. This dual effect aligns with the literature on digital ethics in education, highlighting how technologies both challenge and enable ethical agency (Williamson & Piattoeva, 2022).

4.9.4 SRL and AI attitudes

Students reported relatively high SRL skills across motivational, cognitive, and metacognitive dimensions. Strong intercorrelations among these domains support theoretical models viewing self-regulation as a multidimensional but integrated construct (Zimmerman & Schunk, 2011). However, regression analyses showed that these SRL dimensions did not significantly predict attitudes toward AI, suggesting that acceptance of AI tools may depend more on sociocultural and contextual variables (e.g., peer norms, institutional policies) than on individual learning competencies. This is compatible with the UTAUT, which emphasizes social influence and facilitating conditions (Venkatesh et al., 2003).

A relevant exception was the negative association between cognitive strategies and perceived technological risks. Students with higher use of cognitive strategies tended to perceive fewer risks associated with AI. One possible interpretation is that students with more developed learning skills feel more capable of using AI critically and selectively, which reduces perceived vulnerability. This connects with research showing that digital literacy and critical information skills mitigate perceptions of technological threat (Ng, 2012).

4.9.5 Group differences

The absence of sex differences in attitudes and SRL fits with recent findings indicating narrowing gender gaps in technology-related competencies among younger cohorts (OECD, 2021). Higher metacognitive self-regulation among older students is coherent with longitudinal models of self-regulation development, according to which metacognitive monitoring and control improve with academic experience (Zimmerman & Schunk, 2011). These age-related effects, albeit modest, highlight the importance of developmental trajectories in psychological education.

4.9.6 Educational implications

The findings carry several pedagogical implications. First, educators in psychology should not assume that students' extensive use of AI is accompanied by deep understanding of its limitations, biases, or ethical consequences. Structured instruction on responsible AI use, academic integrity, and data ethics appears necessary. Second, given that many students perceive deterioration of critical thinking, curricular design should integrate activities requiring reasoning, evaluation, and reflection that cannot be easily automated, such as debates, oral examinations, clinical case analysis, and reflective portfolios. Third, rather than banning AI tools, educational strategies may benefit from embracing guided and transparent AI integration, encouraging metacognitively informed use.

4.9.7 Limitations and future directions

This study has some limitations. The sample size was small and predominantly female, with limited geographical diversity, which restricts the generalizability of findings. The design was cross-sectional and based exclusively on self-report measures, which do not capture actual behavioral data or long-term effects. Future research should incorporate larger samples, experimental or longitudinal designs, and multimethod assessment, including performance indicators and qualitative interviews. It would also be valuable to examine discipline-specific effects, as attitudes toward AI may differ between psychology, engineering, and humanities students.

4.10 CONCLUSION

In conclusion, psychology students widely use AI and perceive it as useful and easy to use but express significant concerns regarding critical thinking and ethics. SRL is high but largely independent from AI attitudes. These results underscore the need to integrate AI literacy, ethics, and critical thinking into psychology education, ensuring that technological innovation is accompanied by reflective and responsible learning practices.

Conclusions

Generative artificial intelligence (GenAI), including tools such as ChatGPT, is now widely used by university students for studying, writing, and problem-solving. These tools support activities such as summarizing texts, explaining concepts, drafting assignments, and organizing arguments. As a result, GenAI has become part of everyday academic practice in many disciplines.

At the same time, the educational use of GenAI raises important questions about learning quality, critical thinking, intellectual autonomy, and academic ethics. While GenAI may support efficiency and comprehension, it may also encourage cognitive offloading, excessive trust in automated outputs, and reduced verification of sources and arguments. In this context, students may become confident in AI-generated answers even when these answers are incomplete or incorrect.

This book examines GenAI use in higher education through theoretical and empirical perspectives. It focuses on students' critical thinking, reflective judgment, confidence calibration, and self-regulated learning, while also considering technology acceptance and ethical responsibility. The aim is to clarify under which conditions GenAI supports learning and when it increases risks for reasoning quality and academic integrity.

The first chapter confirms that German pluricentrism remains an insufficiently addressed dimension in German as a foreign language (DaF) education despite its direct relevance for real-life communication, intercultural competence, and professional language use. Although German exists as a pluricentric language with distinct national varieties in Germany, Austria, and Switzerland, the empirical findings demonstrate that students' awareness of these varieties is limited, fragmented, and often conceptually unclear. In particular, many learners remain unfamiliar with the term "national variety" itself and frequently confuse it with regional dialects, which indicates a structural gap in linguistic education and instructional framing (Ammon, 1995; Hägi, 2007; Skubis, 2020).

The survey results provide clear evidence that direct exposure to German-speaking environments is still limited among the student group, and this lack of immersion likely restricts learners' ability to recognize

DOI: 10.1201/9781003795926-5

national lexical and pragmatic differences. Even though learners have alternative access to authentic linguistic input (e.g., digital media), the results suggest that such exposure alone does not guarantee systematic awareness of national norms, codified standards, and context-sensitive vocabulary use. The data further demonstrate that students perform better when lexical items are presented as contrasting pairs, while their accuracy decreases when words appear independently, implying that contextual comparison functions as a compensatory strategy rather than as a sign of internalized pluricentric competence.

The most significant learner difficulty observed in this chapter concerns the ability to generate examples of national varieties. Only a small group of students attempted to provide their own examples of Germanisms, Austricisms, and Helvetisms, which highlights not only limited lexical repertoire but also a lack of confidence and training in productive variation awareness. This aligns with broader observations that teaching materials often present pluricentric language issues in a superficial manner, reinforcing monocentric "Germany-centered" norms instead of supporting structured cross-variety competence (Pusswald, 2007; Skubis, 2022a). The findings reinforce the pedagogical argument that pluricentric competence should be developed early and consistently, especially in receptive skills, because tolerance and comprehension of variation influence students' ability to function in real-life linguistic environments (Hägi, 2007).

GPT-5 demonstrated strong performance in classifying lexical items according to national varieties and produced plausible word sets differentiating German, Austrian, and Swiss usage. These results indicate that generative language models may serve as a valuable supplementary support tool for learners, particularly in contexts where access to authentic regional input, native speakers, or pluricentric teaching materials is limited. The model's ability to provide explanations, categorize vocabulary, and propose additional examples suggests a meaningful potential for integrating GenAI tools into DaF teaching as a form of guided exploration, lexical enrichment, and self-study support (Radford & Narasimhan, 2018; Radford et al., 2019; Roumeliotis & Tselikas, 2023).

At the same time, the chapter underlines that AI-based linguistic competence must not be treated as equivalent to human linguistic and cultural experience. GenAI outputs are shaped by training data, may contain errors or overgeneralizations, and may produce hallucinated or weakly justified classifications, making external verification essential, especially when national terminology has institutional or legal relevance. Therefore, the pedagogical advantage of GPT-5 lies not in replacing authoritative codices, but in offering flexible support that can enhance lexical sensitivity, promote learner curiosity, and expand exposure to linguistic diversity when used responsibly and critically.

Beyond language pedagogy, this chapter also highlights the relevance of pluricentric language competence for international professional communication, including management and global business. Lexical mismatches between national varieties may affect clarity, translation adequacy, and intercultural interpretation, especially in domains requiring terminological precision. In this context, AI-supported language adaptation may support multilingual communication practices by offering region-sensitive vocabulary options and by improving cross-border consistency of corporate messaging.

Overall, this chapter demonstrates that teaching German as a pluricentric language requires a systematic shift in curriculum design, textbook development, and teacher education. In line with previous research, the findings suggest that learners must be prepared not only to master "standard German" as an abstract norm but also to navigate diverse standardized varieties used in real societies and institutions (Ammon, 1995; de Cilia, 2005; Skubis, 2020). Generative AI tools such as GPT-5 can support this transformation by providing accessible exposure to variety-sensitive language use, but their educational value depends on structured pedagogical integration, teacher guidance, and a constant emphasis on critical verification.

The second chapter addressed the diversity of students' attitudes toward generative artificial intelligence (GenAI) and their ways of using it in academic teaching and learning. Although research on artificial intelligence in education has been developing for more than three decades, the emergence and global diffusion of GenAI tools, especially after the release of OpenAI's ChatGPT in November 2022, introduced a new and disruptive dynamic into higher education. Because GenAI is free, widely accessible, and increasingly integrated into everyday learning activities, understanding students' attitudes, behavioral patterns, intentions, and awareness of risks becomes a critical research and practical priority.

To respond to these challenges, the study was designed as quantitative, cross-sectional, and diagnostic-exploratory, and it involved a survey of 309 students from a Polish university, representing both STEM and social science fields and both Bachelor's and Master's degree levels. The research framework combined the affective–behavioral–cognitive (ABC) model with UTAUT/UTAUT2, which enabled a multidimensional interpretation of emotions and motivations, behavioral usage patterns, cognitive assessments, and acceptance-related intentions. This approach was particularly useful because the ABC model allows a comprehensive measurement of attitudes, whereas UTAUT/UTAUT2 explains how these attitudes translate into intentions and usage through constructs such as performance expectancy, effort expectancy, social influence, facilitating conditions, hedonic motivation, and habit.

The findings related to Hypothesis 1 demonstrated that students' affective and motivational attitudes toward GenAI exist and show moderate internal consistency; however, they are not strongly differentiated across demographic and educational subgroups. The main statistically significant differentiating factor was age, with students older than 40 reporting more positive affective-motivational attitudes compared to those aged 20 or younger. Gender did not significantly differentiate overall attitudes, although analyses at the level of individual items revealed that men reported greater enthusiasm when using GenAI and greater willingness to experiment with new GenAI features. At the same time, field of study and degree level did not contribute to systematic differences in affective attitudes. Therefore, Hypothesis 1 was only partially confirmed, and the results indicate that the emotional and motivational dimension of GenAI acceptance is relatively universal across student groups, with age-related differences being the most visible, though not structurally transformative.

In relation to Hypothesis 2, the analyses clearly showed that students did not significantly differ in the frequency or methods of GenAI use depending on age, gender, field of study, or degree level. Neither correlation analyses nor intergroup comparison tests identified significant or meaningful differentiation. This finding suggests that GenAI usage patterns have become normalized and widespread across student categories and do not depend on educational specialization or demographic background. This supports the interpretation that facilitating conditions in the university environment, such as equal access to tools and similar academic expectations, contribute to standardization in usage patterns. Consequently, Hypothesis 2 was not confirmed, and the results emphasize the universal character of GenAI behavioral integration in higher education.

The strongest empirical support was found for Hypothesis 3, which assumed that attitudes toward GenAI are related to the intention to continue using it and to recommend it to other students. Correlation analyses revealed clear, positive, and statistically significant relationships between intention and the affective, behavioral, and cognitive components of attitudes. Importantly, the cognitive component, particularly beliefs that GenAI improves learning effectiveness, supports competence development, increases productivity, and is essential in future professional work, played the dominant role in shaping both continuation intentions and recommendation tendencies. This result aligns directly with UTAUT and UTAUT2, where performance expectancy is treated as the most powerful predictor of acceptance. Although emotional and behavioral factors also contributed, they were supportive rather than dominant, with habit-related behaviors reinforcing readiness for continued use. Moreover, subgroup analyses showed that demographic and educational factors moderated the strength of these relationships, but not their direction, confirming that the acceptance mechanism is stable across groups. Hypothesis 3 was therefore fully confirmed.

The results related to Hypothesis 4 provided strong evidence that students simultaneously perceive GenAI as a valuable tool supporting learning effectiveness, competence development, productivity, and creativity, while also showing high awareness of its limitations and the need for safe and critical use. The descriptive results indicated that mean values were clearly above the midpoint for perceived benefits but even higher for awareness of limitations and safe use principles. Correlation analyses confirmed that awareness of limitations positively coexists with perceived benefits. This means that students do not treat GenAI as an unquestionable epistemic authority; rather, positive acceptance is accompanied by reflective caution. This outcome indicates a mature pattern of GenAI adoption in academic contexts and fully confirms Hypothesis 4.

Taken together, the findings of this chapter show that GenAI has become an integral and normalized element of academic learning practices, reflected in relatively stable emotional attitudes and universal behavioral usage patterns. At the same time, the willingness to continue using and recommending GenAI is strongly driven by cognitive assessments of usefulness and future relevance, which confirms key assumptions of technology acceptance models. The chapter also highlights that students' critical awareness of limitations is not in conflict with acceptance; instead, reflective evaluation coexists with recognition of benefits, suggesting a balanced attitude toward GenAI.

Finally, the results can be interpreted in light of connectivism, which frames learning as a networked process distributed across human and technological nodes. In this context, GenAI functions as an additional cognitive node that can support learning only if students maintain the competence of evaluating, selecting, and verifying information critically. The observed combination of benefit recognition and limitation awareness therefore supports connectivist assumptions, demonstrating that students increasingly treat GenAI as a tool embedded within broader learning networks rather than as a replacement for human judgment. This provides a strong justification for future research aimed at integrating connectivist competencies with

UTAUT/UTAUT2 constructs, in order to better explain not only technology acceptance but also the quality and responsibility of GenAI-supported learning.

The third chapter examined whether long-term use of generative artificial intelligence (GenAI) in academic project work strengthens or weakens students' critical thinking competences and reflective thinking, operationalized as metacognitive monitoring and confidence calibration.

The results show that the impact of GenAI is not inherently positive or negative; it depends on how access is structured. Across the whole sample, critical thinking task performance increased over the three-month teaching cycle, indicating that the course format itself supported competence development. However, competence growth did not automatically translate into stronger reflectivity: students could improve scores while simultaneously becoming more overconfident, which is particularly relevant when GenAI outputs appear convincing regardless of their correctness.

Unrestricted GenAI access produced the most problematic pattern for reflective thinking. Although competence scores improved moderately, calibration worsened markedly, with increased overestimation and poorer alignment between confidence and correctness. This outcome is consistent with automation bias: students may accept GenAI suggestions with reduced verification and increased certainty that is not matched by accuracy, weakening intellectual autonomy even when they are informed about GenAI's possible errors.

Working without GenAI maintained relatively stable reflectivity and cognitive caution, but competence development was slower. This suggests that full exclusion can protect monitoring quality, yet may reduce efficiency in building complex analytical skills required in project management tasks.

The most beneficial outcomes appeared under limited GenAI access. This condition combined the highest competence increase with improved calibration and reduced overestimation, indicating that controlled support can strengthen both critical thinking and reflective responsibility. A usage limit likely preserved the need for independent reasoning and justification while still allowing GenAI to function as a scaffold for structuring, alternative generation, and targeted analytical support.

Overall, the findings confirm the hypotheses and support a key practical implication: educational policies should avoid extreme approaches (total prohibition or unrestricted access). Instead, structured rules that maintain students' responsibility for verification, reasoning quality, and decision-making are the most promising way to balance technological support with intellectual autonomy.

Finally, further research should examine regulation models beyond simple quantitative limits (e.g., task- or stage-dependent rules), investigate mediating mechanisms such as cognitive offloading and automation bias in more detail, and test whether gains in competence and reflectivity persist once GenAI support is withdrawn.

The fourth chapter investigated psychology students' attitudes and perceptions toward AI (with a focus on ChatGPT) and examined how these relate to self-regulated learning, ethical reflection, and perceived impacts on critical thinking in psychology education.

The results indicate that AI use is nearly universal in this cohort, suggesting that generative AI has already become a normalized element of students' learning environments. Students primarily reported using AI for comprehension support, summarizing and organizing material, and increasing efficiency in studying, with a smaller proportion using it for idea generation in written tasks. This pattern positions AI as a cognitive and organizational aid rather than a purely technical tool.

Attitudes toward AI were moderately positive but clearly not uncritical. Students tended to evaluate AI as useful and easy to use, aligning with the logic of technology acceptance models in which perceived usefulness and ease of use relate to stronger behavioral intention. At the same time, perceived risks remained at an intermediate level, demonstrating an ambivalent stance in which convenience and performance benefits coexist with concerns about negative educational and societal consequences.

A key finding is that the majority of students perceived AI as worsening critical thinking. This perception supports concerns about cognitive offloading and surface learning: when AI generates plausible explanations and academic-style text quickly, it may reduce students' motivation to engage in deeper analysis, independent reasoning, and epistemic vigilance. In psychology education, where reflection, evaluation of evidence, and disciplined skepticism are central, such perceived risks become particularly relevant.

Perceptions of AI's influence on ethical self-reflection were mixed, with substantial groups reporting improvement, deterioration, neutrality, or a dual effect depending on the context of use. This suggests that AI can simultaneously function as a trigger for ethical awareness, by raising questions about bias, responsibility, and integrity and as a factor that may weaken responsibility when students feel distanced from authorship or the consequences of their academic work. The coexistence of these interpretations highlights the need for explicit, reflective AI ethics education rather than relying only on compliance-based integrity rules.

Students reported relatively high self-regulated learning across motivational, cognitive, and metacognitive domains, and these components were internally coherent. However, attitudes toward AI were largely independent of self-regulated learning indicators, indicating that acceptance and use may be driven more by contextual forces (availability, peer norms, institutional culture) than by individual learning competencies. One notable exception was that stronger cognitive strategy use predicted lower perceived technological risks, suggesting that students who actively apply learning strategies may feel more capable of using AI selectively and critically, thereby reducing perceived vulnerability.

Group comparisons revealed no significant gender differences in AI attitudes or self-regulated learning despite unequal subgroup sizes. Age differences emerged mainly in metacognitive self-regulation, with older students reporting higher levels, which is consistent with the idea that monitoring and control strategies develop with experience in higher education.

Overall, the findings imply that psychology education should move beyond simply allowing or prohibiting AI tools. The prevalence of use and the simultaneous concern about critical thinking and ethics indicate a need for structured pedagogical integration: clear guidance on responsible use, explicit instruction on limitations and bias, and learning designs that require justification, evaluation, and reflective judgment. Future research should extend these results using larger and more diverse samples, behavioral measures beyond self-report, and longitudinal or experimental approaches to clarify how AI use shapes learning outcomes, critical thinking, and ethical agency over time.

This book shows that GenAI tools are already widely used in higher education and that students generally perceive them as useful and easy to use. At the same time, many students report concerns about academic honesty, weaker critical thinking, and dependence on AI-generated outputs. These findings confirm that students' attitudes toward GenAI are often positive but not uncritical.

The empirical results suggest that the effects of GenAI depend on how it is used. Full and unrestricted use may increase overconfidence and weaken the ability to judge whether an answer is correct. In contrast, limited use may support learning outcomes while maintaining reflective thinking and intellectual autonomy. Students can benefit from GenAI support, but they still need to remain responsible for reasoning, verification, and final conclusions.

Overall, this book suggests that higher education should support responsible GenAI use through clear rules, ethical guidance, and learning tasks that require justification, evaluation of evidence, and independent decision-making. Further research should examine long-term effects and differences across disciplines as revealed risks may not be identical in all educational contexts.

References

Introduction

Castany, R. S. (2025). The challenges of teaching translation technologies in the AI era. *Cadernos de Tradução*. https://dialnet.unirioja.es/servlet/articulo?codigo=10441881

Chamorro-Mera, A. (2025). Gen-AI tools in academia: A cluster analysis of university faculty adoption. *Multidisciplinary Journal for Education, Social and Technological Sciences*, Vol. 12, No. 2. https://doi.org/10.4995/muse.2025.23908

Csaszar, F., Jacobides, M., & Zemsky, P. (2025). The effects of artificial intelligence on management education. *Strategic Organization*. https://doi.org/10.1177/14761270251385484

Halliday, S., Lavis, T., Callaghan, P., & Chur-Hansen, A. (2025). Generative AI in higher education psychology programs: A scoping review exploring the opportunities for its use in assessment methods. *Australian Psychologist*. https://doi.org/10.1080/00050067.2025.2580236

Hayes, S., Earle, S., Dukhan, S. et al. (2025). Perspectives from South Africa on GenAI in higher education: A postdigital dialogue with the global context. *Postdigital Science and Education*, Vol. 7, pp. 1375–1413. https://doi.org/10.1007/s42438-025-00593-6

Law, L. (2024). Application of generative artificial intelligence (GenAI) in language teaching and learning: A scoping literature review. *Computers and Education Open*, Vol. 6, p. 100174. https://doi.org/10.1016/j.caeo.2024.100174

Li, B., Tan, Y. L., Wang, C., & Lowell, V. (2025). Two years of innovation: A systematic review of empirical generative AI research in language learning and teaching. *Computers and Education: Artificial Intelligence*, Vol. 9, p. 100445. https://doi.org/10.1016/j.caeai.2025.100445

Meepung, T. (2025). Fostering innovator skills through integration of creative learning and generative AI. *International Education Studies*, Vol. 18, No. 6, pp. 80–98. https://doi.org/10.5539/ies.v18n6p80

Nawaz, M. A., & Ong, C. E. (2025). Navigating the new frontier: The impact of generative AI on LJMU postgraduate business students' research competencies. *Postgraduate Journal of Management Research*, Vol. 5, No. 2. https://openjournals.ljmu.ac.uk/PJMR/article/view/3419

Pérez, G., Henderson, T., Pierre, T., Marvez, G. R., Vasquez, A., Eshun, P., & Polanco Pino, Y. (2025). Subjective intelligence: A framework for Generative AI in STEM education. *Education Sciences*, Vol. 15, No. 12, p. 1571. https://doi.org/10.3390/educsci15121571

Reider, R., & Lang, S. (2025). GenAI for simulation modeling: A synergistic approach. In: *18th International Doctoral Students Workshop on Logistics, Supply Chain and Production Management.* https://www.researchgate.net/publication/392862266

Skubis, I. (2025a). Exploring the potential and perceptions of social robots in tourism and hospitality: Insights from industry executives and technology evaluation. *International Journal of Social Robotics*. https://doi.org/10.1007/s12369-024-01197-z

Skubis, I. (2025b). Humanoid robots CEOs and leaders in project management: Decision-making, human oversight, team dynamics and ethics. *International Journal of Humanoid Robotics*. https://doi.org/10.1142/S0219843625500082

Skubis, I. (2025c). AI and leadership in the age of automation: A critical analysis of Generation Z's perspectives on humanoid robot leaders. *International Journal of Humanoid Robotics*. https://doi.org/10.1142/S0219843625500069

Skubis, I., Wodarski, K., & Lütge, Ch. (2024). Human-ChatGPT interaction: Prompt analysis on the basis of sex robots' topic – Linguistic, social and ethical considerations of Generative AI. *Linguistic and Philosophical Investigations,* Vol. 23, No. 1, pp. 2467–2485.

Skubis, I., Wodarski, K., & Lütge, Ch. (2025). Ethical considerations, prompt management and linguistic challenges in ChatGPT's responses to controversial topics: A comparative analysis of GPT-3.5 and GPT-4.0 in the case study on sex robot influencers. *Review of Contemporary Philosophy*, Vol. 24, No. 1, pp. 54–82.

Testa, M., Della Volpe, M., D'Amato, A., & Apuzzo, A. (2025). Redesigning education by unlocking the potential of generative AI in academic learning. In: A. Visvizi, K. Kozłowski, I. Calzada, & O. Troisi (Eds.), *Multidisciplinary movements in AI and generative AI* (Business 2025) (pp. 115–134). Edward Elgar Publishing. https://doi.org/10.4337/9781035358663.00015

Chapter 1

Ammon, U. (1995). *Die deutsche Sprache in Deutschland, Österreich und der Schweiz. Das Problem der nationalen Varietäten.* Walter De Gruyter.

Ammon, U., Bickel, H., Lenz, A. N., & Ebner, J. (2004). *Variantenwörterbuch des Deutschen. Die Standardsprache in Österreich, der Schweiz und Deutschland sowie in Liechtenstein, Luxemburg, Ostbelgien und Südtirol.* Walter De Gruyter.

Bang, Y., Cahyawijaya, S., Lee, N. et al. (2023). A multitask, multilingual, multimodal evaluation of ChatGPT on reasoning, hallucination, and interactivity. arXiv preprint arXiv:2302.04023. https://arxiv.org/abs/2302.04023

Botha, J., & Pieterse, H. (2020). Fake news and deepfakes: A dangerous threat for 21st century information security. In: *ICCWS 2020 15th International Conference on Cyber Warfare and Security*. Academic Conferences and Publishing Limited. https://researchspace.csir.co.za/dspace/handle/10204/11946

Brynjolfsson, E., Li, D., & Raymond, L. R. (2023). Generative AI at work. NBER Working Papers 31161. National Bureau of Economic Research, Inc.

Clayton, J. (2023, May 16). Sam Altman: CEO of OpenAI calls for US to regulate artificial intelligence. *BBC News*. https://www.bbc.com/news/world-us-canada-65616866

de Cillia, R. (2006). Varietätenreiches Deutsch: Deutsch als plurizentrische Sprache und DaF-Unterricht. In H.-J. Krumm & P. R. Portmann-Tselikas (Eds.), Begegnungssprache Deutsch – Motivation, Herausforderung, Perspektiven (pp. 51–65). StudienVerlag.

Duden. Deutsches Universalwörterbuch. 7. Auflage, 2011.

Ehnert, R., Fuchs, S., & Hertrampf, D. (2000). Deutsch in Europa – Muttersprache und Fremdsprache (Wittenberger Beiträge zur deutschen Sprache und Kultur. In: Ingrid Kühn and Marianne Lehker (Hgg.), *Regiolekte in der Ausbildung von LehrerInnen* für Deutsch *als Fremdsprache* (pp. 197–222). Peter Lang.

Guo, S., Wang, Y., Li, S., & Saeed, N. (2023). Semantic communications with ordered importance using ChatGPT. arXiv preprint arXiv:2302.07142. https://arxiv.org/abs/2302.07142

Hacker, P., Engel, A., & Mauer, M. (2023). Regulating ChatGPT and other large generative AI models. In: *Proceedings of the 2023 ACM Conference on Fairness, Accountability, and Transparency* (pp. 1112–1123) (FAccT '23), Chicago, IL, USA, June 12–15, 2023 (pp. 1112–1123). ACM. https://doi.org/10.1145/3593013.3594067.

Hägi, S. (2007). Bitte mit Sahne/Rahm/Schlag. Plurizentrik im Deutschunterricht. *Fremdsprache Deutsch. Zeitschrift* für die Praxis des *Deutschunterrichts*, Heft 37, pp. 5–13.

Jarząbek, A. D. (2013). Der plurizentrische Ansatz und das DACH-Prinzip in polnischen DaF-Lehrwerken. *Germanica Wratislaviensia*, No. 138, pp. 173–183.

Pusswald, Ch. (2007). *Das Plurizentrische Modell in der Praxis des DaF-Unterrichts: Eine Analyse anhand des österreichischen Deutsch.* Graz, Dissertation.

Radford, A., & Narasimhan, K. (2018). Improving language understanding by generative pre-training. https://openai.com/research/language-understanding

Radford, A., Wu, J., Child, R., Luan, D., Amodei, D., & Sutskever, I. (2019). Language models are unsupervised multitask learners. https://openai.com/research/language-understanding

Radzik, A. (2012). Interkulturalität in Sprache, Literatur und Bildung. In: Bianca Beníšková (Hgg.), *Die nationalen Standardvarietäten des Deutschen und interkulturelle Kompetenz im DaF-Unterricht* (pp. 13–22). Univerzita Pardubice.

Radzik, A. (2013). Anwendungsorientierte Darstellungen zur Germanistik: Modelle und Strukturen. In: Aleksandra Bednarowska, Magdalena Filar, Beata Kołodziejczyk-Mróz, & Piotr Majcher (Hgg.), *Didaktisierung der dialektalen Varietäten des Deutschen im DaF-Unterricht: Vorschläge aus der alten und neuen Perspektive der Dialektologie* (pp. 375–392). Weidler Buchverlag.

Ransmayr, J. (2006). *Der Status des österreichischen Deutsch an nichtdeutschsprachigen Universitäten. Eine empirische Untersuchung*. P. Lang.

Retti, G. (1999). *Austriazismen in Wörterbüchern. Zum Binnen- und Außenkodex des österreichischen Deutsch*, phil. Diss. Innsbruck (Doktorarbeit).

Roumeliotis, K. I., & Tselikas, N. D. (2023). ChatGPT and open-AI models: A preliminary review. *Future Internet*, Vol. 15, No. 6, p. 192. https://doi.org/10.3390/fi15060192

Russ, Charles V. J. (1994). *The German language today: A linguistic introduction.* Routledge.

Shafer, N. (2018). *Varietäten und Varianten verstehen lernen. Zum Umgang mit Standardvariation in Deutsch als Fremdsprache.* Universitätsverlag Göttingen.

Skubis, I. (2016a). Codificiation of German varieties in dictionaries. In: *The 12th International Conference on European Languages, Literature and Linguistics* (pp. 26–32). «East West» Association for Advanced Studies and Higher Education GmbH.

Skubis, I. (2016b). From monocentric to pluricentric language – Variations of the German language. In: E. Krawczyk-Neifar (Ed.), *Modern language and culture. Where do we go…* (pp. 56–72). Wyższa Szkoła Zarządzania Ochroną Pracy w Katowicach.

Skubis, I. (2017). English and German as pluricentric languages. In: *Continuity and change. And what next?* (pp. 94–110). Wyższa Szkoła Zarządzania Ochroną Pracy.

Skubis, I. (2020). *Pluricentryzm języka niemieckiego w języku prawa karnego Niemiec, Austrii i Szwajcarii.* Wydawnictwo Adam Marszałek.

Skubis, I. (2021). Językoznawstwo jako bezpieczna dyscyplina dla badań nad sztuczną inteligencją. In: B. Fischer, A. Pązik, & M. Świerczyński (Eds.), *Prawo sztucznej inteligencji i nowych technologii* (pp. 169–181). Wolters Kluwer.

Skubis, I. (2022a). Pluricentrism in education and communication – Lexical differences in English and German varieties – Outcomes of the research. In: *Kultura i Edukacja* (pp. 143–164).

Skubis, I. (2022b). The importance of co-teaching in teaching German varieties. In: B. Pituła & M. Kowalski (Eds.), *Co-teaching – Everyday life or terra incognita of contemporary education*? (pp. 223–236). Vandenhoeck & Ruprecht Verlag.

Skubis, I. (2024a). Seksroboty – Zarządzanie Etyką i Zarządzanie Innowacjami w Branży Sextech. *Management and Quality*, Vol. 6, No. 3, pp. 211–232.

Skubis, I. (2024b). The EU guidelines on roboethics and ethics of sex robots. In: Ch. Lütge & A. Kriebitz (Eds.), *Introduction to digital ethics*. Edward Elgar.

Skubis, I., & Kołodziejczyk, D. (2024). *Human vs ChatGPT - Language of advertising in beauty products advertisements*. Taylor and Francis.

Skubis, I., Wodarski, K., & Lütge, Ch. (2024). Human-ChatGPT interaction: Prompt analysis on the basis of sex robots' topic – Linguistic, social and ethical considerations of Generative AI. *Linguistic and Philosophical Investigations*, Vol. 23, No. 1, pp. 2467–2485.

Utri, R. (2013). Standardsprache und Plurizentrik – Am Beispiel des Österreichischen Deutsch. *Zeitschrift des Verbandes Polnischer Germanisten*, Heft 1, pp. 29–42.

Utri, R. (2014). Die Plurizentrizität der Sprachen – Geschichte, derzeitiger Stand, Ausblicke. *Germanica Wratislavienisia,* No. 139, pp. 335–346.

Wołk, A., Skowrońska, H., & Skubis, I. (2021). Multilingual chatbot for e-commerce: Data generation and machine translation. In: *PACIS 2021 Proceedings*, Vol. 232, pp. 1–14.

Wołk, K., Wołk, A., Wnuk, D., Grześ, T., & Skubis, I. (2022). Survey on dialogue systems including slavic languages. *Neurocomputing*, Vol. 477, pp. 62–84.

White, J., Fu, Q., Hays, S., Sandborn, M., Olea, C., Gilbert, H., Elnashar, A., Spencer-Smith, J., & Schmidt, D. C. (2023). A prompt pattern catalog to enhance prompt engineering with ChatGPT. arXiv preprint arXiv:2302.11382. https://arxiv.org/abs/2302.11382

Zhou, C., Qiu, C., & Acuna, D. E. (2022). Paraphrase identification with deep learning: A review of datasets and methods. arXiv preprint arXiv:2212.06933. https://arxiv.org /abs /2212 .06933

Zhuo, T. Y., Huang, Y., Chen, C., & Xing, Z. (2023). Exploring AI ethics of ChatGPT: A diagnostic analysis. arXiv preprint arXiv:2301.12867. https://arxiv.org /abs/2301 .12867

Chapter 2

Acosta-Enriquez, B. G., Arbulú P´erez Vargas, C. G., Huamaní Jordan, O., Arbulú Ballesteros, M. A., & Paredes Morales, A. E. (2024a). Exploring attitudes toward ChatGPT among college students: An empirical analysis of cognitive, affective, and behavioral components using path analysis. *Computers and Education: Artificial Intelligence*, Vol. 7, pp. 1–11 https://doi.org/10.1016/j.caeai.2024.100320

Acosta-Enriquez, B. G., Arbulú Ballesteros, M. A. Huamaní Jordan, O., López Roca, C., & Saavedra Tirado, K. (2024b). Analysis of college students' attitudes toward the use of ChatGPT in their academic activities: Effect of intent to use, verification of information and responsible use. *BMC Psychology,* Vol. 12, No. 255, pp. 1–18. https://link.springer.com/article/10.1186/s40359-024-01764-z

Ajzen, I. (2001). Nature and operation of attitudes. *Annual Review of Psychology*, Vol. 52, pp. 27–58. https://doi.org/10.1146/annurev.psych.52.1.27

Boone, H. N., & Boone, D. A. (2012). Analyzing Likert data. *Journal of Extension*, Vol. 50, No. 2, Article 48. https://doi.org/10.34068/joe.50.02.48

Creswell, J. W., & Creswell, J. D. (2022). *Research design: Qualitative, quantitative, and mixed methods approaches* (6th ed.). SAGE Publications Inc.

DeVellis, R. F. (2017). *Scale development: Theory and applications* (4th ed.). Sage.

Farrelly, T., & Baker, N. (2023). Generative artificial intelligence: Implications and considerations for higher education practice. *Education Sciences*, Vol. 13, No. 11, pp. 1–14. https://doi.org/10.3390/educsci13111109

Field, A. (2018). *Discovering statistics using IBM SPSS Statistics* (5th ed.). Sage.

Fishbein, M. (1967). *Readings in attitude theory and measurement.* Wiley.

Hidayat-ur-Rehman, I., & Ibrahim, Y. (2024). Exploring factors influencing educators' adoption of ChatGPT: A mixed method approach. *Interactive Technology and Smart Education*, Vol. 21, No. 4, pp. 499–534. https://doi.org/10.1108/ITSE-07-2023-0127

Hinkle, D. E., Wiersma, W., & Jurs, S. G. (2003). *Applied statistics for the behavioral sciences*. Houghton Mifflin.

Hollander, M., Wolfe, D. A., & Chicken E. (2014). *Nonparametric statistical methods* (3rd ed.). Wiley.

Huang, X., Zou, D., Cheng, G., Chen, X., & Xie, H. (2023). Trends, research issues and applications of artificial intelligence in language education. *Journal of Educational Technology & Society*, Vol. 26, No. 1, pp. 112–131. https://go.openathens.net/redirector/liberty.edu?url=https://www.proquest.com/scholarlyjournals/trends-research-issues-applications-artificial/docview/2767094132/se-2

Jung, I. (2019). Connectivism and networked learning. In: I. Jung (Ed.), *Open and distance education theory revisited. Implications for the digital era* (pp. 47–55). Springer.

Katz, D. (1960). The functional approach to the study of attitudes. *Public Opinion Quarterly*, Vol. 24, No. 2, pp. 163–204. https://doi.org/10.1086/266945

Maier, Ch., Thatcher, J. B., Grover, V., & Dwivedi, Y. K. (2023). Cross-sectional research: A critical perspective, use cases, and recommendations for IS research. *International Journal of Information Management*, Vol. 70, No. 1. https://doi.org/10.1016/j.ijinfomgt.2023.102625

Muthukrishnan, N., Maleki, F., Ovens, K., Reinhold, C., Forghani, B., & Forghani, R. (2020). Brief history of artificial intelligence. *Neuroimaging Clinics of North America*, Vol. 30, No. 4, pp. 393–399. https://doi.org/10.1016/j.nic.2020.07.004

Rokeach, M. (1968). *Beliefs, attitudes, and values: A theory of organization and change*. Jossey-Bass.

Saka, R. O., Osademe, G. C., & Ononokpono, N. J. (2023). Exploratory research design in management science: A review of literature on conduct and application. *International Journal of Research and Innovation in Social Science*, Vol. VII, No. IV, pp. 1384–1395. https://doi.org/10.47772/IJRISS.2023.7515

Sheskin, D. J. (2020). *Handbook of parametric and nonparametric statistical procedures* (6th ed.). CRC Press.

Svenningsson, J., Höst, G., Hultén, M., & Hallström, J. (2022). Students' attitudes toward technology: Exploring the relationship among affective, cognitive and behavioral components of the attitude construct. *International Journal of Technology and Design Education*, Vol. 32, pp. 1531–1551. https://link.springer.com/article/10.1007/s10798-021-09657-7

Tabachnick, B. G., & Fidell, L. S. (2019). *Using multivariate statistics* (7th ed.). Pearson.

Tamilmani, K., Rana, N. P., Wamba, S. F., & Dwivedi, R. (2021). The extended Unified Theory of Acceptance and Use of Technology (UTAUT2): A systematic literature review and theory evaluation. *International Journal of Information Management*, Vol. 57. https://doi.org/10.1016/j.ijinfomgt.2020.102269

Venkatesh, V., Morris, M. G., Davis, G. B., & Davis, F. D. (2003). User acceptance of information technology: Toward a unified view. *MIS Quarterly*, Vol. 27, No. 3, pp. 425–478. https://doi.org/10.2307/30036540

Venkatesh, V., Thong, J. Y. L., & Xu, X. (2012). Consumer acceptance and use of information technology: Extending the unified theory of acceptance and use of technology (UTAUT2). *Management Information Systems - MIS Quarterly*, Vol. 36, No. 1, pp. 157–178. https://doi.org/10.2307/41410412

Wang, Y., Li, P., Han, Y., & Zhang, B. (2023). Understanding students' cognitive and affective attitude and attitudinal structures toward physical activity: A person-centered approach. *International Journal of Physical Activity and Health*, Vol. 2, No. 3, Article 5. https://doi.org/10.18122/ijpah.020305.boisestate

Williams, C. (2007). Research methods. *Journal of Business & Economic Research*, Vol. 5, No. 3, pp. 65–71.

Williamson, B., & Eynon, R. (2020). Historical threads, missing links, and future directions in AI in education. *Learning, Media and Technology*, Vol. 45, No. 3, pp. 223–235. https://doi.org/10.1080/17439884.2020.1798995

Zawacki-Richter, O., Marín, V. I., Bond, M., & Gouverneur, F. (2019). Systematic review of research on artificial intelligence applications in higher education – Where are the educators? *International Journal of Educational Technology in Higher Education*, Vol. 16, No. 39, pp. 1–27. https://doi.org/10.1186/s41239-019-0171-0

Chapter 3

Bijańska, J., & Wodarski, K. (2024a). *Use of Chatgpt-4 to set the project's reserve budget*. Scientific Papers of Silesian University of Technology. Organization and Management Series. No. 212, pp. 25–40. https://dx.doi.org/10.29119/1641-3466.2024.212.2

Bijańska, J., & Wodarski, K. (2024b). Hard coal production in Poland in the aspect of climate and energy policy of the European Union and the war in Ukraine. Investment case study. *Resources Policy*, Vol. 88. https://doi.org/10.1016/j.resourpol.2023.104390

Butler, H. A., Dwyer, Ch. P., Hogan, M. J. Franco, A., Rivas, S. F., Saiz, C., & Almeida, L. S. (2012). The Halpern Critical Thinking Assessment and real-world outcomes: Cross-national applications. *Thinking Skills and Creativity*, Vol. 7, No. 2, pp. 112–121. https://doi.org/10.1016/j.tsc.2012.04.001

Chirayath, G., Premamalini, K., & Joseph, J. (2025). Cognitive offloading or cognitive overload? How AI alters the mental architecture of coping. *Frontiers in Psychology*, Vol. 16. https://doi.org/10.3389/fpsyg.2025.1699320

Dimitrov, D. M., & Rumrill, P. D. (2003). Pretest-posttest designs and measurement of change. *Work*, Vol. 20, pp. 159–165.

Essel, H. B., Vlachopoulos, D., Essuman, A. B., & Amankwa, J. O. (2024). ChatGPT effects on cognitive skills of undergraduate students: Receiving instant responses from AI-based conversational large language models (LLMs). *Computers and Education: Artificial Intelligence*, Vol. 6. https://doi.org/10.1016/j.caeai.2023.100198

Field, A. (2013). *Discovering statistics using IBM SPSS statistics*. SAGE.

Fleming, S., & Lau, H. C. (2014). How to measure metacognition. *Frontiers in Human Neuroscience*, Vol. 8, Article 443. https://doi.org/10.3389/fnhum.2014.00443

Gerlich, M. (2025). AI tools in society: Impacts on cognitive offloading and the future of critical thinking. *Societies*, Vol. 15, No. 6. https://doi.org/10.3390/soc15010006

Guo, Y, Huang, L., Zhang, C., Li, Q., & Chen, M. (2026). ChatGPT in education: A systematic review of its impact on critical thinking skills and dispositions. *Thinking Skills and Creativity*, Vol. 60. https://doi.org/10.1016/j.tsc.2025.102106

Romeo, G., & Conti, D. (2026). Exploring automation bias in human–AI collaboration: A review and implications for explainable AI. *AI & Society*, Vol. 41, pp. 259–278. https://doi.org/10.1007/s00146-025-02422-7

Schraw, G. (2009). A conceptual analysis of five measures of metacognitive monitoring. *Metacognition Learning*, Vol. 4, pp. 33–45. DOI https://doi.org/10.1007/s11409-008-9031-3

Chapter 4

Akgun, S., & Greenhow, C. (2022). Artificial intelligence in education: Addressing ethical challenges in K-12 settings. *AI and Ethics*, Vol. 2, No. 3, pp. 431–440. https://doi.org/10.1007/s43681-021-00096-7

American Psychological Association. (2017). *Ethical principles of psychologists and code of conduct*. APA.

Azevedo, R., & Taub, M. (2020). The challenge of measuring processes and outcomes while learning from multiple representations with advanced learning technologies. In: P. Van Meter, A. List, D. Lombardi, & P. Kendeou (Eds.), *Handbook of learning from multiple representations and perspectives* (1st ed., pp. 532–553). Routledge. https://doi.org/10.4324/9780429443961-34

Barr, N., Pennycook, G., Stolz, J. A., & Fugelsang, J. A. (2015). The brain in your pocket: Evidence that Smartphones are used to supplant thinking. *Computers in Human Behavior*, Vol. 48, pp. 473–480. https://doi.org/10.1016/j.chb.2015.02.029

Bearman, M., Tai, J., Dawson, P., Boud, D., & Ajjawi, R. (2024). Developing evaluative judgement for a time of generative artificial intelligence. *Assessment & Evaluation in Higher Education*, Vol. 49, No. 6, pp. 893–905. https://doi.org/10.1080/02602938.2024.2335321

Bender, E. M., Gebru, T., McMillan-Major, A., & Shmitchell, S. (2021). On the dangers of stochastic parrots: Can language models be too big? In *Proceedings of the 2021 ACM Conference on Fairness, Accountability, and Transparency* (pp. 610–623). Virtual Conference. https://doi.org/10.1145/3442188.3445922

Borenstein, J., & Howard, A. (2021). Emerging challenges in AI and the need for AI ethics education. *AI and Ethics*, Vol. 1, No. 1, pp. 61–65. https://doi.org/10.1007/s43681-020-00002-7

Bretag, T. (2013). Challenges in addressing plagiarism in education. *PLoS Medicine*, Vol. 10, No. 12, p. e1001574. https://doi.org/10.1371/journal.pmed.1001574

Broadbent, J., & Poon, W. L. (2015). Self-regulated learning strategies & academic achievement in online higher education learning environments: A systematic review. *The Internet and Higher Education*, Vol. 27, pp. 1–13. https://doi.org/10.1016/j.iheduc.2015.04.007

Cotton, D. R. E., Cotton, P. A., & Shipway, J. R. (2024). Chatting and cheating: Ensuring academic integrity in the era of ChatGPT. *Innovations in Education and Teaching International*, Vol. 61, No. 2, pp. 228–239. https://doi.org/10.1080/14703297.2023.2190148

Davis, F. D. (1989). Perceived usefulness, perceived ease of use, and user acceptance of information technology. *MIS Quarterly*, Vol. 13, No. 3, pp. 319–340. https://doi.org/10.2307/249008

Dulonsky, J., & Metcalfe, J. (2009). *Metacognition*. SAGE Publications Ltd.

Fernández-de-Castro, J., Martínez-Bautista, H., Rojas-Muñoz, L. M., & Galindo-Muñoz, R. (2024). Escala de Autorregulación del Aprendizaje: Validación de un instrumento para educación secundaria y media superior. *Revista Complutense de Educación*, Vol. 35, No. 1, pp. 33–43. https://doi.org/10.5209/rced.82444

Flavell, J. H. (1979). Metacognition and cognitive monitoring: A new area of cognitive–developmental inquiry. *American Psychologist*, Vol. 34, No. 10, pp. 906–911. https://doi.org/10.1037/0003-066X.34.10.906

Floridi, L., & Chiriatti, M. (2020). GPT-3: Its nature, scope, limits, and consequences. *Minds and Machines*, Vol. 30, No. 4, pp. 681–694. https://doi.org/10.1007/s11023-020-09548-1

Floridi, L., Cowls, J., Beltrametti, M., Chatila, R., Chazerand, P., Dignum, V., Luetge, C., Madelin, R., Pagallo, U., Rossi, F., Schafer, B., Valcke, P., & Vayena, E. (2018). AI4People-An ethical framework for a good ai society: Opportunities, risks, principles, and recommendations. *Minds and Machines*, Vol. 28, No. 4, pp. 689–707. https://doi.org/10.1007/s11023-018-9482-5

Grassini, S. (2023). Development and validation of the AI attitude scale (AIAS-4): A brief measure of general attitude toward artificial intelligence. *Frontiers in Psychology*, Vol. 14, p. 1191628. https://doi.org/10.3389/fpsyg.2023.1191628

Hadwin, A., Järvelä, S., & Miller, M. (2017). Self-regulation, co-regulation, and shared regulation in collaborative learning environments. In: D. H. Schunk & J. A. Greene (Eds.), *Handbook of self-regulation of learning and performance* (2nd ed., pp. 83–106). Routledge. https://doi.org/10.4324/9781315697048-6

Jobin, A., Ienca, M., & Vayena, E. (2019). The global landscape of AI ethics guidelines. *Nature Machine Intelligence*, Vol. 1, No. 9, pp. 389–399. https://doi.org/10.1038/s42256-019-0088-2

Kasneci, E., Sessler, K., Küchemann, S., Bannert, M., Dementieva, D., Fischer, F., Gasser, U., Groh, G., Günnemann, S., Hüllermeier, E., Krusche, S., Kutyniok, G., Michaeli, T., Nerdel, C., Pfeffer, J., Poquet, O., Sailer, M., Schmidt, A., Seidel, T., … Kasneci, G. (2023). ChatGPT for good? On opportunities and challenges of large language models for education. *Learning and Individual Differences*, Vol. 103, p. 102274. https://doi.org/10.1016/j.lindif.2023.102274

Lund, B. D., Wang, T., Mannuru, N. R., Nie, B., Shimray, S., & Wang, Z. (2023). ChatGPT and a new academic reality: Artificial Intelligence-written research papers and the ethics of the large language models in scholarly publishing. *Journal of the Association for Information Science and Technology*, Vol. 74, No. 5, pp. 570–581. https://doi.org/10.1002/asi.24750

McCabe, D. L., Butterfield, K. D., & Treviño, L. K. (2012). *Cheating in college: Why students do it and what educators can do about it*. Johns Hopkins University Press.

Ng, W. (2012). Can we teach digital natives digital literacy? *Computers & Education*, Vol. 59, No. 3, pp. 1065–1078. https://doi.org/10.1016/j.compedu.2012.04.016

Nicol, D. J., & Macfarlane-Dick, D. (2006). Formative assessment and self-regulated learning: A model and seven principles of good feedback practice. *Studies in Higher Education*, Vol. 31, No. 2, pp. 199–218. https://doi.org/10.1080/03075070600572090

OECD. (2021). *21st-century readers: Developing literacy skills in a digital world*. OECD Publishing.

Panadero, E. (2017). A review of self-regulated learning: Six models and four directions for research. *Frontiers in Psychology*, Vol. 8, p. 422. https://doi.org/10.3389/fpsyg.2017.00422

Perkins, M., Roe, J., Postma, D., McGaughran, J., & Hickerson, D. (2024). Detection of GPT-4 generated text in higher education: Combining academic judgement and software to identify generative ai tool misuse. *Journal of Academic Ethics*, Vol. 22, No. 1, pp. 89–113. https://doi.org/10.1007/s10805-023-09492-6

Rest, J. R., Narvaez, D., Bebeau, M. J., & Thoma, S. J. (1999). *Postconventional moral thinking: A Neo-Kohlbergian approa*. Lawrence Erlbaum.

Risko, E. F., & Gilbert, S. J. (2016). Cognitive offloading. *Trends in Cognitive Sciences*, Vol. 20, No. 9, pp. 676–688. https://doi.org/10.1016/j.tics.2016.07.002

Rudolph, J., Tan, S., & Tan, S. (2023). ChatGPT: Bullshit spewer or the end of traditional assessments in higher education? *Journal of Applied Learning & Teaching*, Vol. 6, No. 1, pp. 342–363. https://doi.org/10.37074/jalt.2023.6.1.9

Selwyn, N. (2019). *Should robots replace teachers? AI and the future of education*. Polity Pre.

Teo, T. (2011). Factors influencing teachers' intention to use technology: Model development and test. *Computers & Education*, Vol. 57, No. 4, pp. 2432–2440. https://doi.org/10.1016/j.compedu.2011.06.008

Venkatesh, V., & Davis, F. D. (2000). A theoretical extension of the technology acceptance model: Four longitudinal field studies. *Management Science*, Vol. 46, No. 2, pp. 186–204. https://doi.org/10.1287/mnsc.46.2.186.11926

Venkatesh, V., Morris, M., Davis, G., & Davis, F. (2003). User acceptance of information technology: Toward a unified view. *MIS Quarterly*, Vol. 27, No. 3, pp. 425–478.

Williamson, B., & Piattoeva, N. (2022). Education governance and datafication: Changing analytics and the digitalization of education. *Education and Information Technologies*, Vol. 27, pp. 3515–3531.

Winne, P. H., & Hadwin, A. F. (2008). The weave of motivation and self-regulated learning. In: D. H. Schunk & B. J. Zimmerman (Eds.), *Motivation and self-regulated learning: Theory, research, and applications* (pp. 297–314). Lawrence Erlbaum Associates Publishers.

Zhai, X. (2022). ChatGPT user experience: Implications for education. *SSRN Electronic Journal*. https://doi.org/10.2139/ssrn.4312418

Zimmerman, B. J. (2000). Attaining self-regulation: A social cognitive perspective. In: M. Boekaerts, P. R. Pintrich, & M. Zeidner (Eds.), *Handbook of self-regulation* (pp. 13–39). Academic Press. https://doi.org/10.1016/B978-012109890-2/50031-7

Zimmerman, B. J. (2002). Becoming a self-regulated learner: An overview. *Theory into Practice*, Vol. 41, No. 2, pp. 64–70. https://doi.org/10.1207/s15430421tip4102_2

Zimmerman, B. J., & Schunk, D. H. (2011). *Handbook of self-regulation of learning and performance*. Routledge.

Index

ABC model 22–29, 51, 54, 66, 67, 72, 82, 83
academic education 21
academic tool 22
affective attitudes 23
affective component 23, 25, 54, 65, 67, 72, 73, 82
affective-motivational attitudes 30–41, 48, 70, 78, 82
age 24, 26, 27, 29, 30, 31, 34, 37–39, 42, 43, 46, 49, 50, 54, 55, 57, 65, 67, 68, 73, 76, 77, 79, 82, 83
AI Act 5
AI-driven tools 3
AI in higher education 113, 117
AI use in psychology education 112, 115, 120, 122
ambivalent attitudes toward AI 123
anonymity 8
artificial intelligence in education 21
attitude models 114
attitudes toward AI 114, 117–119, 121–125
attitudes toward GenAI 22–24, 26, 27, 30, 37, 38, 42, 50, 54, 66–73, 75, 80, 82, 83, 84
Austrian variety 3, 5, 9
Austricisms (A) 7, 10, 12, 15, 19
autonomy, intellectual 87–89, 87–89, 107, 108, 110, 111

Bachelor's degree 24, 29, 30, 33, 37, 45, 48, 63, 71, 73, 78, 81
balance between technological support and autonomy 88, 107, 110
bar chart 10
behavioral component 23, 25, 42, 65, 72, 73, 82
behavioral intentions 24
benefits of GenAI 74, 76–84
bias 4, 18
biomedical engineering 27, 29
Brötchen 11, 13
Brötli 13

chatbots 21
codex (linguistic code) 2
cognitive component 23, 54, 65, 66, 67, 72, 73, 75, 83
Composite Index (CI) 30–37, 41–50
corporate communication 19
correlational analyses 121
correlation analysis 37, 51, 65, 67, 75, 83
co-teaching 7
creativity 22, 24, 28, 66, 75, 76, 79–81, 83
critical thinking 86–91, 93–103, 105–107, 109, 111, 113, 115–118, 120, 123, 125
critical thinking competences 86–91, 93–95, 97, 99, 101, 103, 105–107, 109, 111
cross-sectional research 26
curriculum development 14

D (abbreviation) 5, 7, 8, 10–15, 19, 20
DACHL map 6
DaF 3, 5, 16
data analysis 30, 42, 119
decision-making 87, 91, 95, 110
deep learning models 4
degree level 27, 29, 30, 33, 37, 45, 48, 50, 63, 71, 78, 82–84
demographic characteristics 26, 27, 29, 30, 38, 39, 49
descriptive statistics 30–32, 42–44, 52, 74, 83
design (research) 117, 118, 125
diagnostic-exploratory research 26
dialect 2, 5, 6, 10, 13, 15, 16, 18
digital literacy 124

educational characteristics 22, 23, 27, 29, 30, 38, 42, 49, 50, 51, 54–56, 58, 60, 62, 64, 66–71, 76–78, 82–84
educational implications 125
educational process 87
effort expectancy 24, 27, 28, 82
e-learning 25
ethical and professional considerations 115
ethical reflection 115, 117, 120, 123, 124
evaluation frameworks 4
examples (own examples task) 7, 8, 11, 13, 15, 18

experiment 86–88, 90, 91, 93, 95, 103–106, 109
exposure to German-speaking regions 7, 14, 15, 18

field of study 29, 30, 32, 36, 37, 40–42, 44, 48, 50, 61, 65, 70, 72, 73, 78, 80–84
fine-tuning 4
foreign language teaching 3, 5
frequency of GenAI use 22, 23, 42, 49, 82

GDPR 5
GenAI 21–30, 37–51, 53–56, 58, 60, 62, 64–85, 86–89, 91, 93–95, 103–111
gender 24, 27, 29, 30, 32, 35, 37–40, 42, 44, 47, 49, 50, 59, 65, 67, 69, 71–73, 77, 79, 80, 82–84
gender differences 122, 124
generating examples 7, 8, 13, 15
generative AI 1–20
Generative Pre-trained Transformer (GPT) 4
Germanisms (D) 7, 10, 12, 13, 15, 19
German national varieties 3, 5, 7, 8, 10, 12, 14–16, 18
German variety 3, 7, 9, 10, 11, 15
GFL 1, 5–7, 9, 12, 18
Google Forms 26
GPT-5 3, 7, 8, 12–14, 16, 17
grammar 2, 11, 12, 14, 16
group comparisons 122
group differences 124
GSL 5, 18

habit 25, 27, 28, 54, 67, 72, 73, 82, 83
hallucinations 4
hedonic motivation 25, 27, 28, 66, 72, 73, 82
higher education 86, 88, 90, 92, 94, 96, 98, 100, 102, 104, 106, 108, 110
human oversight 4
hypotheses 22, 23, 30, 38, 42, 49, 50, 51, 54, 67, 73–75, 79, 80–84, 86, 88, 108, 111

identification task 8, 15
innovation 23, 85
intelligent teaching systems 21
intention to continue using GenAI 22, 23, 50, 51, 53–56, 58, 60, 62, 64, 65, 83
intercultural communication 3
international management 3, 17

knowledge gap 3

language barriers 3
language education 1, 3, 14, 16–19
learning process 86
lexical differences 17, 18
Likert scale 30
limitations 14
Limitations 22–24, 74–84
limited AI use 88, 91, 93, 105, 107–110, 108–110
limited-risk AI systems 5
linguistic code 2
localization 14
logistics 27, 29
long-term teaching project 88, 107

management 27, 29
Master's degree 24, 29, 30, 33, 37, 45, 48, 63, 71, 73, 78, 81, 84
mathematical errors 4
mean 30–33, 39, 42–45, 49, 51, 52, 65, 74, 75
median 30, 31, 32, 33, 43, 44, 45, 52, 74, 75
metacognition 116
methodology 7, 18, 89, 117
motivation to learn 27, 40, 41
multiple-choice question 8, 11, 14, 16, 18

national varieties 2, 3, 5–18
NLP (natural language processing) 4, 14, 17
non-parametric tests 30

objectives 117
orthography 2, 11, 14, 16

participants 7
patterns of AI use 122
perceived benefits 22, 23, 79–81, 83, 84
perceived benefits and limitations 22, 23
perceived risks 22, 75
perceptions of AI 113, 115, 117
perceptual tolerance 6
performance expectancy 24, 27–29, 54, 65–67, 71–73, 75, 82–84
personal details 26, 27, 30, 38, 42, 49
phonetics 11, 12, 14, 16
pie chart 9
plagiarism 4
pluricentric language 1, 14–19

pluricentrism 1, 3, 5, 7, 9, 11, 13, 15, 17, 19
prevalence of AI use 122
production engineering 27, 29
productivity 22, 24, 29, 54, 66, 75, 76, 79, 80–83
professional competencies 22, 24
project management 27, 29
project management students 87, 103
prompt engineering 4
psychology education 112, 113, 115–117, 120, 122, 125

quantitative research 26
questionnaire 8, 26, 27, 28, 29

real-time language adaptation 3
reflective thinking 86, 88, 94, 107, 108
regression analyses 119, 121, 124
reliability 5
research challenges 22, 23
research hypotheses 22, 23, 30, 38, 42, 49, 50, 51, 54, 67, 73–75, 79, 80–84
research methodology 22, 89
research objective 88
research results 22, 26, 30, 82–85
results 112, 119, 122, 125
robustness 5

sample size 29, 39, 51, 65, 75
self-regulated learning 112, 113, 115, 117, 119, 121, 123, 125
self-regulation 108
self-reported behaviors 26
Semmel 11, 13
Shapiro-Wilk test 33, 51, 75
smart homes 21
social influence 24, 28, 82
social sciences 27, 29, 30, 32, 36, 44, 48, 61, 70, 72, 78
Spearman's correlation 30, 34–37, 42, 46–49, 51, 53, 55, 56, 58, 60, 62, 64–66, 68–71, 75–78, 83
specialised translation 12
spoken standard 3
standard variety 2
statistical analysis 30, 51, 74
STEM disciplines 29, 32, 36, 44, 48, 61, 65, 70, 72, 78, 80, 81
survey questionnaire 26, 27, 28, 29
survey results 8
Swiss variety 3, 9

teacher training 18
technological support 87, 88, 94, 107, 110
technology acceptance 22, 24, 72, 73, 75, 84, 85
technology acceptance model 114
textbooks 5, 6, 18
theoretical foundations 89
theoretical framework 113, 117
toxicity 5
translation accuracy 3
translation services 14
transparency 5

unified theory of acceptance and use of technology 114, 124
Unified Theory of Acceptance and Use of Technology (UTAUT) 22, 24–29, 54, 65–67, 71–73, 75, 82–85
Unified Theory of Acceptance and Use of Technology (UTAUT2) 22, 24–29, 54, 66, 67, 72, 73, 75, 82–85
use of AI 112, 114, 115, 117, 120, 125
use of AI in teaching 89
use of GenAI 22–27, 38–42, 49–51, 53–56, 58, 60, 62, 64–67, 74–79, 82–84

variety 2, 3, 5–13, 15, 17, 18
variety vs dialect 10, 16
vocabulary 2, 6, 11, 12, 14, 15, 16

willingness to recommend GenAI 22, 28, 51, 65–73, 83
written standard 3

YouTube 9

LEXICAL ITEMS

Abfall 13
Abitur 11, 13, 20
Anzug 13
Apfelsine 11, 13, 20
Aprikose 13

Billet 10-13, 20
Bub 11, 13, 20

Fahrkarte 10, 11, 13, 20
Faschingskrapfen 13
Fleischbrühe 11, 12, 13, 19

Geldbeutel 11, 13, 20
Guggumere 14
Gurke 14
Gurkerl 14
Gewand 13
Grüezi 11
Grüß Gott 11

Härdöpfel 13
Häuserl 11, 13, 20

Jänner 5, 10, 11, 13, 20

Karfiol 11
Kartoffel 5, 13
Kiosk 5
Krapfen 13
Kren 11, 12, 13, 19
Kukuruz 13

Marille 10, 11, 13, 19
Matura 11, 12, 13, 20
Mist 6, 13
Müll 13

Nidel 11, 13, 20

Obers 5, 10, 11, 13, 14, 20

Paradeiser 5, 13
Pflaume 13
Portmonee/Portemonnaie 11-13, 20

Rahm 13, 14
Rauchfang 13

Sackerl 14
Sahne 5, 10, 11, 13, 14, 15, 20
Salär 11, 13, 20
Säckli 14
Schlagobers 13
Schlagrahm 13
Schlagsahne 13
Schornstein 13
Spital 11
Straßenbahn 11

Trafik 5
Tram 11
Treppe 10, 11, 13, 20
Tumbler 11, 13, 20
Tüte 14

Vélo 11

Zwetschge 13
Zwetschke 13

For Product Safety Concerns and Information please contact our EU representative GPSR@taylorandfrancis.com Taylor & Francis Verlag GmbH, Kaufingerstraße 24, 80331 München, Germany

Printed and bound by CPI Group (UK) Ltd, Croydon, CR0 4YY
14/09/2026
02216243-0016